Springer Series on Cultural Computing

Cultural Computing is an exciting, emerging field of Human Computer Interaction, which covers the cultural impact of computing and the technological influences and requirements for the support of cultural innovation. Using support technologies such as artificial intelligence, machine learning, location-based systems, mixed/virtual/augmented reality, cloud computing, pervasive technologies and human-data interaction, researchers can explore the differences across a variety of cultures and cultural production to provide the knowledge and skills necessary to overcome cultural issues and expand human creativity.

This series presents monographs, edited collections and advanced textbooks on the current research and knowledge of a broad range of topics including creativity support systems, creative computing, digital communities, the interactive arts, cultural heritage, digital culture and intercultural collaboration.

This Series is abstracted/indexed in Scopus.

Suman Gupta

Collective Principles and the Formation of the Internet

Cultural Influences and Historical Impacts (Beginnings to 2010)

Springer

Suman Gupta
Faculty of Arts and Social Sciences
Open University
Milton Keynes, UK

ISSN 2195-9056 ISSN 2195-9064 (electronic)
Springer Series on Cultural Computing
ISBN 978-3-031-90469-1 ISBN 978-3-031-90470-7 (eBook)
https://doi.org/10.1007/978-3-031-90470-7

This Springer imprint is published by the registered company Springer Nature Switzerland AG
The registered company address is: Gewerbestrasse 11, 6330 Cham, Switzerland

To John Seed
historian, poet, contrarian, rambler, gourmet

Acknowledgements Many conversations have fed this book, especially with Richard Allen, Ayan-Yue Gupta, Milena Katsarska, John Seed, Peter H. Tu, and Cheng Xiao. As ever, my colleagues at the Open University ensured a stimulating and accommodative working environment. I am grateful to Wayne Wheeler at Springer for seeing this through to publication.

I look forward to being upbraided for and regretting the lapses in this book, for which I alone am responsible.

Competing Interests The author has no competing interests to declare that are relevant to the content of this manuscript.

Contents

Chapter 1
Introduction: Internet Polity and Guiding Concepts

Abstract The introductory chapter opens with a brief statement of the context and theme of this study. Two nodal terms are unpacked to clarify the methodology and structure of the book. The first is *polity*: a general theory of polity underpins observations about the 'Internet Polity' here. This is elaborated in Aristotelian terms and via formulations of 'global polity'. The extent to which *ideology* might be associated with *polity* is also considered. The other nodal term is *internet*: a section is devoted to sharpening the everyday senses of 'internet', and proposing distinctions from 'Internet Technology' and 'Internet Infrastructure'. Notes on the relationship between technical communication and ordinary language follow. The chapter ends with an overview of the two parts of the book.

Five decades after its technological structure started being erected, and three decades after access to it started burgeoning, the internet has become a habitual feature of global everyday life. It remains nevertheless a structure in the making and concentrates hopes as well as misgivings. Of late, misgivings seem to have the upper hand. And yet, those are usually laced with a commitment to reorient the internet for a greater good or to resuscitate its tarnished promise. Hopes for social progress remain entrenched in perceptions of the internet while escalations of social conflicts are pinned upon it.

There is a constant proliferation of surveys concerning the usage of and public attitudes towards the internet that underscore these opening observations. Surveying is naturally undertaken for cohorts in specific contexts, at large scale for political states. A 2022 Pew report gives an indicative overview, covering '19 advanced economies in North America, Europe, the Middle East, and the Asia–Pacific region' (Wike et al. 2022). This report confirms, like other such reports, that internet usage across all segments of peoples is growing towards a terminal point. Users now access the internet through a range of gadgets, such as personal computers, smart phones, television sets, gaming kits. The Pew report, like most others, both assumes and confirms that attitudes towards the internet inform broad social commitments: e.g., in relation to 'democracy', 'privacy' and 'security', 'political extremism', 'misinformation' and 'media manipulation', 'tolerance' or 'inclusiveness'. Thus, the internet is construed

S. Gupta, *Collective Principles and the Formation of the Internet*, Springer Series on Cultural Computing, https://doi.org/10.1007/978-3-031-90470-7_1

both as a proxy for existing social norms (i.e., surveying usage of and attitudes to the internet reveal general social attitudes) and, at the same time, as a social intervention (i.e., the internet is itself responsible for prevailing social attitudes). Along the latter line, it is regarded as both generator of and recourse against security and privacy vulnerabilities, social inequalities ('digital divides'), reduced human capacities (amidst increasingly 'smart' systems). It seems possible that such surveys reflect prevailing perceptions of the internet and also mould those perceptions.

Academic and polemical publications about the internet's social import are legion, veering between enthusiasm and alarm about the prospects. As the twenty-first century has progressed, a significant number of these maintain that the internet has gone off course. For some, that is primarily due to protectionist measures by powerful political states and international alliances, effectively dividing the internet and controlling various citizenry through it. For others, the global dominance of certain profit-making corporations plays a stronger role, curtailing creative freedoms and manipulating consumers through the internet. There are well-evidenced studies of how internet-based facilities could, by design or inadvertently, serve to exacerbate antisocial proclivities and have deleterious political consequences. There are passionate debates about the internet as a source of very large-scale data on every aspect of individual and social activity, and the extent to which those are capitalized and by whom. Relatedly, modifications in the technological structure of the internet, especially in terms of security layering and the integration of automation, are contemplated with great expectations and even greater unease. To give indicative citations for these strands of research and commentary would belie the immense richness of each. At any rate, general accounts now plausibly suggest that the internet is geopolitically divided by powerful states (e.g., Giacomello 2005; Mueller 2010, 2017; O'Hara and Hall 2021) and, in collaboration or competition with states, divided by global corporations catering to and competing for markets via consolidated platforms (e.g., Zittrain 2008; Srnicek 2017; Dijck et al. 2018; Deibert 2020; Terranova 2022; Muldoon 2022; Lehdonvirta 2022). The idea that the internet is divided naturally seems to go against the grain of what the term 'internet' stands for. It follows that such accounts conceive of the cohesive internet of the past (say, the 1990s) as being a different formation from the contested and divided internet that has come to prevail (after 2000). In numerous manifesto-like pronouncements, these developments are considered socially deleterious and come with calls for revitalizing, renewing, reclaiming, resetting, etc. the internet in the future. None speak of eschewing the internet; these are not technophobic but emphatically technophilic accounts.

This study does not contribute directly to one or the other of these current debates but is motivated by all of them. Together, these show that a politically active and committed collective of global scope has grown on the internet and is mediated by its technological structure. Of course, like most persons now, members of this collective use the internet for their real-world engagements. But their collective character is distinguished beyond their real-world interests through engagement, along diverse lines, with the internet itself as a political arena with distinctive principles and commitments at stake. It is because a 'virtual world' apropos of the internet is widely discerned and talked about now that the qualification of 'real world' becomes necessary and makes sense—and is used accordingly here. The collectivity that has grown around the internet seems to actuate definite social commitments, and the internet provides the ground for an organized society. There are well-developed expressive modalities and social practices to bolster the sense of collectivity. I consider this collective formation as the *Internet Polity* here. The idea of an Internet Polity naturally draws upon and is concerned with all the discussion strands outlined briskly here.

The following pages are devoted to examining how this Internet Polity was formed and has developed since, and what its structuring principles and expressive features are and how those get modified. This is a history of the social dimension of the internet from, roughly, 1970 to 2010, presented with a distinctive historiographical rationale. History is itself a somewhat variegated discipline, and the history of the internet is correspondingly so too. Mainstream history has generally focused on a top-down perspective of political and economic forces and agents (exceptional individuals and ideologues) working upon society. These generally take the form of national histories, socio-political histories, socio-economic histories, imperial histories, etc. Much of the history of the internet as currently available is in this mould. These are accounts of political, economic, industrial forces drawing upon the work of exceptional technologists, entrepreneurs, and visionaries to act upon society. This is prodigiously covered ground, and much appears there that is relevant to understanding the Internet Polity. I gratefully and often call upon such histories below.

However, alongside mainstream history, several searching and different approaches to history have appeared over the years: history of ideas, history from below/bottom-up history, cultural history, subaltern history, people's history and the like. These are all squarely in the discipline of history because they follow consistent historiographical principles of evidence and reasoned argument to capture the past in terms of the present. Attempts to grasp the internet's place in social life from these perspectives have generally been narrowly focused and with uneven ideological investments (several from the 1990s onwards are discussed in subsequent chapters). This book takes such an approach. It is not a mainstream history of the internet; it is an alternative history of the internet in terms of its social uptake and collective purchase. Accordingly, Part I is a history of ideas: it tracks the development of certain political ideas which are grounded in the technological structure of the internet in this period. This history of ideas is effectively also a history of the social developments that gradually centred on the internet. Part II is a cultural history/social history: it traces the development of a social discourse that makes the internet a collective space and facility. Both parts follow a chronological order; build upon brief accounts of the relevant mainstream histories of the Cold War, post-Cold War, 1990s privatizations, and post-9/11 in relation to the internet. Both parts then add layers of the history of ideas and cultural/social history upon that received mainstream history of the internet.

Accordingly, two arguments occupy respectively the two parts of this study.

- The first, in Part I, focuses on the technological structure that is the internet in its most material sense—its protocols, hypertext systems, security controls. The argument is that this structure is composed of technological features which were developed in terms of the social or political norms followed by their developers. With usage, those norms have acquired the position of social first principles for the collectivity that has formed on the internet. These principles have largely underpinned the exchanges within and life of what is dubbed the *Internet Polity* here. They tacitly guide activities, expressions, and doings for this collectivity on the internet. The technological features and the principles grounded through their usage are discussed in a historicist vein, from their inception to the more-or-less stable form they have acquired, and then to their emerging remit.
- The second argument, in Part II, concerns the development of the distinctive vocabulary and the concordant linguistic practices that have become centred in internet usage. These constitute the discourse that evinces the Internet Polity as such. The linguistic domain of the internet is, obviously, an extremely complex field, already intensively researched. In fact, this part focuses on one dimension of the discourse: the dissemination of and interconnections between catchwords and catchphrases anchored to the internet, again with a historicist perspective. This argument consists in analysing the emergence of catchwords, and the adaptations and shifts they went through, propelled by internet usage. Tracking the careers of these catchwords is a way of apprehending how an Internet Polity discourse was formed and continues to be negotiated.

Together and relatedly, the two arguments serve to conceptualize and describe the Internet Polity, i.e., the collective that works with regard to and within the internet and inhabits the internet. Attempts to present a general description of the Internet Polity as such and in these terms are yet to be made.

Along with this historicist perspective, both arguments (Parts) are held together by a methodological emphasis on language usage. Throughout, this study pays close attention to linguistic features, especially the use of words and phrases, and their contexts. Whether in relation to technological features or social arrangements, this study tracks the emphases and manoeuvres involved in lexical choices. Connotative shifts in words, naming practices, the appointment of standardized terms and definitions, associations made between words, the formation of registers, the appearance of neologisms, frequency patterns in word usage, routinized constructions, informal and formal vocabularies, unorthodox syntax and the like call for pause throughout and glue this study together. This interest in linguistic nuances is related to the historicist perspective in question. The idea is that shifts in lexical usage trace residues of the past in the present along a continuous line, and equally attend to agglomerations of the present upon the past in an ongoing way. This methodological emphasis is especially productive for this study, it is argued, because the internet is largely a system for processing language for outcomes that are availed in linguistic forms. I dwell upon this point later in this chapter, in contemplating the relationship between technical terms and ordinary-language terms. Looking closely to language usage is the key to describing the Internet Polity here.

To proceed with these arguments, it is expedient to give initial explanations for some of the guiding concepts and terms employed already. The following two sections do so, with the first elaborating on the concept of a 'polity', and the second clarifying my handling of the term 'internet'. A further section then offers some preliminary observations on the relationship between technical and ordinary language. The final section gives an overview of the two parts and summaries of the chapters in each.

1.1 Nodal Term: Polity

My understanding of a 'polity', as in Internet Polity, is in the main derived from an Aristotelian emphasis that remains in the current term 'politics'. However, I do not take 'polity' as being equivalent to Aristotle's use of the term '*politeía*' (πολιτεία), usually understood as an ideal regime or constitution characterized by the rule of many to maximize collective virtues (on the term and its translations, see Cherry 2009, Bates 2014). Idealistic accounts of the internet or the Internet Polity are of little interest in this study.

The English word 'politics' and equivalent words in European languages are rooted in the Aristotelian formulation of *politikí* (πολιτική). That formulation immediately evokes a centre and scope for considering the norms of ruling and being ruled. The *pólis* (πόλις)—or city-state—is indelibly centred in the philosophy and practice referred as 'politics'. Here, I take the implicit gesture towards a scope and centre in 'politics' (*politikí*) to be the core of the term 'polity': i.e., the extent of a collective formation to which norms of ruling and being ruled, of organized collective life, applies. For Aristotle, this scope and centre was the *polis*. That the *polis* is thus implicit in politics was not an inconsiderable matter for Aristotle, and his own discussion of norms and practices followed accordingly. The opening paragraphs of his treatise on *Politics* made this clear. Aristotle conceived of levels of collectivity as developing through a chronological process, from individual to household to village to city-state, driven by a natural human drive towards politics ('man is by nature a political animal' [Aristotle 1932: 9]). However, when this process fulfils the natural drive by culminating in the city-state, the city-state assumes the highest level of conceptual priority:

> the city-state is prior in nature to the household and to each of us individually. For the whole must necessarily be prior to the part; since when the whole body is destroyed, foot or hand will not exist except in an equivocal sense [...]. It is clear therefore that the state is also prior by nature to the individual; for if each individual when separate is not self-sufficient, he must be related to the whole state as other parts are to their whole [...] (11 [I.i.12])

Without dwelling upon the Aristotelian concept of 'nature', this could be regarded as saying: politics accounts for the processes and practices of regulation with the highest level of coherent social collectivity in view. For Aristotle that was the city-state. As more complex levels of regulated collectivity have obtained since then, the somewhat narrow centring of the city-state for politics has been extended or taken as a point of departure, but never quite lost. Indeed, complex levels of collectivity were developing in Aristotle's lifetime. Imperial expansion at the time already made his *pólis*-centredness conservative and small (on the slippages between Aristotle's *pólis* and empire, see Dietz 2012). In any case, widening scopes and recentrings of collectivity have inevitably reorientated and reconfigured politics since. Such configurations can be traced with reference to, for instance, rearticulated ideas of *citi*zenship for the currently centred nation-state/federal state or sovereign state, and the more abstract and contested formulations of world state or transnational state or cosmopolis. I think of each of these levels of collectivity as representing a scope for politics and political arrangements, and as being polities—each level describes a polity.

The regulated collectivity that has emerged via and within the scope of the internet is thus an Internet Polity. This polity appears to be in the region of those contested formulations of world state, transnational state, or cosmopolis. However, the latter have been more salient in theory than in practice. Current global or transnational political arrangements are grounded on the precedence of nation-states. The internet has been formed for practice and taken up in practice, and the Internet Polity has had a complex and, in some ways, incommensurable relationship with nation-states. The Internet Polity has developed with regard to a technological formation. This has occurred through *doings* online rather than by the will of constitutional enactments and regime-based agreements. In relation to the internet, such formal enactments and agreements have usually appeared after the fact. These are observations which are fleshed out in subsequent chapters. At this initial stage, we may take it as a plausible assertion that the Internet Polity's distinctive existence is imbued in *functioning* collectively. In this area, concepts and norms often struggle to stay abreast of practices and performances.

The global scope of the Internet Polity could be given more nuance by calling upon globalist—or globalization led—conceptions of polity, especially in the field of International Relations. These have usually departed from Kenneth Waltz's (1979) structuralist account of international politics. Waltz proposed models with predominantly nation-states as key units of the international domain, organized according to the relationships of the internal components of each and in relation to each other, in terms of hierarchical or anarchical templates. The departures from this account have variously sought to introduce fluidities within this structure in view of globalizing developments, either to build upon or to reconfigure it. The precedence of the nation-state as foregrounded unit in international politics has thus been questioned and diluted. The part played by other international actors (especially global corporations and transnational agencies) has come to be more judiciously centred. Fine-grained levels of inter-subject or inter-group relations (networks, assemblages) have been foregrounded in the picture. Some of these efforts have discerned the emergence of a 'global polity' accordingly (e.g., Ougaard and Higgott 2002; Neuman and Sending 2010). Their grounding in real-world preconceptions poses some challenges for apprehending an Internet Polity in the way proposed above. In brief, the internet appears as a facility for the functioning of real-world society rather than collectivizing in a way that is both distinctive and woven into real-world society.

However, Olaf Corry's *Constructing a Global Polity* (2013) appears most serviceable for conceptualizing an Internet Polity, both because of its critique of prior formulations (in Chaps. 1–3) and because of its flexible conceptualization of 'polity' and 'global polity' (in Chap. 4). In Corry's formulation: a polity arises 'whenever a set of subjects become oriented towards one or more common governable objects or entities'—'governance-objects' (86):

> A polity thus defined requires a shared understanding that something can and should be governed, but no affinity between actors is necessary (and so a polity is not a society in the 'thick' sense of shared values or norms), nor necessarily an ability for one agent to coerce the others (and so is not a hierarchy). Only a shared discursive frame positing a particular object as governable and in need of governance defines a polity. This definition does not restrict itself to a particular kind of actor so long as there are more than one of them and they are oriented towards the governance of the same object, which in turn could be any kind of object: territorial or social, or a mix of human, technological and natural elements. (87)

When such a governance-object ceases to exist, Corry explains, so does the polity. The constitutive terms of this formulation follow: 'The governance-subjects of a certain polity are the actors for whom a certain governance-object is salient to such a degree that it is co-constitutive of their identities' (90); 'The ordering principle of polities can be called "object-orientation" because actors are structured into a polity through their common identification with a governance-object' (92). Insofar as such a conception of polity has a global scope, or forms a 'global polity', the global 'can best be understood as denoting subjects or objects constituted with reference to the world as one place' (100). These are admirably lucid and consistent formulations and immediately lend themselves to characterizing an Internet Polity. In these terms, the Internet Polity consists of the internet as a 'governance-object', with actors who consider the internet as co-constitutive of their identities and addressable in a shared discursive frame, and who understand the internet as coterminous with the world as one place. That last clause might raise some eyebrows. Nevertheless, we can take it that even localized and narrow investments in the internet tend to be presented 'in terms of a discourse of the world as a singular place of action' (100).

The constitution of the internet as a 'governance-object' occupies Part I of this study. In a couple of chapters there, I argue that its technological formation has been built upon features (protocols, hypertext, and security layering) which gel with how actors regard it. Thus, an 'object-orientation' has formed towards the internet and a sense of social collectivity. The latter builds upon social and political first principles which correspond to the norms with which those technological features were designed. I dub these, respectively, the principles of 'minimal-gradual-mechanical standardization', of 'precedent individuation', and of 'targeted collective regulation'. Together these offer a groundwork for contemplating the Internet Polity as an organized formation. In Part II of this study, I explore the 'discursive frame' through which the object-orientation of the Internet Polity has developed and been articulated—I call this the *Internet Polity discourse*.

Before moving on from the concept of 'polity', let me pause on the related concept of 'ideology'. A study on the Internet Polity is apt to raise questions like: 'does it have an ideological character?'; 'what ideologies play in it'; 'does studying it involve an ideological agenda?'. Such questions are addressed to some degree as the study progresses. Nevertheless, an anticipatory note on this study's approach to ideology seems prudent. Various stages in the development of the internet, beginning from the Cold War period, have been strongly associated with real-world ideologies and political commitments. Liberal capitalist regimes and libertarian enthusiasts have made strong claims through and upon it. At the same time, the internet has evidently proved serviceable to every kind of real-world ideological move and political alignment, including warring and incommensurable ones: revolutionary and democratic socialist, left and right anarchist, moderate and fundamentalist theocratic, conservative and liberal ethnonationalist, etc. The internet is thus understood as a facilitating environment, and sometimes as a catalyst, and at times even as formative for real-world political actions. The phrase 'internet politics' is employed in all those senses at present (e.g., by Chadwick 2006; Chadwick and Howard 2009). This study, however, does not quite focus on the extent to which real-world politics is mediated and modified by the internet. The purpose here is to describe some features of the Internet Polity as such, where the internet offers a scope for organized collectivity and the doings and lives of those therein. Accordingly, an initially stand-offish rather than invested approach to ideology, not immediately imbricated in real-world political positions, is expedient.

Michael Freeden's *Ideologies and Political Theory* (1996), and his subsequent publications, offers a methodology for studying ideologies. This suggested that the various real-world ideologies we live amidst are composed of a finite set of political concepts. Such concepts are signified by weighty norm-bearing words like 'liberty', 'democracy', 'power', 'authority', 'rights', 'equality', 'justice', etc. In signifying political concepts, these words are imbued with a range of contextual, cultural, and intensional (more than intentional) content which gives them their distinctively political orientation. In brief, such words appear as the 'outward forms' of political concepts (Freeden 1996: 49). The political concepts and words signifying them could be considered the building blocks of all ideologies. Some such loaded words and their underpinning concepts are combined and permuted to form one or another ideology.

This is how that works. The words are used according to a linguistic rationale (i.e., in terms of lexical and syntactic rules); at the same time, rationales for connecting political concepts are layered upon the linguistic rationale. Generally, these loaded words are implicitly ambiguous and open to interpretation because the political concepts in question are inevitably contestable. If they are considered carefully, numerous contradictory and unresolvable inferences are possible. However, for social contingencies, where it is necessary to make decisions and act in a coherent and purposeful way, such ambiguity and irresolution is not helpful. This is where ideologies and ideological differences arise. Each ideology adopts a particular sense of the relevant political words and understands the concerned political concepts in one definite and practical way. An ideology thus involves *decontesting* inherently contestable political words and concepts for purposeful application. Moreover, an ideology then links the chosen decontested words and concepts to each other, so as to formulate general principles and concordant systems. The latter offer an ideological basis for responding consistently and coherently to a range of existing and potential contingencies. They come to articulate an ideological worldview. Naturally, within an ideology, the balance and linkages of deconstested words and concepts are constantly modified to enable application to changing circumstances. Thus, decontestation could be considered an ongoing process, which serves to garner consensus among adherents of an ideology.

Ideologies differ from each other by fixing and linking decontested political words and concepts in different ways, to obtain different sets of general principles and concordant systems—that is to say, to extend different ideological worldviews. That could lead to contradictory decisions and actions by different ideological formations for a given contingency. Freeden's argument about the pragmatic and systematized decontestations of political words-concepts involved in forming ideologies offers an analytical framework for differentiating ideologies. By this framework, examining the role of ideologies in any given situation does not involve implicitly subscribing to an ideology or assuming an ideological position. The idea of *decontestation* is the crux of this approach. In Freeden's words:

> A word may be related to many meanings and to changing meanings. Ideologies, however, display precisely the converse features. They aim at cementing the word-concept relationship. By determining the meaning of a concept they can then attach a single meaning to a political term. Ultimately, ideologies are configurations of *decontested* meanings of political concepts. (76)

Freeden conceived of this analytical framework as being principally of academic interest. The framework is not meant to help determine what the appropriate political pathway or preferred ideological approach should be (though he obviously preferred a liberal position). The analytical framework offers tools for examining the political world, not for acting upon it.

I have dwelled upon Freeden's analytical framework not so much to employ it explicitly, but to endorse it in a general way for the purposes of this study. It forms a kind of backdrop for arguments made in subsequent chapters. At any rate, I wish to disavow commitment to or motivation from any one ideology at this opening stage. In subsequent chapters, the ideological investments that have led developers towards certain technologies and appeared in the Internet Polity discourse are naturally discussed. Historical contexts are set out at several points in this study as ideological confrontations, compromises, or accommodations. In Part I, the account of technological features and corresponding social and political first principles cover both contestations and decontestations of words-concepts. In examining relevant catchwords in Part II, such contestations and decontestations are explicitly negotiated. But it is far from clear to me whether these amount to the Internet Polity possessing a distinctive ideological worldview. It is possible that the Internet Polity simply mirrors the play of diverse ideologies in our all-too-real world.

1.2 Nodal Term: Internet

I have been using the term ‘internet’ (with lower-case initial) somewhat loosely so far. Obviously, ‘internet’ is the nodal word for this study: i.e., it is the term in relation to which technical terms, collective principles, popular catchwords, and indeed a cultural vocabulary are elaborated here. To do that systematically, it is useful at this initial stage to register the current senses of this nodal term and to set some rigorous senses for its use in this study.

The *Oxford English Dictionary* (OED 2023) now defines ‘internet’ as a noun and a verb. The dominant noun usage is defined with two senses:

1. Originally (with lower-case initial): a computer network comprising or connecting a number of smaller networks, such as two or more local area networks connected by a shared communications protocol; an internetwork; *spec.* such a network (called *ARPANET*) operated by the United States Department of Defense. In later use (usually **the internet**): the global network comprising a loose confederation of interconnected networks using standardized communication protocols, which facilitates various information and communication systems such as the World Wide Web and email. Also: the resources accessible via this global network, *esp.* the World Wide Web.
2. With *the.* The users of the internet considered collectively; (hence) preferences, characteristics, or attitudes of these users, attributed to the internet itself.

In this general definition, there are already some complexities and slippages. Sense 1 makes a distinction between earlier and later usage that is, obviously, redolent of a historical shift in the technology from confined to global accessibility. Though Sense 1 underlines the lower-case initial, the examples of usage given show that ‘Internet’ with the upper-case initial was more common in that sense. The use of the definite article ‘the’ in Sense 2 was, the examples also show, not unusual in the earlier usage and seems to conflate Sense 1 with Sense 2. The verb senses in the OED involve a distinction between transitive and intransitive usage.

For the purposes of this study, I use the term ‘internet’ with some distinctions that are not clear in the OED definition or other such dictionary definitions.

The current everyday usage of the term ‘internet’ appears to conflate several senses and is often considered switchable with ‘digital’ and ‘online’—I include these in the term ‘internet’ where appropriate. In this everyday form, it refers to:

- a technological structure or equipment (as in, e.g., ‘the internet is not working’, ‘blocking the internet’, ‘my internet is slow’);
- a facility (e.g., ‘use the internet’, ‘search the internet’, ‘buy off the internet’); and
- a collectively shared space or environment (e.g., ‘I am on the internet’, ‘I am online’, ‘my digital life’, ‘their digital footprint’).

That last sense seems close to the OED Sense 2 but is not quite so: that is about users’ attributions, and this is about a perceived collective presence.

Importantly, in everyday usage now, these three senses are conflated, i.e., they usually work inextricably together, often slide into each other or switch from one to the other seamlessly. That is particularly the case where 'internet' is used as a qualifier, as in 'digital business', 'internet services', 'internet banking', and so on. Such usage implicates all three senses, and the communicative context usually determines which is to be foregrounded. Thus, for instance, 'internet banking' could be taken as the technological structure for banking, the facility offered by the internet as a banking outlet, the space in which banking happens (as in 'British banking'). The conflation of the senses of facility and collective space is of particular interest in thinking about the Internet Polity. Arguably, the idea of an organized social formation is grounded in these senses of being somewhere and using something/doing something. To some degree, this feature of the term is analogous to the term 'shop', which could evoke both a space (a building or retail area) and a facility (where things are bought and sold). The verb form of 'internet' ('internetting', 'internetted') is however not quite analogous to the verb form of 'shop' ('shopping'). The former generally involves doing something technical with regard to the technological structure, while the latter has to do with utilizing the facility. My use of the term 'internet' here (with lower-case initial) is generally in this current everyday manner, with three conflated senses which may be distinguished by the contexts in which employed.

The nuances of using a lower-case initial or an upper-case initial call for a pause. The connotations and merits of 'Internet' v 'internet' have been intermittently raised, especially in relation to institutional style guides, since the 1990s (see Long 2004; Martin 2016; Bromwich 2016). Of late, the lower-case initial is increasingly standardized, but for much of the history of the internet both were used in inconsistent ways and generally the upper-case initial was preferred. It was often considered that 'Internet' referred to a specific and well-defined technological structure and was preferred by the technically minded, while 'internet' signified how users utilize and interact with that structure and was preferred by those interested in its social effects. In practice, though, the distinction was unevenly registered, and both lower-case and upper-case initials were employed to both ends. Now that distinction is conflated in the everyday use of 'internet' and this study uses the lower-case spelling, unless in naming a concept or category, as in 'Internet Polity'.

The initial usage of the term 'internetwork' by the developers of ARPANET became the 'internet' in naming the protocol that enabled communication between networks (beginning with the first draft, Cerf et al. 1974, discussed in Chap. 2). In a standardizing and formal vein, as opposed to the everyday senses, the US Federal Networking Council's definition on 24 October 1995 has a noteworthy official and historical weight:

> 'Internet' refers to the global information system that—
>
> (i) is logically linked together by a globally unique address space based on the Internet Protocol (IP) or its subsequent extensions/follow-ons;
> (ii) is able to support communications using the Transmission Control Protocol/Internet Protocol (TCP/IP) suite or its subsequent extensions/follow-ons, and/or other IP-compatible protocols; and
> (iii) provides, uses, or makes accessible, either publicly or privately, high level services layered on the communications and related infrastructure described herein. (FNC 1995)

This definition appeared as the internet was becoming programmatically commercialized and shortly after the World Wide Web was launched in the public domain in 1993. This was, then, a timely definition. In fact, it was as much an announcement as a definition, saying: the internet's 'global' reach is established; consensus on its protocols reached; its functionality for both 'public and private' providers set. I return to this juncture variously in later chapters.

Notably, this definition focused on one dimension of the technology and therefore shaped future usage of the term: it was conceived predominantly at the level of computer programming (protocols). The definition did not allude to material devices and the undergirding infrastructure. It took the material technology as preceding step-by-step and lying alongside the internet by this definition, in the 'related infrastructure'. The programming 'software' which is built upon the material 'hardware' was centred. Accordingly, in discussions of the internet, since then software have tended to dominate public perceptions and the hardware taken for granted. This emphasis in the FNC's 1995 definition began to shift gradually only a decade later (see Chap. 6). For the purposes of this study, I refer to the technological structure captured by such definitions, with that emphasis on programming, as *Internet Technology.*

That the FNC (1995) definition of 'internet' emphasized the software dimension of Internet Technology is understandable. The definition was not offered as an engineering standard but as a public and market standard. In fact, for computing generally, software was what professional and lay users engaged with in a hands-on way, whereas the hardware was received or provided—had a given character and involved much beyond the ken of most users. For Internet Technology particularly, software was the obvious ground on which the Internet Polity gradually formed itself. Even as Internet Technology was emerging in the early 1970s, Theodor H. (Ted) Nelson, one of the progenitors of hypertext systems (on which more in Chap. 3), had complained:

> Among the many odd things that have resulted from the collision of computer people with educators, publishers and others have been the respectful imitation of computer ways by those who didn't quite understand them. [...]
>
> The most dismal of these practices has been the adoption of the term 'software' for any intellectual or artistic property. This wholly loses the distinction [...] between:
>
> - hardware (programmable equipment);
> - software (programmes, detailed plans of operation that the hardware carries out);
> - contents or data (material which is worked on by, moved in or presented by the hardware under control of the software).
>
> In other words, hardware and software together make an environment; data or contents move and appear in that environment. (Nelson 1974: DM5)

From an engineering perspective such as Nelson's, it is difficult to think of hardware and software independently of each other. The two dimensions form a *hardware-software environment*; that the two dimensions are separable is after the fact of this environment. For the general consumer or user, the working of the software subsumes the view, though obviously dependent on the hardware as a backdrop.

The hardware-software environment calls for a separate term from both the ordinary-language 'internet' and the more formal but programme-centred 'Internet

Technology'. However, such a term is not quite consensually available. In some circles, the term 'Cyberspace' has occasionally served as such, especially for those concerned with policies and practices that extend across this environment. Policies for securing the internet against illegal usage obviously need such a term and often employ 'Cyberspace' to situate the hardware-software environment amidst real-world polities. The US Army and Marine Corps (2013) joint policy document *Cyberspace Operations* offers a useful example of this:

> Cyberspace can be described in terms of three layers: physical network, logical network, and cyber-persona. The **physical network** layer of cyberspace is comprised of the geographic component and the physical network components. It is the medium where the data travel. The **logical network** layer consists of those elements of the network that are related to one another in a way that is abstracted from the physical network, i.e., the form or relationships are not tied to an individual, specific path, or node. A simple example is any Web site that is hosted on servers in multiple physical locations where all content can be accessed through a single uniform resource locator. The **cyber-persona** layer represents yet a higher level of abstraction of the logical network in cyberspace; it uses the rules that apply in the logical network layer to develop a digital representation of an individual or entity identity in cyberspace. The cyberpersona layer consists of the people actually on the network. (Executive Summary, v-vi)

Broadly, in this description, the 'physical network' corresponds to hardware, the 'logical network' to software, and the 'cyber-persona layer' situates both in relation to persons in the 'real world'. The environment comprised of all these is dubbed 'Cyberspace'. However, with a broader view of Internet Polity discourse, the term 'Cyberspace' seems too historically loaded to be glibly pinned down thus. Its accruing and shifting connotations after being coined in William Gibson's cyberpunk fiction in the early 1980s are not easily wiped away simply by defining it thus (the career of the term is detailed in Chap. 5).

It is therefore prudent to appoint a different term for this hardware-software environment here. Accordingly, for present purposes, the term *Internet Infrastructure* will be used to refer to the overall technological system of hardware and software that supports and manifests the internet. Internet Technology is included within this. Various hardware components of the Internet Infrastructure are obviously not solely or necessarily for the purpose of operating Internet Technology: for instance, a region's electrical grids or satellite transmission system are as much part of the Internet Infrastructure as are the physical gadgets which offer internet connections and portals.

With the terms 'internet' in everyday usage, 'Internet Technology', and 'Internet Infrastructure' in hand, the groundwork for describing the Internet Polity is laid. Before moving on to that, I turn to a few notes on the general relationship between ordinary-language terms and technical terms. Much hinges on this relationship in delineating the social and political first principles and discourse of the Internet Polity.

1.3 Ordinary Language and Technical Communication

A term that is used in a fuzzy way in ordinary-language exchanges may well be used in a precise and well-defined manner in technical communication (in which I include both natural science and engineering terms). Conversely, terms coined with precise senses for the latter may disperse with looser connotations in the former. Such well-defined technical terms have been appointed mainly to refer to objects and conditions that are understood as being out there in the material world, i.e., which can be observed repeatedly and in the same way. Thus, these terms are used to systematize observations and formulate the principles governing them in a mutually agreed manner by scientists and engineers. In the natural sciences, this is undertaken predominantly for rigorous description and inferring underpinning concepts. Engineering draws upon that natural-science terminology and, further, appoints technical terms to develop applications and affordances that employ the resources of the material world, i.e., tangible products. These endeavours may take the path of redefining existing ordinary-language terms for consistent systematic usage or appointing new terms for that end.

The development of a technical vocabulary for the programming dimension of computer engineering, and especially for Internet Technology, is distinct from the larger area of engineering. For Internet Technology, the resources of the material world and tangible products are not as significant as for engineering in general (which includes the rest of the Internet Infrastructure). In the main, the rationale for technical terms in computer programming derives emphatically from the resources of the social world—that is, the world of information, communications, transactions—and realize intangible products. In appearance, the appointment of this technical vocabulary is much like that of other areas of engineering. It also consists in redefining ordinary-language terms for consistent and well-defined usage or in coining new terms (with a penchant for acronyms and collocates). But that occurs with the resources of the material world put at a remove and those of the social world foregrounded. In fact, the technical vocabulary of computer programming both extrapolates from and intervenes within ordinary-language circuits continuously. It hones the rationales of ordinary-language usage, and terms are defined to sharpen, realize, and actualize their applicatory logic. Concurrently, this technical vocabulary serves to nudge ordinary-language usage itself towards acclimatization with its applicatory logic. The engineering involved in computer programming is inevitably also an engineering of the social world.

What all that comes down to is that the technical vocabulary of computer programming, and especially of Internet Technology, evinces a distinctive self-perpetuating rationale that reflects upon ordinary language. Forming a 'programming language', laying out a 'protocol', developing a 'platform', setting 'domain names', determining a 'policy', etc. in this technical vocabulary is a matter of defining terms in serviceable and precise ways that nevertheless resonate with ordinary-language senses, and then of establishing a functioning order between those terms. Once established, the vocabulary grows with more terms being defined and added to the functioning order of the technology. The growing vocabulary is also itself the driver for the developing scope and reach of the technology. One may say: the development and grounding of Internet Technology is contained in the generation and uptake of its technical vocabulary.

Any foundational text of computer programming gives a clear sense of how this process of building a technical vocabulary is established. Let me pause, for instance, on the most significant foundational text of Internet Technology: the draft Transmission Control Programme (TCP) of December 1974 (Cerf et al. 1974), where the term 'internet' was first employed. The TCP (1974) draft consisted significantly in an ordering of terms, capitalized, and construction of their logical connections—as in the opening passages:

> To provide for unique names at each TCP, we concatenate a NETWORK identifier, and a TCP identifier with a port name to create a SOCKET name which will be unique throughout all networks connected together.
>
> A pair of sockets form a CONNECTION which can be used to carry data in either direction [i.e. full duplex]. The connection is uniquely identified by the <local socket, foreign socket> address pair, and the same local socket can participate in multiple connections to different foreign sockets.
>
> Processes exchange finite length LETTERS as a way of communicating; thus, letter boundaries are significant. However, the length of a letter may be such that it must be broken into FRAGMENTS before it can be transmitted to its destination.

Each capitalized term is both a fixing of a technical definition and a way of establishing a relation to other capitalized terms. These can then, altogether, be visualized as a system of terms and logically manipulated as a system (e.g., by introducing symbolic functions or by presenting graphic maps). This fixing and establishing of terms is done by departing from their ordinary-language senses. At the same time, each capitalized term's defined and established content, which makes them technical terms, nevertheless maintains some consonance with ordinary-language content too. The technical fixing of SOCKET, CONNECTION, LETTERS, FRAGMENTS allows some, however limited, purchase for ordinary-language decoding according to the familiar everyday usage of 'socket', 'connection', 'letters', 'fragments'. Where such everyday terms are laden with material-world denotation (e.g., if 'socket' and 'connection' suggest electrical wiring in one's home), that is given an abstract turn without entirely removing their everyday associations. Possibly, the real-world referents in ordinary-language work as metaphors for their technical content.

Contemplated as a whole, we may say that the relationship between technical-language precision and ordinary-language fuzziness is, at some level, constitutive of how the technical vocabulary of computer programming works. This technical vocabulary is functionally specialized within computer engineering circuits, and at the same time, it allows for an exploitable hint of ordinary-language resonance in wider non-technological or user activities. Arguably, such technical vocabulary studiedly enables some degree of instinctive entry while, at the same time, withholding the underpinning knowledge and control among techies. Bernadette Longo's *Words and Power* (2021) offers the most careful history of the technical vocabulary of computer programming from the 1940s to the 1960s, with reference to glossaries and dictionaries. The detailed account in this shows how the vocabulary emerged through such word-listings: first to facilitate communication between computing specialists across professional and academic contexts, then to standardize professional practices according to applied areas, and finally to institute pedagogic practice for 'computing science' as an academic discipline (especially Longo 2021: Chap. 6). In Chap. 5 of this study, the development of specifically a vocabulary for Internet Polity discourse through dictionaries and glossaries, mediating between technical terms and everyday usage, is discussed.

This study on the Internet Polity is not particularly focused on unpacking technical vocabulary. However, the intricate and peculiar relationship of technical vocabulary and everyday usage is of particular interest here. This study is eventually concerned largely with the everyday usage that enlivens the Internet Polity. The relationship between technical and everyday terms imbues the vocabulary of Internet Polity discourse with a sort of split character. On the one hand, the technical vocabulary articulates how the engineers achieved their objectives. On the other hand, echoes of the technical vocabulary in ordinary-language usage give a sense of what came of the resulting services and applications. In the following Part I, two chapters (Chaps. 2 and 3) give reasonably careful attention to technical terms, not in the spirit of translating them into ordinary language but by mediating between their technical connotations and ordinary-language suggestions. These mediations demonstrate that specific social and political principles were extended from the norms followed in constructing Internet Technology and became grounded in the formation of the Internet Polity. In Part II, three chapters (Chaps. 4 to 6), I concentrate on internet-related catchwords, which also and constantly mediate deliberately between technical and everyday terms. Pondering those give a closer sense of how an Internet Polity discourse emerged and settled as a sphere of everyday interactions and shaped social and political life online and beyond.

1.4 Parts and Chapters

This study has two parts with six chapters after this one.

The main argument of Part I (Chaps. 2 and 3) is that the core features of Internet Technology were developed according to certain norms, depending upon the developers' social circumstances. In collective and habitual usage later, as the Internet Polity was formed, those norms assumed the position of social and political first principles. That means that the Internet Polity's collective practices and arrangements, social structures and commitments, ethical and cultural precepts came to be premised on these principles. This occurred either by trying to subscribe to all of them or, where they work against the grain of each other, trying to find a functional balance or making pragmatic compromises. Three features are discussed in two chapters: internet protocols, hypertext systems, and security controls. As noted earlier, the corresponding first principles that came to be assumed through application are dubbed here as: 'minimal-gradual-mechanical standardization', 'precedent individuation', and 'targeted collective regulation'. Part I is devoted to tracking the development of these technological features and concordantly elucidating what these principles are and how they evolved.

By way of honing the method followed in Part I, Chap. 2 opens by making a distinction between *why-do-it* and *how-to-do-it* questions for analysing technological developments. In relation to Internet Technology, *why-do-it* questions are foregrounded here; *how-to-do-it* solutions are discussed insofar as they illuminate *why-do-it* considerations. The chapter then moves on to a brief overview and perspective of the Cold War context in which Internet Technology initially developed. The bulk of the chapter addresses the *why-do-it* and therefore *how-to-do-it* moves involved in early computer networking and internetworking. Particular attention is given to steps in the development of the TCP/IP suite, mainly covering a period from the 1960s to the 1980s. The principle of minimal-gradual-mechanical standardization is inferred from those moves or, more precisely, is found to be implicit in those moves.

The Cold War context outlined in Chap. 2 is complicated in Chap. 3 by a brief account of civil rights and anti-war movements over the same period, with their bearing upon computing circles in view. This chapter then turns to the development of hypertext systems from a *why-do-it* perspective, with conditional attention to various *how-to-do-it* solutions. First, the concept of hypertext is outlined in relation to *information* and *knowledge* management, and the principle of precedent individuation is explained. Then phases in the development of hypertext systems are considered. The earlier concepts and attempts are outlined. With those early aspirations in mind, the features of the dominant system that emerged, the World Wide Web (WWW), are outlined. The discussion of hypertext systems closes with an account of the developers' introductions to WWW and anticipations of a 'semantic Web'. The chapter then takes up security controls as a feature in Internet Technology. It is averred that these were not quite conceived and designed in the way protocols and hypertext systems were but came to be instilled through gradual and pragmatic interventions. Changing philosophies of security are taken on board, and the early development of security controls that came to be integrated with Internet Technology recalled. The principle of targeted collective regulation is clarified in the process.

Part II (Chaps. 4 to 6) explores the linguistic dimensions of the discourse that materialized the Internet Polity, from the late 1980s onwards. It is argued that this distinctive discourse, with an accruing and shifting vocabulary, spread quickly when internet services were privatized in the 1990s. The three principles shaping Internet Technology were variously negotiated as this discourse developed, and they were grounded as social and political first principles for the Internet Polity. Methodologically, as stated earlier, the arguments here are traced via a number of catchwords, in terms of their contexts, careers, and interlinks. The three chapters of Part II largely focus on the development and consolidation of the Internet Polity discourse (roughly up to 2010), with the final chapter pushing towards—or rather, opening up—a path for investigating the post-formation Internet Polity in the twenty-first century.

Notes on the relationship between the two parts of this study, and on the concept of catchwords, introduce Chap. 4. This is followed by an outline of the 1990s historical context in which the internet was made available to large-scale uptake. A sketchy account of global regime-changes in favour of privatization leads into a summary of the strategies that led to the commercialization of Internet Technology. Through the 1990s, perceptions of the internet were powerfully shaped by two catchwords that are discussed in the latter part of Chap. 4. 'Information superhighway' presented a top-down perspective of the internet. It referred principally to the internet as a policy and strategy area of the real-world polity represented by the USA government and relevant corporations. 'Cyberspace' offered a kind of bottom-up perspective for internet developers and users. The term evoked a new world to take into possession, which could be designed and structured in original and unprecedented ways. The career of the two catchwords through that decade is tracked here, and the corresponding implications for the Internet Polity.

Taking a wider view, but still with a predominant focus on the 1990s, Chap. 5 describes how a distinctive vocabulary for Internet Polity discourse developed and how cultural significance was attributed to collective activities on the internet. A brief discussion of the nodal term's usage—of 'internet', and coterminously words with 'e' and 'digital' prefixes—sets up the chapter. An account of computing and internet dictionaries and glossaries fleshes out the vocabulary that consolidated Internet Polity discourse. Several phases of dictionary making are covered: of computing terms for professionals, of computing terms for lay users, of hacker slang/jargon/techspeak, of internet terms, of internet slang (and relatedly cyberlexicography). Turning next to attributions of cultural collectivity via Internet Technology, the overlaps and distinction between 'technoculture', 'cyberculture', and 'digital culture' are unpacked. After pausing on the rise of popular 'online communities' and academic 'internet studies', a final section of Chap. 5 discusses the normative shifts that took place around the term 'hacker'.

Moving to the post-2000 period, Chap. 6 begins by reflecting upon the complexities of the internet itself becoming the salient repository of sources, medium of investigation, and often the object in historicist accounts. Debates on technological determinism are pondered here. As events, 9/11 and the 2000 dot-com crash are pegged as turning points. A broad argument is proposed about the condition of the Internet Polity thereafter. It is argued that it became *contained* in two moves during the 2000s, with developments in Internet Infrastructure after the dot-com crash and, from around 2010, the commodification of data. This containment involved, first, a space of the internet opening beyond the erstwhile Internet Technology. This space incorporated data exchanges between 'smart' objects, unsupervised systems, and machine-learning capacities. Second, much of the Internet Polity discourse and collective life became concentrated in very large platforms, which have global reach, local penetration, and data-management standards. This move facilitated the burgeoning data market and fed into the first move. The two moves are outlined by focusing on two sets of catchwords. The first is addressed via the connotations of 'Internet of Things' and 'smart' objects, and the second by pausing on 'social networking sites' or 'social media platforms'. This chapter, and the study, concludes by briefly reconsidering the formative social political first principles of the Internet Polity.

References

Aristotle (1932) Politics (trans: Rackham H). William Heinemann and Harvard University Press, London and Cambridge MA

Bates CA Jr (2014) The centrality of *Politeia* for Aristotle's *Politics*: Aristotle's continuing significance for social and political science. Social Sci Inf 53(1):139–159. https://doi.org/10.1177/0539018413510364

Bromwich JE (2016) Bulletin! The 'internet' is about to get smaller. New York Times, 24 May. https://www.nytimes.com/2016/05/25/business/media/internet-to-be-lowercase-in-new-york-times-and-associated-press.html

Cerf V, Dalal Y, Sunshine C (1974) RFC 675: specification of internet transmission control programme. Network Working Group. https://datatracker.ietf.org/doc/html/rfc675

Chadwick A (2006) Internet politics: states, citizens, and new communication technologies. Oxford University Press, Oxford

Chadwick A, Howard PN (eds) (2009) Routledge handbook of internet politics. Routledge, Abingdon

Cherry KM (2009) The problem of polity: political participation and Aristotle's best regime. J Politics 71(4):1406–1421. https://doi.org/10.1017/s002238160999003x

Corry O (2013) Constructing a global polity: theory, discourse and governance. Palgrave Macmillan, Basingstoke

Deibert RJ (2020) Reset: reclaiming the internet for civil society. September, Tewkesbury

Dietz MG (2012) Polis and empire: Aristotle's politics. Am Polit Sci Rev 106(2):275–293. https://doi.org/10.1017/S0003055412000184

van Dijck J, Poell T, de Waal M (2018) The platform society: public values in a connective world. Oxford University Press, Oxford

FNC (Federal Networking Council, US) (1995) FNC resolution: definition of internet. 24 Oct. https://www.nitrd.gov/historical/fnc/internet_res.pdf

Freeden M (1996) Ideologies and political theory: a conceptual approach. Clarendon, Oxford

Giacomello G (2005) National governments and control of the internet: a digital challenge. Routledge, Abingdon

Lehdonvirta V (2022) Cloud empires: how digital platforms are overtaking the state and how we can regain control. MIT Press, Cambridge MA

Long T (2004) It's just the "internet" now. Wired, 16 Aug. https://www.wired.com/2004/08/its-just-the-internet-now/

Longo B (2021) Words and power: computers, language, and U.S. cold war values. Springer, Cham

Martin KC (2016) Should you capitalize the word Internet? Oxford Dictionaries Blog, 5 April. https://web.archive.org/web/20190401111733/https://blog.oxforddictionaries.com/2016/04/05/should-you-capitalize-internet/

Mueller ML (2010) Networks and states: the global politics of internet governance. MIT Press, Cambridge MA

Mueller ML (2017) Will the internet fragment? Sovereignty, globalization and cyberspace. Polity, Cambridge

Muldoon J (2022) Platform socialism: how to reclaim our digital future from Big Tech. Pluto, London

Nelson TH (1974) Computer Lib/dream machines: new freedoms through computer screens—a minority report. Online at https://archive.org/details/computer-lib-dream-machines

Neuman IB, Sending OJ (2010) Governing the global polity: practice, mentality, rationality. The University of Michigan Press, Ann Arbor MI
O'Hara K, Hall W (2021) Four internets: data, geopolitics, and the governance of cyberspace. Oxford University Press, Oxford
Ougaard M, Higgott R (eds) (2002) Towards a global polity. Routledge, London
OED (Oxford English Dictionary) online (2023). https://www.oed.com/
Srnicek N (2017) Platform capitalism. Polity, Cambridge
Terranova T (2022) After the internet: digital networks between capital and the common. Semiotext(e), South Pasadena CA
US Army and Marine Corps (2013) Cyberspace operations. Joint Publication 3-12(R), 5 Feb. https://irp.fas.org/doddir/dod/jp3_12r.pdf
Waltz KN (1979) Theory of international politics. Addison-Wesley, Reading MA
Wike R, Silver L, Fetterolf J, Huang C, Austin S, Clancy L, Gubbala S (2022) Social media seen as mostly good for democracy across many nations, but U.S. is a major outlier. Pew Research Centre, 6 Dec. https://www.pewresearch.org/global/2022/12/06/social-media-seen-as-mostly-good-for-democracy-across-many-nations-but-u-s-is-a-major-outlier/
Zittrain J (2008) The future of the internet and how to stop it. Yale University Press, New Haven CT

Part I
Collective Principles in Internet Technology

Chapter 2
Internet Protocols and Minimal-Gradual-Mechanical Standardization

Abstract To clarify the method followed in Part I, this chapter opens by making a distinction between *why-do-it* and *how-to-do-it* questions for analysing technological developments. In relation to Internet Technology, *why-do-it* questions are foregrounded here; *how-to-do-it* solutions are discussed insofar as they illuminate *why-do-it* considerations. The chapter then moves on to a brief overview of the Cold War context in which Internet Technology initially developed. The bulk of the chapter addresses the *why-do-it* and therefore *how-to-do-it* moves involved in early computer networking and internetworking. Particular attention is given to steps in the development of the TCP/IP suite, mainly covering a period from the 1960s to the 1980s. The norm of minimal-gradual-mechanical standardization is inferred from those moves or, more precisely, is found to be implicit in those moves. The implications of its being functionally taken as a first principle for the emerging Internet Polity in due course are considered.

2.1 How-to-do-it and Why-do-it

My argument in this and the next chapters (Part I) is that, from the 1960s to the 1990s, the developers of Internet Technology followed certain social and political norms through the various stages of constructing it. They adhered to these norms loosely and yet consistently due to their shared social circumstances and convictions. These were not programmatically enjoined or explicitly formulated as hard-and-fast rules. Indeed, through consecutive stages, the various developers often understood and employed them with different emphases. That these norms were effectively grounded in Internet Technology meant that working with and on the internet entailed conforming with them. This was not by their being enforced but by gradual habituation and as a matter of convenience. Consequently, these norms have assumed the character of social and political first principles for the organized collectivity that has developed on the internet, i.e., the Internet Polity. As first principles, these are more implicit than explicit, and they appear now to be less context-dependant and more context-defining. They have a pragmatic rather than conceptual thrust. These

S. Gupta, *Collective Principles and the Formation of the Internet*, Springer Series on Cultural Computing, https://doi.org/10.1007/978-3-031-90470-7_2

are the first principles on which the Internet Polity's organization and discourse are premised; they are embedded in Internet Technology and constitutive of the Internet Polity. They need not be regarded as cohering into a distinct political ideology. In terms of Freeden's (1996) understanding of ideology (discussed in Chap. 1), their underpinning work does not necessitate the decontestation of words-concepts such that any existing ideological formation is actively opposed or challenged. Rather, they work to tacitly and inevitably structure the many ideological investments that are played out on the internet. They operate as an unavoidable and seemingly neutral substrate which accommodates all sorts of ideological investments amidst the Internet Polity—though, of course, claims of neutrality are almost always suspect.

In Part I, I lay out these first principles of the Internet Polity by considering the development of the main components of Internet Technology: the protocols, hypertext system, and security controls. The argument here is about Internet Technology and does not extend to the wider area of Internet Infrastructure. In tracing the first principles that were grounded in the development of Internet Technology, I employ a reasonably consistent mode of argument. In short, I focus on the *how-to-do-it* questions that the developers resolved only insofar as they implicate *why-do-it* considerations—where *doing-it* refers to conceptualizing, constructing, instituting, and maintaining Internet Technology. *How-to-do-it* questions are for reaching workable solutions for given tasks, while *why-do-it* questions concern the causes and consequences preceding and proceeding from those tasks. *Why-do-it* considerations may be finessed and modified as *how-to-do-it* steps are clarified. Sometimes, the scope of *why-do-it* consequences become wider or finds unexpected tangents as *how-to-do-it* problems are resolved.

For Internet Technology, particular *how-to-do-it* questions (such as, how to route messages? how to name domains?) have definite answers, which are effectively the realization of technological solutions. The definite answers lead to the (usually short-term) closure of implementing a solution, though the direction of that solution could be built upon by actively posing further *how-to-do-it* questions. *Why-do-it* questions do not necessarily have definite answers. Such questions (e.g., why route messages? why name domains?) may be answered variously and lead to further and wider considerations.

In general, *why*-questions are apt to lead seamlessly into further *why*-questions, potentially in lengthening chains (Feynman's [1983] witty demonstration of this might be recalled). Let me stress though that in my emphasis on *why-do-it* as a form of questioning, I am not looking to the rationales of *why*-questions generally, which have exercised philosophers often (influentially Bromberger 1992, recently Skow 2016). Much more modestly, the thrust of *how-to-do-it* and *why-do-it* here is on the *do-it*. The *do-it* gives the limiting context for such questions here, and that context is Internet Technology. In the previous chapter, I argued that although an engineering pursuit, Internet Technology draws more upon social than material resources. Resolutions to *how-to-do-it* questions in this context involve, so to speak, crafting the facility or affordance that is the internet with those resources purposively harnessed and systematized—there is a functional end, not a searching scope. *Why-do-it* questions in this context lead into searching exploration of those harnessed and systemized social resources. They push towards delving the social import of Internet Technology, i.e., of both the resources utilized and the resolutions achieved. The argument followed in this and the next chapter moves back and forth between *how-to-do-it* and *why-do-it* considerations, with a particular interest in the latter and delineating the former only to the extent needed for the latter to be articulated. The norms that guided the developers of Internet Technology and became ensconced as first principles for the Internet Polity are intricately woven with the *why-do-it* considerations.

In some respects, the emphasis on *why-do-it* as a social process enjoins a historicist approach to the Internet Polity for this Part. The many valuable histories of the internet, which I draw upon opportunistically as the argument proceeds, have generally and very understandably given primary attention to the impressive *how-to-do-it* aspect of Internet Technology. These have usually taken the *why-do-it* considerations as before-the-fact causes and after-the-fact consequences. The historicist emphasis of this argument, however, is on those first principles being grounded within Internet Technology, and thereby providing a structural basis for the collective form of the Internet Polity. The familiar metaphors to describe this structural basis are of the internet as an 'environment' or as having an 'architecture'.

Various strands in the *why-do-it* to *how-to-do-it* developments of computer programming and the pre-Internet Infrastructure, in the decades immediately before and following the Second World War (detailed in Longo 2021 and Akera 2007), both prepared the ground for and became constitutive elements of Internet Technology. Here I do not dwell on that prior groundwork. I begin by focusing on the core content of networking and Internet Technology from the 1960s and onwards. Of primary interest in this chapter are the *why-do-it* assumptions at the heart of Internet Technology, the digital networking mechanisms and the initially distinct Transmission Control Protocol (TCP) and Internet Protocol (IP) suite. Arguably, that is where the main thrust of a social and political first principle of the Internet Polity was rooted. The *why-do-it* considerations underpinning hypertext systems and security controls are addressed in the next chapter, covering a period which precedes and overlaps with the period discussed in this. I argue that each of these aspects of Internet Technology accordingly make available specific first principles of the Internet Polity. Together these principles may appear to work for contrary or complementary ends, but they do not negate each other at any point. Rather, they function conjointly so that all the principles stay active and are mutually negotiated. Very briefly, the following are the principles in question: the TCP/IP suite grounds a principle of *minimal-gradual-mechanical standardization*; hypertext builds upon a principle of *precedent individuation*; and security controls embed *targeted collective regulation*. Together, these are concretized in the organization of the Internet Polity and are variously refracted in the space and facility that is the internet.

Before taking up networking and the TCP/IP suite in this chapter, a few reflections on the Cold War context from which they emerged seem expedient. Histories of Internet Technology have routinely presented the Cold War as its formative social context. The social and political principles grounded in Internet Technology and structuring the Internet Polity now seem rather distant from that formative context.

And yet, that is the context which formed the developers' circumstances and convictions. No doubt those developers' own ideological stakes and investments can be traced in a linked-up fashion. That is, however, not the path taken here. What follows is a sketchy and generalized account of some political facets of the Cold War period which may help to frame the *how-to-do-it* and *why-do-it* considerations in question. These are sketchy framing observations, more suggestive for the argument that follows than directly linked. More such sketchy observations on the Cold War juncture, complicating those in this chapter, appear in the next chapter.

In this chapter, sections on networking mechanisms and the TCP/IP suite follow immediately after this brief pause on the Cold War as social context.

2.2 The Cold War?

The official development of networking and internetworking was centred in the USA and Western Europe over the later Cold War period. It was undertaken predominantly with public monies and through public institutions, both military and academic. As a project funded by and conceived initially in the US Defense Advanced Research Projects Agency (DARPA) in the 1960s, it would be natural to expect that some clear Cold War military objective underpinned it.

A straightforward connection between Cold War strategy and the development of networking and Internet Technology was taken as received knowledge in the early 1990s, putatively to ensure the resilience or 'survivability' of communications in the event of a nuclear attack (e.g., Rheingold 1994: 71, 74). The impetus of 'survivability' played an obvious part in, especially, Paul Baran's contribution to designing packet-switching. The Cold War impetus was noted in Hafner and Lyon's (1996: Chap. 1) history of the internet, amidst a short picture of the Cold War setup for computing research. However, the popular view taken later has been that Cold War military objectives and strategies had a limited role in the formation of Internet Technology, and certainly not a structuring role. Looking back to Robert Taylor's directorship of ARPA's Information Processing Techniques Office in the critical period from 1965 to 1969, another historian of the internet John Naughton (1999) observed:

> Years later the myth spread that what drove ARPA to build the world's first computer network was the desire to provide a communications system that could survive a nuclear attack on the United States. The record suggests otherwise: Bob Taylor simply wanted to make the taxpayer's dollar go further. (Naughton 1999, 85)

In a popular vein, *The New Hacker's Dictionary* (Raymond 1996) announced that any military objective in ARPANET 'is a myth'; it 'was conceived from the start as a way to get most economical use out of then-scarce large-computer resources'.

Despite those quick dismissals of Cold War imperatives, steps towards Internet Technology are aptly understood as structured by Cold War research investments by the US military establishment. A few years before histories of the internet started appearing, Stuart Leslie (1993) analysed military sponsorship of university research across the applied sciences and technology through this period. These investments determined research priorities and targeted specific institutions (Leslie focused on MIT and Stanford). Military investments effectively superseded those made by industries, which universities had depended upon after the Second World War. Leslie's study detailed the resulting transformations in university-based research as a gradual and unmistakable creep of militarization rather than as a straightforward imposition of military objectives:

> Everyone recognized that the postwar university had changed dramatically, and not necessarily for the better. Sociologist Robert Nisbet, along with many other conservatives, blamed the federal government for creating what he called the 'higher capitalism,' the system of contracts and project grants that seemed to have undermined the traditional structure and values of the university. What Nisbet and others did not fully recognize was how the increasing predominance of one patron, the military, was indelibly imprinting academic (and industrial) science with a distinct set of priorities, and how those new priorities would in turn set the future direction for much of American science. (Leslie 1993, 8)

Leslie's study explored a broad spectrum of science and technology research, but not computing; relatedly, Jessica Wang (1999) later investigated the Cold War legislative and policy moves that moulded such research.

With particular attention to computing, the most detailed account of military investments in and contracts for research came from Arthur Norberg and Judy O'Neill (1996) shortly after Leslie's study. This covered the development of most steps in Internet Technology and Internet Infrastructure under the aegis of the Defense Department. The impetus for such research from the early 1960s was, they observed, a utilitarian one: i.e., large-scale information management for 'command-and-control' purposes. They explained the phrase thus:

> *Command and control* denotes a set of activities associated, in military contexts, with rapidly changing environments. These activities include the collection of data about the environment, planning for options, decision making, and dissemination of decisions. Increasing the amount of strategic information that could be controlled would improve the command decisions needed in a rapidly changing environment; and computer technology had the potential for controlling greater amounts of information and presenting it in effective ways to aid decision making. The military services regarded computers as important components of modern warfare. (Norberg and O'Neill 1996, 9)

The use of networking (especially ARPANET) was shown to have followed a strategy for integrating different strands of military-sponsored research, which gradually focused on experimental application in 'testbeds' (269–271). These command-and-control information resources were used in warfare, notably the Vietnam War. Paul Edwards' (1996) study of the technological and cultural developments around computing delved that wartime use to some extent—more on this in the next chapter. Edwards also pointed to the utilitarian military approach:

> [C]omputers can automate and accelerate important military tasks. The speed and complexity of high-technology warfare have generated control, communications, and information analysis demands that seem to defy the capacities of unassisted human beings. (Edwards 1996, 65)

However, beyond this narrow military focus, he found complex ideological interests at work, of considerably wider import. These interests converged, Edwards argued, on propagating a 'closed world' perspective, where every social observation came to be interpreted in narrow ways to produce a distinctive and persistent Cold War capitalist cultural discourse. Computing entered the cultural imaginary, he maintained, to normalize and propagandize the militaristic 'closed world' outlook in the USA. Insofar as historicizing the internet itself went, soon after Janet Abbate (1999) presented a careful account of how Cold War military strategies undergirded both ARPANET and the internet. Her account focused on the norms that went into the technological design of networking and internetworking, i.e., 'military values, such as survivability, flexibility, and high performance, over commercial goals, such as low cost, simplicity, or consumer appeal' (2).

Informative as such studies of the Cold War context of computing and Internet Technology are, let me propose a somewhat different approach to lead into my argument below. To grasp why the Cold War context may have planted *general* social and political first principles through Internet Technology calls for a broader sense of that formative period—one that is less single-mindedly centred on military strategies and mores. The military emphasis gives a straightforwardly confrontational cast to the ideological and geopolitical Cold War front. With that military emphasis, the social formations along that front—USA and Western Europe v. USSR and Eastern Europe—are considered segregated from and uncooperative towards each other, though not involved in open hostilities. To be precise, the military perspective allows that there were constantly simmering or open hostilities at the peripheries (Latin America, Middle East and South-East Asia, Africa), always tending to spill into the centred frontline, but nevertheless not quite doing so. Those peripheries were the proxy 'hot' zones for the centred Cold War alignments. The 'hot' zones kept the Cold War front on the cusp of barely contained crises which both reified and threatened ruptures in the 'Iron Curtain'. There were also, of course, numerous fissures within each alignment: diplomatic rows and dissenting eruptions which threatened to 'boil over' into regime change or 'freeze' diplomatic relations. Nevertheless, the centred front remained 'coldly' separated, desisting from penetrating into each other. Overarching political-military histories of the period (such as Gaddis 2005; Westad 2007; Black 2015; Fink 2022) have generally concretized those confrontational metaphors and metonyms—Cold War, iron curtain (wall), *détente* and crisis, freeze and boil—while conveying the immense complexity of the machinations and their global scale. However, for the modest purposes of contextualizing general principles in the emergence of Internet Technology, perhaps a more micro-historical or everyday sense of the period is needed.

Histories of and sources from areas around and beyond military strategies present a nuanced picture of the Cold War. Such areas include trade (e.g., Jackson 2001; Cain 2013), media reportage (e.g., Fainberg 2021; Lovejoy and Pajala 2022), cultural activities (e.g., Richmond 2010), academia (e.g., Tsvetkova 2021), tourism (e.g., Pedersen and Noack 2019). This nuanced picture is not simply of two ideological alignments segregated from each other in a constant state of confrontational readiness. Rather, it is a picture of two alignments which work with embargos and exceptional agreements, restrictions and permissions, obstructions and allowances, sealed borders with selective gateways, painful mutual awareness, and carefully graded remoteness. Diplomatic missions and news reporters were maintained on both sides. Some degree of cultural and academic exchange and cooperation was possible amidst many degrees of carefully policed separation. While most were unable to cross the borders between the alignments at will, there were allowances for some to do so for business, work, or even leisure, and those allowances were not confined to the governing elites and their agents. Mutual suspicion and watchfulness about each other were bolstered by surveillance within both alignments; at the same time, a kind of desire for the other, cross currents of curiosity and influences were variously manifested. Overall, the Cold War around its centred boundaries could be regarded as a game designed for both sides to maintain (or secure) their integrity while each side tries to not only get an advantage over the other but also to perform any advantage it has for the other.

If considered as a structure of communications, rules, or conventions, the Cold War game extended distinctive kinds of cooperative exchanges across both alignments and also enabled competitive exchanges between them. The latter meant that the game was supported by carefully controlled mechanisms of mutual support and understanding, e.g., in terms of the availability of research and analyses, translations and exchanges, reportage. Only with those was it possible for both sides to try and obtain an advantage over and perform that advantage to the other, even in the well routinized hostile or confrontational tenor. The global theatre of the Cold War could be thought of as largely consisting in performances of opposed sides which are not far off from the performances of ruling and opposition parties in a parliament, though with much larger stakes. In various ways, the concepts underpinning Internet Technology seemed to concretize the rules of the game that structured Cold War communication. They structured a mutually sustained balance of both enabling cooperation within an alignment and enabling competition between alignments. Paul Baran, credited as one of the inventors of packet-switching, was in fact decidedly working for 'survivable' communications in the event of a nuclear attack. For his work, that Cold War military objective was a direct impetus. However, Baran's sense of the Cold War was obviously cognizant of the rules of the game outlined here, and he understood his contribution to networking accordingly. As he observed in an interview:

> Not only would the US be safer with a survivable command and control system, the US would be even safer if the USSR also had a survivable command and control system as well! There was never any desire for classification of this work. Classification tended to be limited to analysis of vulnerabilities; how many sites would be damaged, what our assumptions were of the other guy's capabilities versus our capabilities. They were about the only things that ever got classified. (Quoted in Naughton 1999: 105–106)

The point we can take away from this is not that there was extraordinary freedom of disclosure, but rather that there was a clear distinction between what needed to be and what did not need to be classified. The kind of 'survivable' communications methods that led to networking and the TCP/IP suite did not need classification; information about one side's material strengths and weaknesses did. The former were considered within the area of the rules of the Cold War game that both sides should have; the latter were in areas which actuated the possibility of one side getting an advantage over the other, which involved actually playing the Cold War game. Having said that, it is worth noting that Baran's views on what was or was not classified should be read with circumspection. Classified research became a sensitive political issue by the late 1960s, of which more in the next chapter.

The rationale of what I have been calling the Cold War game, which makes good sense as a context for developing Internet Technology, is conceptually not far from commercial rationales. It is a matter of shifting from two alignments trying to obtain and demonstrate an advantage over each other to multiple alignments doing so simultaneously. The modes of demonstrating an advantage involve different measures: for the bipolar ideological context, in terms of weapons capabilities, territorial and outer space control, economic or cultural superiority; and, for the multipolar commercial context, in terms of stock value, quality and quantity of production, market share. The pertinent regulatory and contractual regimes are obviously of different orders. Nevertheless, the rationale of cooperation and competition slides fairly smoothly from the bipolar Cold War to multipolar business activity. In fact, this overlapping rationale has been so obvious that Internet Technology, developed accordingly, is sometimes regarded as the most successful 'dual-use' technology—that is, simultaneously for military and commercial advantage (e.g., Stowsky 2003: 21).

A further consequence of this way of viewing the Cold War context is self-evident. The rationale of Internet Technology, as argued above, seemed consistent with the rules of the Cold War game, so that its development was not particularly covert (as Baran, among others, noted). However, that rationale also effectively and eventually gave one side of the Cold War a distinct advantage, especially *after* the Cold War. Internet Technology was developed primarily in the possession of the USA and Western Europe; in fact, it failed to be developed in the Soviet Union and the Eastern Block (see Peters 2016). The commercial exploitability of Internet Technology was inherent in the capitalist economic arrangements of the former and not so in the socialist state-controlled and planned economic arrangements of the latter. Eventually Internet Technology seemed to offer a decided advantage for capitalist over socialist arrangements, not so much in Cold War competition as by post-Cold War 'normalization'. Internet Technology may not have helped win the Cold War for capitalism, but it did serve to consolidate post-Cold War capitalism.

2.3 Networking and the TCP/IP Suite

With the Cold War game in mind, it is instructive to note the *why-do-it* indications amidst the *how-to-do-it* instructions in early documents tracking developments from networking to internetworking.

2.3.1 Networking

As an initial position, for computer networking, the situation that needed to be addressed could be put as follows. A great deal of information I is stored and processed for making inferences to advance knowledge in a computer C. At a given time, a computer C_1 stores and processes information I_1, computer C_2 does that with information I_2, and so on. Some aspects of I_1 are relevant to I_2 (and each of those to I_3, I_4, I_5 in respectively C_3, C_4, C_5 and so on); it is likely that if I_1 and I_2 can be pooled, both I_1 and I_2 can inform each other and lead to stronger inferences. That was the key *why-do-it* push, which leads to the key *how-to-do-it* consideration: how to make I_1 in C_1 and I_2 in C_2 available to each other so that advance of knowledge is facilitated? Moreover, how to extend that facility so that any set of I_n in any C_n can become mutually available to each other and may, further, combine to process inferences on scale and at speed? This key *why-do-it* push articulates an ideological principle: *knowledge advances if information is pooled and worked on cooperatively or collectively*. This might sound obvious but let me put some caveats around it.

First, if the *why-do-it* push is seen thus, it is taken for granted that advancing knowledge is a primary objective of networking. That is a view that scholars and educators are likely to hold, but others might, for instance, hold commerce or entertainment as the primary objectives of networking. Indeed, such a view was to have a decisive effect on the development of the internet later, reorienting Internet Technology in various ways. This knowledge-based approach to *why-do-it* was perfectly understandable for the social class of those developers attending to the *how-to-do-it* challenges—all from a highly educated, technically adept, professional stratum. A different perspective for that stage might be that the key *why-do-it* push was: *knowledge is best conserved if all information and processes are accessible in different and distributed locales*. That was the basis of Baran's bid to increase the 'survivability' of information in the event of a nuclear attack.

Second, it has not always been regarded as self-evident that pooling and cooperation necessarily advance knowledge. This is in fact a modern conception of knowledge, especially centred in the applied sciences. Conventional approaches had often focused on the synthesis of information in individuals as the key to advancing knowledge. Of course, knowledge was always regarded as accruing—growing additively—but the business of advancing it depended on individual syntheses. This conventional idea has had a powerful impetus in the humanities and in mathematics.

My laborious way of pausing on these *why-do-it* principles underlines the extent to which they are choices rather than inevitable conditions.

The *how-to-do-it* challenges that followed from this key *why-do-it* push involved three issues. (1) How might engineering such collective availability of information stored in computers bear upon the content of that information? (2) How can this be achieved given that computers have variations in their capacities and specifications (the hardware)? (3) How can this be engineered given that the information is held and processed through different programming languages and operating systems (the software)?

In the most straightforward way, each of these issues argued for introducing common standards to facilitate connectivity. In fact, standardization is the key to networking and internetworking, but not in a straightforward way. Most obviously, standardization could have meant mandating restrictions on the information content and processing choices made available: e.g., appointing a standard vocabulary and syntax for information storage, fixing limits to the intent for which information is processed, putting content restrictions on storage and retrieval. Similarly, this could have gone in the direction of mandating hardware and software for networking purposes and decreeing a timetable for compliance. Such rigid standardization practices could be regarded as purposive pathways for developing connectivity under a centralized authority. The technology was developed, however, in terms of a deliberately flexible and hesitant subscription to standardization. The leading ideas were that such connectivity must be achieved without bearing upon the content of the information and processing choices and with minimum disturbance of the existing integrity of the hardware and software in use—and certainly without requiring large-scale or immediate replacements. Standardization should take place by consensual and convenient adoption, as a preferred choice, rather than by mandating. Moreover, it was decided that any standardization achieved incrementally should not need to be policed and enforced in a continuous way. It should preferably be self-regulating.

Achieving connectivity with these resolutions became the *how-to-do-it* challenge. In other words, the principle that guided the technological steps seemed determined to keep standardization minimal, slow, adoptive, and unpoliced insofar as possible. Emphatic imposition of standards would be deferred or held off; the scope of what is standardized would be narrow; standards would be enabled without modifying the existing basis of the infrastructure, and without being checked and ensured by some ruling authority. Instead of conceiving of standardization as applied to a restricted domain of collective usage, here standardization was conceived from its inception as gradually enabling a continuous expansion towards all possible domains of usage. In this *how-to-do-it* approach, then, the *why-do-it* reasoning could be put as follows: *in a network, enforced centralized standardization is likely to have a limited scope and unpredictable effects whereas adoption-by-choice is likely to have a wider scope and enabling effect*. Once adopted, standards would then simply be maintained by design rather than by auditing. Potentially, networking should be universally extendable and not confined to or at the behest of select groups, authorities, and purposes. Let me dub this a principle of *minimal-gradual-mechanical standardization.*

That developers of computer networking and Internet Technology subscribed to the principle of minimal-gradual-mechanical standardization was usually evident in the *how-to-do-it* methods they employed. They rarely stated it explicitly. In a pragmatic spirit, justifications for implicitly abiding by the principle mostly consisted in cost-effectiveness and expediency, which were constant refrains in *how-to-do-it* proposals. One of the rare statements of the principle appeared in the influential paper 'Towards a Cooperative Network of Time-Shared Computers' by Thomas Marrill and Lawrence Roberts (1966). This was shortly after they conducted the first experiment in linking two computers, the MIT Lincoln Labs TX-2 computer in Lexington MA to

System Development Corporation's Q32 computer in Santa Monica CA, in October 1965. For any message protocol for connectivity in a network, they felt:

> If a protocol is adhered to between two computers in the network, say A and B, it is not absolutely necessary that the same protocol be established between C and D, nor even between A and D. Since the motivation for the network is to overcome the problems of computer incompatibility without enforcing standardization, it would not do to require adherence to a standard protocol as a prerequisite of membership in the network. Instead, the network should be designed for maximum flexibility. If a protocol which is good enough to be put forward as a standard is designed, adherence to this standard should be encouraged but not required. (Marill and Roberts 1966, 428)

The principle was repeated in a footnote on possibly standardizing display languages for monitors: 'As in the case of message protocol, adherence to a proposed standard should be encouraged but not made mandatory' (429). At this nascent stage of computer networking, standardizing connectivity protocols was unlikely to have appeared to be prohibitively costly. Technical considerations of efficiency, adaptability, and (I think this always comes in) elegance in *how-to-do-it* most likely played here; equally, those were considered coeval with an ideological disinclination to enforce standards. The developers clearly regarded this as a matter of choice for users, since, even if an adequate standardized protocol were to be proposed, they felt that 'this standard should be encouraged but not required', 'a proposed standard should be encouraged but not made mandatory'. Encouraging but not enforcing adherence to standards when it becomes feasible captures the principle of minimal-gradual-mechanical standardization well. A similarly straightforward statement of the principle was to appear a couple of decades later, when the World Wide Web (W3) was introduced in 1992. A paper by the developers observed that, 'In general the philosophy of the W3 initiative is not to force any more standards or common practices upon the world than absolutely necessary' (Berners-Lee et al. 1992: 457), and explained how the protocol only renders those features essential which enable flexibility and openness. W3 has been a salient component in the consolidation of Internet Technology, and I pause on it in Chap. 3.

By and large, *how-to-do-it* steps in developing Internet Technology sought to maintain consistency with the principle of minimal-gradual-mechanical standardization, albeit with small gaps and allowances left here and there. Each step in achieving connectivity accordingly worked with the understanding that the integrity of the information would be maintained while differences of hardware and software are accommodated—within networks and then across networks. I now outline some of the principal *how-to-do-it* steps to consider where they actualized minimal-gradual-mechanical standardization.

Packet-switching is the obvious *how-to-do-it* step to begin with, of which a sketchy account goes as follows. Information is generally captured and usually communicated between users in *analogue* form, i.e., as continuous signals. When we see/hear and send/receive information through images and sounds (let us generically call these *messages*), we apprehend continuous signals carried in energy waves. For example, a message composed of words is apprehended as visible sequences of signs (letters) or as audible sequences of phonemes. Insofar as elaborately linked circuits of currents (through wires or airwaves) are employed to send/receive those images and sounds over long distances or across wide areas, it seems natural to pass the information along in analogue form, with the integrity of messages undisturbed in transmission. That is to say, such signals would be transmitted much as they are transmitted and received through electrical pulses of variable amplitudes. At the inception stage of computer networking, such analogue transmission was slow and called for cumbersome infrastructure of circuitry and sending/receiving equipment. That was especially so where numerous strands of signals needed to be transmitted simultaneously with their integrity as messages maintained. It involved hefty volumes of continuous signals being passed from circuit to circuit, as and when space became available on those circuits (*circuit-switching*).

Transmitting messages in *digital* signals rather than analogue signals turned out to make for more efficient usage of the capacities of computer networks. Instead of transferring the message directly as continuous analogue signals, this involves converting the message into binary digital signals, i.e., into time-separated sequences of 1s and 0s. That could then be transferred as sequences of electrical pulses with two amplitudes, standing for 1 and 0, which are speedily processed by a computer programme. The sequences could then be thought of as composed of digital *bits* of 1s and 0s, which in turn could be organized into convenient *packets* (or segments or bunches) of bits. The size of the packets could be set such that the maximum number of packets is directed (routed) through whatever network circuits have capacity and are available. So, a number of messages could thus be disassembled into digital packets; the packets sent by using available capacities of circuits fully (analogous to packing more small and regular items into a bag than large and irregular items); and then received and reassembled to retrieve the messages at the appropriate destinations. The main thing to ensure is that the relevant packets from the sending computers are reassembled at the receiving computers so that the message is delivered to the intended recipient. To achieve this, suitable instructions for disassembling and reassembling the packets are needed at the sending and receiving ends, and a system for locating the receivers and senders (*addressing*) needs to work alongside those instructions. These instructions and the system of locating are the *protocols* that the computer network adopts.

Effectively, whereas the earlier slower process involved maintaining the integrity of messages as continuous analogue signals amidst circuit-switching, this process involves disassembling and reassembling the message by passing digital packets quickly through available circuits, or *packet-switching*. In this process, the integrity of the message is broken by disassembling for transmission but re-established by the reassembling at the receiving end.

My sketchy *how-to-do-it* account of packet-switching above has already presented the obvious *why-do-it* rationale: packet-switching made for faster and less cumbersome transmitting of information given the capacities of the network at the time, i.e., the limitations of the hardware or of the transmission and processing power in hand. The move from analogue to digital was, therefore, driven by cost saving in hardware terms. That advantage was naturally of the time; with the development of those capacities, it would in principle have become possible to develop analogue computing for general consumption further. But in the technological state that prevailed then, digital computing became comprehensively standardized, albeit without departing from the principle of minimal-gradual-mechanical standardization—that is to say, by adaptation. At our stage of technological development, the *why-do-it* advantage in moving from circuit-switching to packet-switching, and perhaps also generally from analogue to digital, no longer seems as material. Indeed, engineers have never quite stopped contemplating the possibilities of analogue computing. The advantages that analogue optical computing present over digital for optimization problems have been under the spotlight with Microsoft's 2023 announcement of the availability of its Analogue Iterative Machine for testing (Microsoft website, AIM Project 2023).

The point is, however, that the *how-to-do-it* outcome that was packet-switching, and the move to digital computing, have had a seminal part in the development of Internet Technology. The obvious *why-do-it* argument at the time, of maximizing hardware capacities cost-effectively, should not obviate consideration of collateral *why-do-it* considerations of somewhat broader import. Packet-switching was also consistent with the principle of minimal-gradual-mechanical standardization in that it involved no intervention from outside the mechanical network on the content or substance of messages being transmitted. No question of appointing vocabularies or curtailing formats for the purposes of information sharing and exchange arises. In fact, an interesting space in the interstices of communication was thus opened, which is quite difficult to characterize in received semiotic terms. Let me call this the *interim space.* The transmission of information/messages through this space could be likened to *translation* or *transliteration* from, for instance, ordinary language to, so to speak, a processing language (packets of bits + instructions). But, in fact, this is not translation or transliteration in a semiotically received sense. Lexical and syntactical relations are not converted meaningfully but arbitrarily fragmented. The closest the packet disassembling-reassembling process in this interim space comes to being understood in received semiotic terms is as involving a modal change. But this is not a modal change with semiotic content. Apart from modality, until around 1970 the areas of semiotics that might have been called upon to conceptualize the interim space would have referred to codes or cryptography, which featured occasionally in scholarly papers (usually referring to the Morse Code or Braille). It seems possible that the terms 'analogue'/'digital' have intrigued philosophers and cognitive scientists since then (such as, Katz 2008; Maley 2011; Beck 2018) because of the inadequacy of semiotics for describing the interim space opened by packet-switching.

Let me underline the appearance of this *interim space* in information sharing and exchanges. The implications of this are rather larger than packet-switching. In fact, this is at the heart of networking and Internet Technology. It is difficult to say whether this interim space was discovered for or constituted by technological manipulation at this stage. The interim space thereafter expanded as quietly manipulable at the interstices of information. It obviated the need for coercive standardization, but it also concentrated technological ingenuity in line with the principle of minimal-gradual-mechanical standardization. Focusing on it allowed for technological intervention that minimized the remit of standardization between networked computers and between programming languages and operating systems, and then between networks and the user communities involved.

The obvious materialization of the interim space as a technical device appeared in ARPANET's Interface Message Processor (IMP). The IMP was conceived and realized as an interim computer: a composite of hardware connections and software protocols capitalizing on the interim space. This enabled networking between computers (called *host nodes* at the time) without necessitating changes in the integrity of their existing hardware and software. The IMP was designed to interface with host nodes so that the information could be disassembled at the sending host and reassembled at the receiving host according to their respective operating systems, given that all host nodes have implemented the IMP protocol. Its function was described succinctly in J.C.R. Licklider and Robert Taylor (1968)—Taylor was director of ARPA's Information Processing Techniques Office 1965–1969 when IMP was developed, Licklider before that in 1962–1964:

> For each node there is a small, general-purpose computer which we shall call a 'message processor.' The message processors of all the nodes are interconnected to form a fast store-and-forward network. The large multiaccess computer at each node is connected directly to the message processor there. Through the network of message processors, therefore, all the large computers can communicate with one another. And through them, all the members of the supercommunity can communicate-with other people, with programs, with data, or with selected combinations of those resources. The message processors, being all alike, introduce an element of uniformity into an otherwise grossly nonuniform situation, for they facilitate both hardware and software compatibility among diverse and poorly compatible computers. The links among the message processors are transmission and high-speed *digital* switching facilities provided by common carrier. This allows the linking of the message processors to be reconfigured in response to demand. (Licklider and Taylor 1968, 32)

This gives a reasonable sense of the IMP in the interim space which actuates unrestricted communications and information sharing in the 'supercommunity'. It was conceived as narrowing or containing the space for standardizing whereby users could work with otherwise diverse standards, 'introducing an element of uniformity into an otherwise grossly nonuniform situation'… 'among diverse and poorly compatible computers'. In line with the principle of minimal-gradual-mechanical standardization, this meant that otherwise the nonuniform situation and diversity would be maintained. The element of standardization was effectively concentrated in the IMP, which rendered it unnecessary to impose wider standards on the information or on the network of host nodes. The minimization of standardizing rested ultimately in a very simple instruction in its main manual, Report Number 1822 *IMP Specifications* (Bolt Beranek and Newman Inc. initially developed 1969): '*Each participating host* [in the computer network] *will be responsible for the design and construction of its own special unit to mate to the standard Host/IMP interface unit*' (Sect. 2.3/2-13, 1976 version, italics in original). The only standardizing that the IMP called for which had some impact on the information transmitted concerned the size of packets and the scale of book-keeping necessary. The IMP protocol also materialized concepts which were to become centred in the development of the TCP/IP suite, such as naming/addressing and layering, which I come to soon.

The *why-do-it* push of the principle of minimal-gradual-mechanical standardization was thus already ensconced into the practicalities of networking before becoming integrated into Internet Technology. The principle was bolstered by packet-switching.

It worked by containing the *how-to-do-it* focus on an interim space of digital transmission. The materialization of this interim space as a technical device, IMP, narrowed the scope of standardization while maintaining diversities and incompatibilities in line with that principle. The larger ideological commitment to collectivizing advancement of knowledge appeared to give credence to the technological exploitation of this space.

2.3.2 *Internetworking*

For the next step to be considered—i.e., the development of the TCP/IP suite—the focus moved more emphatically on software, weighing in on one side of the IMP's composite hardware-software function. Insofar as the hardware side of computing in relation to the Internet Infrastructure went, both scaling-up and scaling-down moves worked in tandem. Scaling-up of computer networks involved setting up a hierarchy of hosts and servers and expanding their capacities through enhanced materials and energy usage. Scaling-up in this sense is a continuous process unfolding in concert with broadcast telecommunications. This process has been almost exponential in keeping with Moore's Law (Moore 1965) and indeed continues to be so. The most important facet of hardware development corresponding with that scaling-up of networks was the scaling-down of the material computer as a unit for use, i.e., the emergence of microcomputers, desktop computers, and mobile devices (see Campbell-Kelly and Garcia-Swartz 2015). These developments are seminal to Internet Infrastructure, and I discuss one facet of this later (in Chap. 6, re smartphones). Each step in the scaling-up cum scaling-down of the Internet Infrastructure was also a step of developing concordant software and diversifying the possibilities of offering applications and enhancing usage. The development of scaled-down material computers was possible with the convergence of specific devices (plasma and LCD display, microprocessor, mouse, etc.). Those were utilizable in tandem with proliferations and convergences in programming languages and applications, which occupy a more considerable space than Internet Technology in the history of software (see Tracy 2021). General histories of computing naturally trace a combined hardware-software process, in which Internet Technology is but one nexus amidst many *how-to-do-it* considerations (e.g., Ceruzzi 1998 or, more up-to-date, Haigh and Ceruzzi 2021; Bardini 2000; Rankin 2018).

Sticking with Internet Technology and the principle of minimal-gradual-mechanical standardization, the next significant developmental step consisted in networking a diversity of computer networks by producing a protocol that could be adopted between them. This is where the development of TCP/IP comes in, which is the core of Internet Technology. Developing this core involved giving the interim space a particular non-material or intangible technological emphasis. Insofar as the interim space that was materialized in IMP is seen from the perspective of Internet Technology, the immaterial aspect of IMP—the protocol—was foregrounded. That involved a few more *how-to-do-it* turns which nuanced the *why-do-it* considerations in question. And, in fact, this was a decisive move in the direction of standardization, but again in keeping with the practices and, importantly, the spirit of minimal-gradual-mechanical standardization.

The use of the term 'protocol' is itself worth a pause here. That this is a push towards standardization was evident in one of its earliest usages in this context, in Marill and Roberts (1966), quoted above. Their definition of 'message protocol' was: 'a uniform agreed upon manner of exchanging messages between two computers in the network' (428)—in relation to which in fact they had suggested that 'If a protocol which is good enough to be put forward as a standard is designed, adherence to this standard should be encouraged but not required' (428). So, in recommending a standard that is 'uniform and agreed upon', they, in the same move, also recommended its non-coercive implementation. On the currency of the term 'protocol' among developers of networking and internetworking, Naughton (1999) observed:

> Why 'protocol'? It seems an unlikely term to have figured in the vocabularies of engineering students, even bright ones, at the time. Vint Cerf [a co-author of TCP 1974], one of the students involved in the NWG [Network Working Group], told Peter Salus that it had originated in a conversation between Steve Crocker and Jon Postel [also in the NWG], who had thought of it in terms of diplomats exchanging handshakes and information. It was only later that they discovered its etymology (the word comes from the Greek, and means the first page of a document bearing the title, name of the author, scribe and so on). (Naughton 1999, 137)

'Handshake' has been used in computing to designate a signal between computers and programmes to initiate a connection since at least 1965 (the first cited instance in the OED); the 3-way-handshake was the standard procedure in TCP to initiate data transmission. That Cerf associated 'protocol' with diplomacy was neither fortuitous nor mistaken. In fact, the diplomatic protocol is a useful metaphor for understanding the *why-do-it* dimensions of protocols in the interim space of networking. The protocol in diplomatic circles refers to, by the OED sense 6:

> The official rules of etiquette to be observed by the head of state and other dignitaries in ceremonies and relations with the representatives of other states; the procedure governing diplomatic occasions, affairs of state, etc.; the observance of this.

In a succinct way, this definition conveys what various textbooks of diplomacy (such as Berridge 2002) lay out at length. Diplomatic protocols include norms of different strengths: from rigid to flexible, rule to convention, formal to informal, recorded to off-the-record. In brief, the diplomatic protocol incorporates all the norms that enable dialogue to proceed between parties with different interests without compromising those interests. The protocol offers no restrictions on the position that each party holds and does not change the substance of their communications and negotiations. It works at the interstices of communications to keep negotiation going even amidst seemingly incommensurable differences. Precisely how the diplomatic protocol works to that end is not relevant here (on this see, for instance, Brown and Levinson 1987: 1). That it works in that manner is relevant; to that extent, it provides a useful analogy for the *why-do-it* aspect of computing protocols.

The TCP/IP suite offered a set of instructions for the interim space between networks to enable communications to take place without introducing standards in the messages/information, or in the programming languages and computer specifications of networks. In other words, it presented standard practices to enable exchanges without interfering in the exchanges or in the parties involved in exchanges, much like the diplomatic protocol. The TCP/IP thus smoothly extended the minimal-gradual-mechanical standardization principle already grounded in networking technology to realize Internet Technology.

By way of leading up to the TCP, Vinton G. Cerf and Robert E. Kahn presented the paper 'A Protocol for Packet Network Intercommunication' (1974), detailing some of the design considerations. A brief practical account of how minimal-gradual-mechanical standardization in the interim space would work appeared here:

> It would be extremely convenient if all the differences between networks could be economically resolved by suitable interfacing at the network boundaries. For many of the differences, this objective can be achieved. However, both economic and technical considerations lead us to prefer that the interface be as simple and reliable as possible and deal primarily with passing data between networks that use different packet-switching strategies.
>
> The question now arises as to whether the interface ought to account for differences in HOST or process level protocols by transforming the source conventions into the corresponding destination conventions. We obviously want to allow conversion between packet-switching strategies at the interface, to permit interconnection of existing and planned networks. However, the complexity and dissimilarity of the HOST or process level protocols makes it desirable to avoid having to transform between them at the interface, even if this transformation were always possible. Rather, compatible HOST and process level protocols must be developed to achieve effective Internetwork resource sharing. The unacceptable alternative is for every HOST or process to implement every protocol (a potentially unbounded number) that may be needed to communicate with other networks. We therefore assume that a common protocol is to be used between HOSTs or processes in different networks and that the interface between networks should take as small a role as possible in this protocol. (Cerf and Kahn 1974: 638)

The resolution not to interface between networks at all the boundaries of networked computers and processes—e.g., having something like IMP for all internet boundaries—was based on 'economic and technical considerations'. The cost and material implications were discouraging due to the sheer quantity of implementation ('a potentially unbounded number'). So, a deep level of standardization involving hardware-software at all interfaces was put aside on economic grounds. The obvious *why-not-do-it* argument came down to cost, with technical feasibilities and indeterminacies in view. The flip side of that argument is that the resolution was premised on a solution that is unlimited or open as to the networks to be internetworked. Internetworking was conceived as unlimited in application, for all 'existing and planned networks'.

Interestingly, the cost argument made good sense *because* the *why-do-it* condition was already assumed to be all-embracing. With hindsight this seems an obvious choice, but the commitment to be all-embracing was not necessarily so as a prospect. Where Cerf and Kahn start by saying, 'It would be extremely convenient ...', one might have asked, 'For whom?' The answer could have gone in various directions: 'For those using networks for specific purposes'; 'For those using compatible networks'; 'For those authorized to use networks'; 'For existing official networks', 'For us computing researchers', etc. The answer 'For all networks now and to come'—as Cerf, Kahn and their colleagues blithely took it—was a big commitment. It foresaw and allowed for conveniences which could not be anticipated yet. The answer was imbued with an abstract universality in conceiving the technology, amidst the obvious utilitarian perspective, that gives it an ideological character. Any of those other answers could have led to differently nuanced solutions or different modes of complex or extensive standardization. The *a priori* assumption that internetworking's standardizing impetus has a limitless scope also argued in the self-same moment for a very restrained scope of standardization—i.e., by 'a common protocol' where 'the interface between networks should take as small a role as possible in this protocol'. Focusing on the common protocol was a refinement of the principle of minimal-gradual-mechanical standardization for internetworking over that principle's application in computer networking.

There are numerous levels at which the draft TCP that appeared at the end of 1974 (Cerf et al. 1974), and its various refinements towards the TCP/IP suite till, let's say, the finalization of the Domain Name System [DNS] (in Mockapetris 1987a, b), carried forward the subscription to minimal-gradual-mechanical standardization amidst its inevitable standardizing thrust. Most developers sought to maintain it but also, at times, to potentially compromise it in the same moves. Let me refer to two obvious areas here: addressing/naming and protocol layering.

Addressing, in the sense of putting an address on a letter (Cerf et al. 1974: 3 offered a helpful comparison of the TCP to a post office), and naming, in the sense of being able to identify a destination, are obviously critical for transmitting information/messages through the interim spaces of Internet Technology. Jonathan Postel (1978: 5) made the distinction admirably succinctly: 'A name indicates what we seek. An address indicates where it is'. The issue of addressing and naming was complicated by the fact that, given the all-embracing approach, a global or universal system would be implicated in internetworking, and that might necessitate some kind of regulation extrinsic to the protocol. Having any administration centred outside the automated processing of the TCP/IP suite seems to go against the grain of the principle of minimal-gradual-mechanical standardization.

There were various levels of addressing involved—for packet, message, portal—in the disassembling-reassembling process and in ensuring that communications reach their intended destinations without errors and collisions, i.e., *routing*. Much of Cerf and Kahn (1974) was devoted to pre-emptively clarifying the addressing system for the TCP. Insofar as addressing destination portals for routing went, they noted that two global possibilities arise: 'The two important cases here are that the destination port may have a global and unchanging address or that it may be globally unique but dynamically reassigned' (645). The addressing system for the TCP/IP suite was taken up by Postel in his specifications for the Internet Protocol, 1978 onwards, as a separated layer with TCP—more on this soon. He started by assuming that different networks would have different addressing schemes which could change.

As it happened, in this regard an extrinsic authority did need to be instituted outside the TCP/IP suite almost immediately. The move can be clearly pinned down in Postel's drafts of the Internet Message Protocol (in March 1979 and August 1980). For routing, Postel proposed a process called the 'message processing module' or MPM. In March 1979 he simply proposed that:

> We require each MPM to know completely only the addressing format of its own network. In addition, the MPM must be able to select an output link for each message addressed to another network or host. This does not preclude more intelligent behavior on the part of a given MPM, but at least this minimum is necessary. Each network has a unique name and number. (Postel 1979: 5)

In the August 1980 draft, after consultations, he added a further sentence to that: 'such names and addresses are registered with a naming authority and may be listed in documents such as Assigned Numbers' (Postel 1980b: 5–6). The document referred to one he had produced in January 1980 (Postel 1980a). It is a small but politically noteworthy adjustment: it brought in, albeit temporarily, exactly the kind of extrinsic authority that goes against the spirit of minimal-gradual-mechanical standardization.

Further, more effective interference to minimal-gradual-mechanical standardization came for naming. As Postel's (1978) distinction quoted above anticipated, it became expedient to have not just have an *address* identifier for each network portal (an IP address) but also a linked *domain name*. Such a name would have the advantage of making immediate sense for internet users to identify destinations. The insertion of domain names came to have considerable implications for the interim space on which Internet Technology focuses. Whereas the disassembling-reassembling process (the fragmentation) in packet-switching ensured that the integrity of messages/information would be unaffected in the interim space, domain naming opened a little fissure of possibly influencing such integrity. Naming was impossible without some obvious semantic relation—in ordinary language—to at least the communicators of information/messages, if not the information/messages themselves. That meant allowing an ordinary-language hint about information/messages *within* the interim space. This became evident soon after efforts at formalizing a domain naming scheme were taken up (Su and Postel 1982 onwards). Efforts to systematize domain names moved in several steps from having an actively maintained and ever-growing index (regulated by that naming authority mentioned above) to having a system allowing for mechanical assignment of domain names. This became the Domain Naming System (DNS) which was developed to its functional form in 1987 by Paul Mockapetris. In principle, this took away the centralized naming authority and reiterated the mechanical thrust of minimal-gradual-mechanical standardization. Effectively, DNS allowed for decentralized regulation. In process and practice though, that meant existing real-world authorities got a small foothold in the interim space where Internet Technology operates. This was enabled by the following assumptions about usage made in Mockapetris (1987a), which effectively allocated responsibility for locally regulating domain names and for organization-client relationships in relation to domain names:

- The administrative boundaries used to distribute responsibility for the database will usually correspond to organizations that have one or more hosts. […].
- Clients of the domain system should be able to identify trusted name servers they prefer to use before accepting referrals to name servers outside of this 'trusted' set. (Mockapetris 1987a, 4)

For the organizational responsibility, the part played by a local system administrator was also laid out (5). Naturally, these assumptions and allocations of responsibility implicated more than technological design features which could maintain minimal-gradual-mechanical standardization. Two existing political-economic relationships were fused into the design: the employee or subsidiary relationship of a local systems administrator to an organization, and the relationship of organization to clients based on a concept of 'trust'.

Nevertheless, domain-name administration might well have been a largely mechanical business were it not for the fact that domain names contained ordinary-language indications (e.g., corresponding to naming kinds or functions of organizations in ordinary language, such as academic, governmental, commercial). Organizations and users could invest their political and economic interests into capitalizing those indications. The indications were as much within as, so to speak, adjacent to the interim space of Internet Technology: i.e., between the mechanics of interim space transmissions and the rationales of organizations'/users' communicative exchanges. As such, DNS made explicit a mode of information segmentation which could be read as knowledge organization. More importantly, domain names could be invested with brand value, collective-identity value, commercial value, intellectual-property value and the like. Any selected term combined with generic terms in a domain name—calling upon terms which have ordinary-language familiarity—is apt to carry such value-laden significance. As the uptake of services and provisions built upon Internet Technology burgeoned from the 1990s onwards, especially after domain naming converged with the World Wide Web protocols (the problems were described well in Berners-Lee 1999: 126–129), such investments became more competitive and, at times, conflictual (see, for instance Paré 2003; Komaitis 2010; Ng 2012; Khoury and Abdallah 2013). Concurrently and naturally, domain-name regulation became an intensive area of legislation and judicial activity, and the focus of numerous international and national regulatory bodies (Bettinger and Waddell 2015 offers a helpful overview of both, covering national law in 31 countries). DNS cannot be said to have directly compromised the principle of minimal-gradual-mechanical standardization rooted in the TCP/IP suite, and yet it opened a kind of onslaught on the interim space by authorities from the sidelines.

Now I reel back to the 1970s to offer a few observations on protocol layering in relation to minimal-gradual-mechanical standardization. In response to the first drafts of the TCP, Postel (1977) made the following complaint and opened the protocol to being conceived as a suite:

> We are screwing up in our design of Internet protocols by violating the principle of layering. Specifically we are trying to use TCP to do two things: serve as a host level end to end protocol, and to serve as an Internet packaging and routing protocol. These two things should be provided in a layered and modular way. I suggest that a new distinct Internetwork

> protocol is needed, and that TCP be used strictly as a host level end to end protocol. I also believe that if TCP is used only in this cleaner way it can be simplified somewhat. A third item must be specified as well – the interface between the Internet host to host protocol and the Internet hop by hop protocol. (Postel 1977)

He recommended separating the functions being served by the protocol into separate and interdependent layers of protocols (a suite). These could then be adjusted, as and when needed, relatively independently from each other. Moreover, that could be done without calling for an overall redesigning of Internet Technology or, on a larger scale, Internet Infrastructure. The observations that followed were along the *how-to-do-it* line (the processing of the separate functions and interdependencies of the layers), without dwelling further on the *why-do-it* considerations.

However, Postel's principle of layering had a *how-to-do-it* mechanics which was redolent with *why-do-it* underpinnings. In brief, it meant organizing as a protocol layer the coherent elements that perform a distinct function. Then, arranging those layers in a hierarchical sequence one on top of another. This is done so that only those aspects of the layer beneath that impinge on the work of the layer above are available to the latter (sort of, on a mechanical need-to-know basis). Organizing the protocol suite thus answers some immediate *why-do-it* calls. This arrangement meant, as noted already, that adjustments could be made at layers without having to rework the overall TCP/IP suite or Internet Infrastructure. In general, the former is likely to be less costly than the latter. A protocol layer could be adjusted to improve its specific functioning, or the layered structure could be reworked easily to upgrade the end-result of the process. Again, this could result in greater cost-effectiveness in maintenance or delivery of services. Moreover, further layers could be introduced so as to customize usage in specific locales or for particular services: e.g., for security purposes (whereby risks are reduced, including in cost terms). It was soon observed that while there are obvious advantages in layering, there are also some problems and disadvantages (Cooper 1983: Chaps. 3–5; Crowcroft et al. 1992; Calvert 1993). Some of these problems were matters of processing and some of uneven effects on users, and fixes or alternatives have followed their identification. But essentially the TCP/IP layering became the internet standard by 1994 (Russell 2014: 257).

Perhaps more significantly than justification in terms of cost and convenience, the *why-do-it* drive for such protocol layering comes from the fact that it is in tune with the principle of minimal-gradual-mechanical standardization. With hindsight, that might well appear to be its main *why-do-it* consideration. Layering encourages incremental adjustments in parts while discouraging general adjustments to the TCP/IP suite or more generally to Internet Technology as a whole. This mechanism contains or restricts standardization moves within the TCP/IP protocols' mechanical process and allows only limited space for standardizing interventions by any extrinsic authority. It also slows down the overall evolution of Internet Technology. At the same time, protocol layering does allow sufficient space for coherent extrinsic adaptations and activities by, for instance, allowing layers to be implemented according to demand or need, typically locally. Thereby space is maintained for organization-level standardizing drives to be fulfilled without affecting the general integrity of

Internet Technology. A contrary way of seeing that is: layering could offer a potential mechanism for compromising the principle of minimal-gradual-mechanical standardization, at least locally if not across the global scope of Internet Technology. In principle, that could also become pervasive if a global alignment appears with sufficient wherewithal for imposing extrinsic and precipitate standardization layers on Internet Technology without dispensing with its prevailing structure.

As it happened, layering was at the heart of the most explicit debate about standardization in internetworking from its early development. In 1977, the International Organization for Standardization (ISO) set up a subcommittee (SC16), Open Systems Interconnection (OSI), to devise standards for diverse connected networks. As Hubert Zimmerman (1980), who led deliberations to develop OSI protocols, put it:

> The basic objective of SC16 is to standardize the rules of interaction between interconnected systems. Thus, only the external behaviour of Open Systems must conform to OSI Architecture, while the internal organization and functioning of each individual Open System is out of the scope of OSI standards since these are not visible from other systems with which it is interconnected. (Zimmerman 1980, 425)

To this end, a layering structure different from those of the TCP/IP suite were proposed (comparing these is still a standard textbook way of introducing the concept of layering). The determination to bring about standardization at, so to speak, the public surface rather than the mechanical innards of internetworking turned into an acrimonious standoff between OSI proponents and TCP/IP proponents. This was cast, perhaps unfairly, as a confrontation of two philosophies of standardization: OSI's focused on the top, as it were, of the external behaviour and therefore with an idea of legitimate and transparent public utility; TCP/IP's philosophy gelled with the principle of minimal-gradual-mechanical standardization, which operates in the interim space and discourages the imposition of any normatively determined set of standards. Andrew Russell's (2014) history of the philosophy of open standards in communication technologies from the nineteenth century onwards, offers a considered and detailed account of this acrimonious confrontation (Chaps. 7 and 8). Interestingly, he characterized the OSI side as organizationally democratic and consultative and the TCP/IP side as autocratic and design centred, and he argued that the latter prevailed because of this. Subsequently, as legislation to regulate the internet gathered pace through the later 1990s—mentioned above in relation to addressing/naming—the operation of layering has come under some juridical and policy scrutiny. Arguably, the OSI and TCP/IP confrontations drew legislative and juridical attention to protocol layering. The tenor of such scrutiny is indicated in various papers (such as Solum and Chung 2003) emphasizing the need for the layering principle to be respected in internet law, and pleading for a better understanding of protocol layering among policy makers (such as Christopher Yoo 2013).

2.4 A First Principle

Standardization involves appointing rules that are uniformly followed in practice. This can be done either to restrict or to open up. If some select group is required to abide by such rules, then standardization becomes a way of setting up and regulating the group according to those rules. This is a restrictive form of standardizing. If it is anticipated that as many as possible and potentially all groups and persons will come to follow such rules by choice, then standardization becomes a path towards universalizing or pervasively grounding those rules. Those rules may then become habitual in work and life. This is an open form of standardizing. The restrictive form of standardization is likely to be maintained at the behest of some centralized authority, such as an organizational management or government executive, and designed accordingly. It will probably involve constant policing and regulation, and group membership would be availed by permission. The open form of standardizing is likely to be released from such centralized authority, even if developed by one, and designed accordingly. This will probably involve a decentred approach and invite adoption. That latter is, in fact, the idea behind minimal-gradual-mechanical standardization.

The above discussion suggests that networking and internetworking technologies were, from their inception and consistently, thought of in terms of minimal-gradual-mechanical standardization. They were designed to be opened up from the beginning. So long as the technology development and usage were within relatively confined circles (for academic, military, and industrial usage), this principle was followed without needing painstaking elaboration. It simply seemed to be the way to go for the developers, according to their circumstances. However, the more networks multiplied and internetworking spread, the more pressing the need for careful elaboration of standards became. Protocols for domain naming and layering were modes of elaboration in design, just as the confrontation between the OSI and TCP/IP sides called for elaboration through advocacy. Inevitably, elaborations of the design according to minimal-gradual-mechanical standardization also revealed fissures through which such standardization could be enforced to some degree. Persistent attempts to keep to minimal-gradual-mechanical standardization paradoxically also clarified plausible ways of inserting more restrictive forms of standardization in pockets. Amidst the decentred mechanism, it became possible for centralizing authorities to get a foothold here and there.

These approaches to standardization have a bearing on cost calculations and rationalizations. For restrictive forms of standardization governed by some centralized authority, the costs are conditional to the purposes of the authority. Costs can be kept within budget by restriction, and budgets can be focused according to the authority's purposes (the authority can plan accordingly). Costs are a secondary consideration following the primacy of the authority's purposes. We could think of this approach as having a governmental character. For open forms of standardization designed to follow a minimal-gradual-mechanical process in a decentred manner, costs become the primary grounds of rationalizing and seeking legitimacy for every step. Constant growth of uptake calls for constant accounting of costs upwards which need to be realized either from the sponsors (even when those are governments) or from the users. Every move in minimal-gradual-mechanical standardizing needs to be justified to sponsors and users in terms of cost-effectiveness, as directly or indirectly enabling either savings or profits or both. We may think of this approach to standardizing as having a commercial character. The above discussion suggests that in this sense the development of networking and internetworking was commercial from inception.

For an overall sense of how minimal-gradual-mechanical standardization was grounded in Internet Technology, a visual metaphor is helpful. Since the early 1990s, the overall structure of Internet Technology has often been represented in terms of layers which have an hourglass model. At one broad end, all existing and emerging application layers from various sources are placed; these pass through limited options of the transfer layer (typically TCP, which is more standard and connection-based, and in some instances UDP or User Datagram Protocol, which is connection-less); then through the Internet layer (IP); then broadening out to the layer of interface protocols with various networks (such as Ethernet, X.25, LTE, 5G, etc.); and reaching the destinations of the circuits and devices that users access directly. The stability of the narrow 'waist' of the 'hourglass' in Internet Technology protocols has been a subject of considerable interest. That interest has grown as the source-protocol and destination-protocol layers, and the ones above and beneath them, have constantly widened and become increasingly diverse. If Internet Technology is regarded as an evolving structure, the stability of this narrow waist should be considered as supportive to its evolutionary principles (a perspective usefully elaborated in Akshali and Dovrolis 2011). It is generally held that this enables 'interoperability', allowing different systems, networks, and languages to be used across each other.

In the terms being used here, the narrow waist of the Internet Technology hourglass could be regarded as the juncture at which the principle of minimal-gradual-mechanical standardization is maintained. It works to instil minimal-gradual-mechanical standardization across the information exchange and data transmission field that is the internet. The application layers above and network interface layers beneath the waist allow for directly implementing a range of designed and monitored standardizations according to the wants/needs of sources and destinations. Of course, the 'hourglass' concept for Internet Technology is a pure visual metaphor and does not map on to a real spatial arrangement. It is little more than a metaphor for an operational constriction in processing. The constriction is only understandable if the widening ranges of protocols before and after are considered in a relational way. The IP at the waist is not an inflexibly fixed node: the current IP version 6 has been introduced in 2017 to supersede IP version 4 introduced in 1980 (with the TCP/IP suite), mainly allowing for more addresses as the layers above and below have multiplied. Nevertheless, the principle of minimal-gradual-mechanical standardization across the internet field remains ostensibly conceivable there.

My characterization of minimal-gradual-mechanical standardization above as a social and political first principle of the Internet Polity calls for some clarification. The minimal-gradual-mechanical standardization that Internet Technology was designed in terms of became a received way of doing things when a collectivity started growing through internet usage. For using the internet as a facility and inhabiting it as a space, its technological structure was experienced as pragmatically premised on such standardization. Minimal-gradual-mechanical standardization was not foregrounded as a rule, which would have contradicted its tenor. Rather, subscription to it, through habituation by usage, was simply collectively found to be and taken as expedient. Though not explicitly foregrounded as a constitutional tenet of the Internet Polity, such an approach to standardization functioned as a first principle of the Internet Polity in various ways. To name a few:

- The Internet Polity was premised on an always hesitant and occasionally resistant stance towards the extrinsic – 'real-world' – exertion of authority and mandated standard-setting on Internet Technology. In fact, that stance often gave definition to the Internet Polity as such, as an organized collective. This should not be misconstrued by characterizing the polity as implicitly resistant to governmental power. Minimal-gradual-mechanical standardization as the default condition of the internet also enjoined compliance with localized self-standardizations (e.g., as in forming an online community) or targeted standardizations (e.g., as a condition to avail of a service) rather than generalized mandated standardizations. In holding extrinsic interference on the general apparatus of Internet Technology at arm's length, the Internet Polity adopted multiple internally operable standards. On the one hand, the tenets of the Internet Polity seemed to have an uneasy relationship with legislation and policing by governmental executives. On the other hand, correspondingly its tenets seemed inviting to communities/networks and business organizations/markets formed upon shared interests and courting consuming desires. The latter, being 'self-regulated' or 'market tested', were taken as consistent with minimal-gradual-mechanical standardizing processes.
- Familiar political words-concepts which are variously decontested in our social ideologies, are often given a specific added nuance in the Internet Polity. Such nuancing does not quite amount to such words-concepts being decontested to form a distinctively Internet Polity ideology. As observed in the Introduction, the internet accommodates a spectrum of ideologies. What I mean by nuancing is a matter of emphasis which does not necessarily obstruct that accommodativeness. For instance, as a first principle, minimal-gradual-mechanical standardization sets certain parameters for declarations of 'freedom', such as: if a standard emerges through choice and collective adaptation, that is an acceptable limit to 'freedom'; if a standard is extrinsically mandated on Internet Technology, there's a curtailment of 'freedom'; if a local layering on Internet Technology restricts access to an organization's space, there's a test of 'freedom'; and so on. Similarly, words-concepts such as 'belonging', 'identity', 'citizenship' are also nuanced according to minimal-gradual-mechanical standardization. Sanguinary notions of these (available by birth) seem against the grain of such standardization: no privilege in the Internet Polity can precede engagement with the technological structure. Thus, the Internet Polity is constituted in terms of 'access', 'membership', 'digital literacy', 'participation' and the like instead.

There are other such examples. A first principle naturally casts a cohesive trace through the prevailing terminology and conceptual nodes of a polity's discourse, and minimal-gradual-mechanical standardization does so for the Internet Polity discourse.

- While having a collective integrity, the Internet Polity is obviously very far from dissociated from our 'real-world' polities. Indeed, it is not distinctly demarcated from existing polities but penetrates through and permeates across them. Persons who conceive of themselves as members or inhabitants in the Internet Polity are also citizens under actually existing states, employees of actually existing organizations, party to actually existing social groupings and so on. These latter collectives have their interests as internet collectives too. The Internet Polity is, therefore, not merely formed through a process internal to collective engagement with Internet Technology. At the same time, it is also constituted by the bearing of, or rather the incursions of, actually existing collectives as party to internet collectivity. Thus, there is a dialectical relationship between the Internet Polity and actually existing polities. We may say: minimal-gradual-mechanical standardization works as a first principle of the Internet Polity because it is considered as such in actually existing polities. The first principle is therefore constantly reiterated and reified for the internet from our actually existing social and political world. Every demand for legislating and policing standards for the internet from outside the resources of Internet Technology is an acknowledgement of taking minimal-gradual-mechanical standardization as an embedded first principle of the Internet Polity. So are demands to exert localized or targeted control by non-technological means, or—the ultimate mandate—blocking the internet by recourse to the underlying hardware.

The extension of minimal-gradual-mechanical standardization as a social and political first principle of the Internet Polity is variously discerned in its social history and discourse. That will be apparent in Part II. This is, however, one among other social and political first principles, which together coalesce to structure the Internet Polity. I turn next to two further first principles grounded in Internet Technology: of *precedent individuation* through hypertext systems and *targeted collective regulation* through security controls.

References

Abbate J (1999) Inventing the internet. MIT Press, Cambridge MA

Akera A (2007) Calculating a natural world: scientists, engineers, and computers during the rise of U.S. cold war research. MIT Press, Cambridge MA

Akshali S, Dovrolis C (2011) The evolution of layered protocol stacks leads to an hourglass-shaped architecture. ACM SIGCOMM Comp Commun Rev 41(4):206–217. https://doi.org/10.1145/2043164.2018460

Bardini T (2000) Bootstrapping: Douglas Engelbart, coevolution, and the origins of personal computing. Stanford University Press, Stanford CA

Beck J (2018) Analog mental representation. WIREs Cogn Sci 18(9):e1479. https://doi.org/10.1002/wcs.1479
Berners-Lee TJ, Cailliau R, Groff J-F (1992) The world-wide web. Comp Netw ISDN Syst 25:454–459. https://doi.org/10.1016/0169-7552(92)90039-S
Berners-Lee, T (1999) Weaving the web: the original design and ultimate destiny of the world wide web. Harper, New York
Berridge GR (2002) Diplomacy: theory and practice, 2nd edn. Palgrave Macmillan, Basingstoke
Bettinger T, Waddell A (eds) (2015) Domain name and law practice, 2nd edn. Oxford University Press, Oxford
Black J (2015) The cold war: a military history. Bloomsbury, London
Bolt Beranek and Newman Inc. (1976) Interface message processor: specifications for the interconnection of a host and an IMP, report number 1822. Advanced Research Projects Agency, Cambridge MA
Bromberger S (1992) Why-questions. On what we know we don't know: explanation, theory, linguistics, and how questions shape them. University of Chicago Press, Chicago, pp 75–100
Brown P, Levinson SC (1987) Politeness: some universals in language usage. Cambridge University Press, Cambridge
Cain F (2013) Economic statecraft during the cold war: European responses to the US trade embargo. Routledge, Abingdon
Calvert KL (1993) Beyond layering: modularity considerations for protocol architectures. In: 1993 International conference on network protocols. San Francisco CA, pp 90–97. https://doi.org/10.1109/ICNP.1993.340929
Campbell-Kelly M, Garcia-Swartz DD (2015) From mainframes to smartphones: a history of the international computer industry. Harvard University Press, Cambridge MA
Cerf VG, Kahn RE (1974) A protocol for packet network intercommunication. IEEE Trans Commun com 22(5 May):637–648
Cerf VG, Dalal Y, Sunshine C (1974) RFC 675: specification of internet transmission control programme. Network Working Group. https://datatracker.ietf.org/doc/html/rfc675
Ceruzzi PE (1998) A history of modern computing, 2nd edn. MIT Press, Cambridge MA
Cooper GH (1983) An argument for soft layering of protocols. M.S. Thesis, MIT Laboratory for Computer Science, Cambridge MA. https://apps.dtic.mil/sti/citations/ADA133948
Crowcroft J, Wakeman I, Wang Z, Sirovica D (1992) Is layering harmful? IEEE Network Magazine January, 20–24. https://ieeexplore.ieee.org/document/120719
Edwards PN (1996) The closed world: computers and the politics of discourse in cold war America. MIT Press, Cambridge MA
Fainberg D (2021) Cold war correspondents: Soviet and American reporters on the ideological frontlines. Johns Hopkins University Press, Baltimore MA
Feynman R (1983) Interview 'stretching, pulling and pushing'. BBC Fun to Imagine, July 15. https://www.bbc.co.uk/programmes/p014blpr
Fink CK (2022) Cold war: an international history, 3rd edn. Routledge, New York
Freeden M (1996) Ideologies and political theory: a conceptual approach. Clarendon, Oxford
Gaddis JL (2005) The cold war: a new history. Penguin, Harmondsworth
Hafner K, Lyon M (1996) Where wizards stay up late: the origins of the internet. Touchstone, New York
Haigh T, Ceruzzi PE (2021) A New History of Modern Computing. MIT Press, Cambridge MA
Jackson I (2001) The economic cold war: America, Britain and East-West trade 1948–63. Palgrave Macmillan, Basingstoke
Katz M (2008) Analog and digital representation. Mind Mach 18(3):403–408. https://doi.org/10.1007/s11023-008-9112-8
Khoury JS, Abdallah CT (2013) Internet naming and discovery: architecture and economics. Springer, Cham
Komaitis K (2010) The current state of domain name regulation: domain names as second class citizens in a mark-dominated world. Routledge, Abingdon

Leslie S (1993) The cold war and American science: the military-industrial-academic complex at MIT and Stanford. Columbia University Press, New York
Licklider JCR, Taylor RW (1968) The computer as a communication device. Sci Technol 76:21–38
Longo B (2021) Words and power: computers, language, and U.S. cold war values. Springer, Cham
Lovejoy A, Pajala M (eds) (2022) Remapping cold war media: institutions, infrastructures, translations. Indiana University Press, Bloomington IA
Maley CJ (2011) Analog and digital, continuous and discrete. Philos Stud 155(1):117–131
Marill T, Roberts LG (1966) Toward a cooperative network of time-shared computers. In: American federation of information processing societies: proceedings of the AFIPS '66 Fall Joint computer conference, November 7–10, 1966, San Francisco CA. Spartan Books, Washington DC, pp 425–431. https://doi.org/10.1145/1464291.1464336
Microsoft website, AIM Project (2023) https://www.microsoft.com/en-us/research/project/aim/
Mockapetris P (1987a) Domain names—concepts and facilities. RFC 1034. Network working group, November. https://datatracker.ietf.org/doc/html/rfc1034
Mockapetris P (1987b) Domain names—implementation and specification. RFC 1035. Network working group, November. https://datatracker.ietf.org/doc/html/rfc1035
Moore GE (1965) Cramming more components onto integrated circuits. Electronics 38(6):114–117
Naughton J (1999) A brief history of the future: the origins of the internet. Phoenix, London
Ng J (2012) The domain name registration system: liberalisation, consumer protection and growth. Routledge, Abingdon
Norberg AL, O'Neill JE, Freedman KJ (1996) Transforming computer technology: information processing for the pentagon, 1962–1986. Johns Hopkins University Press, Baltimore MD
Paré DJ (2003) Internet governance in transition: who is the master of this domain? Rowman and Littlefield, Lanham MA
Pedersen SB, Noack C (2019) Tourism and travel during the cold war: negotiating tourist experiences across the iron curtain. Routledge, Abingdon
Peters B (2016) How not to network a nation: the uneasy history of the soviet internet. MIT Press, Cambridge MA
Postel JB (1977) Comments on internet protocol and TCP. IEN 2, 15 August. https://www.rfc-editor.org/ien/ien2.txt
Postel JB (1978) Draft internetwork protocol specification. IEN 28, February. https://www.rfc-editor.org/ien/ien28.pdf
Postel JB (1979) Internet message protocol. IEN 85, RFC 753, March. https://www.rfc-editor.org/rfc/rfc753
Postel JB (1980a) Assigned numbers. IEN 127, RFC 762, January. https://www.ietf.org/rfc/rfc762.txt.pdf
Postel JB (1980b) Internet message protocol. IEN 113, RFC 759, August. https://datatracker.ietf.org/doc/html/rfc759
Rankin JL (2018) A people's history of computing in the United States. Harvard University Press, Cambridge MA
Raymond ES (1996) The new hacker's dictionary, 3rd edn. MIT Press, Cambridge MA
Rheingold H (1994) The virtual community: finding connection in a computerised world. Secker & Warburg, London
Richmond Y (2010) Cultural exchange and the cold war: raising the iron curtain. Pennsylvania State University Press, University Park PA
Russell AL (2014) Open standards and the digital age: history, ideology, and networks. Cambridge University Press, Cambridge
Skow B (2016) Reasons why. Oxford University Press, Oxford
Solum LB, Chung M (2003) The layers principle: internet architecture and the law. Available at SSRN: https://ssrn.com/abstract=416263 or https://doi.org/10.2139/ssrn.416263
Stowsky J (2003) Secrets or shields to share? New dilemmas for dual use technology development and the quest for military and commercial advantage in the digital age. Res Policy 33(2):257–269. https://doi.org/10.1016/j.respol.2003.07.002

Su Z-S, Postel JB (1982) The domain naming convention for internet user applications. Network working group. RFC 819. https://www.rfc-editor.org/pdfrfc/rfc819.txt.pdf

Tracy KW (2021) Software: a technical history. ACM Books, New York

Tsvetkova N (2021) The cold war in universities: U.S. and soviet cultural diplomacy, 1945–1990. Brill, Oxford

Wang J (1999) American science in an age of anxiety: scientists, anticommunism, and the cold war. University of North Carolina Press, Chapel Hill NC

Westad OA (2007) The cold war: a world history. Basic, New York

Yoo CS (2013) Protocol layering and internet policy. University of Pennsylvania Law Rev 161(6 May):1707–1771

Zimmerman H (1980) OSI reference model—the ISO model of architecture for open systems interconnection. IEEE Trans Commun com-28(4 April):425–432

Chapter 3
Hypertext and Precedent Individuation/ Security Controls and Targeted Collective Regulation

Abstract The Cold War context outlined in this chapter is complicated by a brief account of civil rights and anti-war movements over the same period, with their bearing on computing circles in view. This chapter then turns to the development of hypertext systems from a *why-do-it* perspective, with conditional attention to various *how-to-do-it* solutions. First, the concept of hypertext is outlined in relation to *information* and *knowledge* management, and the principle of precedent individuation is explained. Then phases in the development of hypertext systems are considered. The earlier concepts and attempts are outlined; then the features of the dominant system from the 1990s, the World Wide Web (WWW), are described. The chapter thereafter takes up security controls as a feature in Internet Technology. These were not quite conceived and designed in the way protocols and hypertext systems were. They came to be instilled through gradual and pragmatic interventions. Changing philosophies of security are taken on board, and the early development of security controls that came to be integrated with Internet Technology recalled. The principle of targeted collective regulation is presented in the process.

3.1 Other Side of the Cold War

The *why-do-it* impetuses that attach to the two technological features taken up in this chapter, hypertext systems and security controls, are somewhat different from those for the internet protocols. For these, the developers worked more directly in terms of *why-do-it* considerations and the *how-to-do-it* steps were devised accordingly. They studied existing social practices carefully and sought to change them, usually as much for idealistic as pragmatic reasons. However, while attention to social practices was upfront, the political implications of the technological interventions were not necessarily so. The *why-do-it* factors were usually expressed in upbeat normative terms which obscured their political thrust. For the purposes of this study, it is expedient to restate the *why-do-it* factors in terms of the political tenets that they came to instantiate for the Internet Polity. It is suggested in this chapter that, analogous to *minimal-gradual-mechanical standardization* appearing as a first principle

S. Gupta, *Collective Principles and the Formation of the Internet*, Springer Series on Cultural Computing, https://doi.org/10.1007/978-3-031-90470-7_3

through the TCP/IP suite, further first principles surfaced through the other features of Internet Technology, namely: a principle of *precedent individuation* built upon hypertext systems and a principle of *targeted collective regulation* grounded in security controls. Collective engagement with the internet meant capitalizing on these technological features, whereby an Internet Polity was structured by the interplay of these three first principles.

By way of leading into this argument, as in the previous chapter I turn again to the historical backdrop for Internet Technology development. The following observations are on further dimensions of the Cold War period to those outlined earlier. These might have a bearing on the *why-do-it* considerations taken up in this chapter. Their relevance may or may not be immediately apparent to all readers, and I do not present these observations as having a direct causal connection to hypertext systems and security controls. I leave it to readers to unpack their significance.

The 1960s–1970s period outlined earlier is associated as much with international Cold War fissures and confrontations as with a wave of related anti-establishment protests: a weaving together of student, anti-war, and civil liberties movements. Though it has become conventional to think of these as centred within countries in North America and Western Europe, these were in fact global in scale, taking place variously in countries in Eastern Europe, Asia, Africa, and Central and South America. To a great degree, these were responsive to the 'hot' peripheries of the international Cold War, especially the Vietnam War, but also other decolonizing movements and civil wars. Almost invariably, these could be regarded as a kind of warming up of the Cold War within the spheres of numerous countries. They involved a confrontation of the ideological polarities of capitalism and socialism *within*. Insofar as North America and Western Europe go, of particular interest here is the centring of such confrontations in universities and among academic constituencies. The spaces where Internet Technology was being developed in the 1960s and 1970s were often within university precincts. The developers were predominantly students and researchers with university affiliations. If the military were mapping their strategies and investments in terms of an international Cold War grid at the time, in the civil sphere there was a searching interrogation of political ideals and governmental norms. It is unlikely that the developers of Internet Technology were untouched by these circumstances, even if not directly invested in these movements.

While the Cold War context of the development of Internet Technology has been extensively considered in histories, these anti-establishment protests have received negligible attention. Soon after the first substantial histories of the internet appeared, Rosenzweig (1998) wrote a review article discussing these (covering Hafner and Lyon 1996; Norberg et al. 1996; Hauben and Hauben 1997; Edwards 1996). He felt:

> Although the Internet may be heralded as an entirely novel development, its historians have generally followed some well-worn paths in the history of technology. These conventional approaches are often illuminating, but the full story will only be told when we get a history that brings together biographical and institutional studies with a fully contextualized social and cultural history. The rise of the Net needs to be rooted in the 1960s – in both the 'closed world' of the Cold War and the open and decentralized world of the anti-war movement and the counterculture. Understanding these dual origins enables us to better understand current

> controversies over whether the Internet will be 'open' or 'closed' – over whether the Net will foster democratic dialogue or centralized hierarchy, community or capitalism, or some mixture of both. (Rosenzweig 1998, 1531)

As it happens, though much has been written about decentralized democracy and anti-establishment activism through the internet since, the anti-war movement and counterculture have received relatively little commentary in the history of Internet Technology.

For computing as a broader field, some attention has been given to that direction, especially in relation to cybernetics. In the Cold War period, hefty investments with great expectations were made in the USA (see Kline 2015; Rid 2016). Over this period, the Soviet Union continued with concerted investments in planned industrialization, especially in cybernetics (see Gerovitch 2002; Peters 2016). These were underpinned by what may be regarded as a state-led top-down standardization principle. The Soviet centralized approach was variously assumed in other socialist countries, most ambitiously in Chile's short-lived Cybersyn Project (see Medina 2014). The focus of cybernetics on feedback-loops in interconnected technological, biological, and social systems seemed particularly promising for top-down standardization, i.e., to enable regulatory management and towards designed egalitarianism. However, cybernetics was equally promising for, and in some ways more effectively synthesized with, the principle of minimal-gradual-mechanical standardization in market-led environments. In fact, the popular and wide-ranging description of the field by its most influential exponent at the time, Norbert Wiener (1961 [1948]), leaned towards the former. He saw standardized formats and practices as available for controlling biological and social systems, rather than having to be incrementally embedded in the interim space of data transfers and exchanges. The focus of cybernetics research on realizing learning machines merged naturally with projects on automation. The promise of cybernetics was therefore equally of interest on all sides of the Cold War, a conceptual and technological space for qualified cooperation and outright competition. As a term, 'cybernetics' generated a host of 'cyber' catchwords associated with 'internet' which I discuss in Part II.

Within North America and Western Europe, socialist intellectuals associated with the New Left student movements and anti-war and civil liberties protests (such as Herbert Marcuse, Ernest Mandel, Jean-François Lyotard) expressed an interestingly ambiguous attitude towards cybernetics and automation. On the one hand, they felt that such technologies were developed to consolidate and perpetuate capitalism in increasingly repressive ways, to normalize unchecked consumption and militarization. On the other hand, they also felt that such technologies could be liberated from their capitalist moorings and become the foundation for an egalitarian society. There are few records of deliberative engagements between cyberneticians or computing specialists and New Left political theorists. A brief exchange between the cybernetician Abraham Moles and Guy Debord representing the revolutionary Situationist collective in 1963 offers a rare and instructive instance of such engagement. A letter from Moles and a response from Debord were published in the *Internationale situationniste* (no. 9, 1964). Moles (1964) suggested that the collective's account of the prevailing alienating 'situations' was limited by its political and artistic perspective and that technology could offer new kinds of situations. Debord's (1964) response consisted in a string of invective with a refusal to acknowledge that Moles had offered an argument at all, pegging him as a mere manager. The conversation was cited in the influential 1966 pamphlet from Situationist students, *On the Poverty of Student Life*, as indicative of the horrors of the future 'cybernetized university' (Members of the Situationist International and Students of the University of Strasbourg 2000 [1966]: 7).

As the student movements and anti-war protests gathered pace through the 1960s and into the 1970s, military-sponsored research in universities was strenuously challenged. Reportedly, researchers in most applied science and technology centres kept their distance from these, but some notable instances of resistance to military-led research by scientists and engineering groups are on record, even in the elite university circle where the US military invested heavily (covered in Leslie 1993: Chap. 9; Wisniowski 2003). Insofar as military-sponsored university research in computing went, that was recognized as having a significant part to play in the Vietnam War (Edwards 1996: Chap. 4; Harrison 1988). Anti-war students and researchers were aware of this: Stuart Leslie (1993: Chap. 9) detailed actions at both MIT and Stanford raising concerns about their role in the Vietnam War. In Stanford, this was directed specifically against the Computation Centre of the Stanford Research Institute in 1971. The protest organizers demanded its closure and began a demonstration before the building, which came to be known as the April Third Movement (documents at the April Third Movement reunion website 1970–1971). Recalling Paul Baran's observations about classified research quoted earlier, this period also saw demands for the discontinuation of such research in universities—traditionally a space for public interest research—and some reluctant capitulation by managements (covered in Leslie 1993: 241–246; for a discussion at the time, Vallance 1969). The effects of these interrogations and demands were short-lived, and the structuring of technological research and sponsorship returned to much as it was by the later 1970s and remained so through the 1980s.

Whether such debates had any general effect on technology researchers, and specifically computing researchers, is difficult to determine. In at least one instance they did: namely, for artificial intelligence researcher Joseph Weizenbaum, who developed the elementary natural language processing ELIZA programme in the late 1960s at MIT. His book *Computer Power and Human Reason* (1976) gave a lucid exposition of the basics of computing and of his field. It concluded with warnings about the overweening ambitions of artificial intelligence research. The use of computers in war, obviously with the Vietnam War in mind, came up for feelingly pronounced rage:

> In modern warfare it is common for a soldier, say, the bomber pilot, to operate at an enormous psychological distance from his victims. He is not responsible for burned children because he never sees their village, his bombs, and certainly not the flaming children themselves. Modern technological rationalizations of war, diplomacy, politics, and commerce (such as computer games) have an even more insidious effect on the making of policy. Not only have policy makers abdicated their decision-making responsibility to a technology they do

not understand – though all the while maintaining the illusion that they, the policy makers, are formulating policy questions and answering them – but responsibility has altogether evaporated (Weizenbaum 1976, 239)

The ambition and incomprehension surrounding these technologies, he decided, underlined the soundness of the critique of 'instrumental reasoning' in Max Horkheimer's *Eclipse of Reason* (1974 [1947]), which built upon Marxist principles in analysing contemporary capitalist culture (see Weizenbaum 1976: 249–250). The politically leftward turn that Weizenbaum took stayed with him, but he may well have been more the exception than the rule among computing researchers.

None of this appears to have had a direct bearing on the development of Internet Technology. Insofar as the Rosenzweig (1998), in the review quoted above, anticipated that 'The rise of the Net needs to be rooted in the 1960s—in both the "closed world" of the Cold War and the open and decentralized world of the anti-war movement and the counterculture' (1531), the effects of the above were mainly indirect. Rosenzweig felt that the distinct role played by technically savvy enthusiasts after its initial development is where this took place. In the loose communities of hobbyist users and hackers, a distinct countercultural computing movement developed, and that eventually burgeoned into various radical utopian efforts which sought entry into the mainstream (Hauben and Hauben 1997 gestured in this direction; Turner (2010) gave an updated picture). Of these too, I have more to say in Part II.

The Internet Technology features described below were sieved through these interrogations, discussions, revisionings, and retrenchments. At any rate, the social and political principles grounded in these features—to do with individuality and collectivity—were most passionately debated amidst the student movements and anti-war protests. In that sense, they contributed to the formation of and have an ongoing relevance to the Internet Polity.

3.2 Hypertext Systems

The *why-do-it* accounts from developers of hypertext were largely presented to advocate for their own efforts. These were typically based on large claims about how the human brain works, teleologies of technology and history, potted accounts of biological and social evolution, sweeping generalizations on cognitive-communicative apparatuses and the like. Nothing similar is attempted here. Such advocatory claims were, in fact, usually designed to rise above or elide political implication. The view taken here is that their *why-do-it* rationales were politically expedient, even if not obviously invested in a political agenda. The first principle that emerged from it and was assumed in the Internet Polity was possible because the developers were inevitably working amidst the social norms of their contexts.

A general description of hypertext systems is needed at this stage. I focus on that first. The steps taken by the specific developers are discussed after that. No distinction is made between 'hypertext' and 'hypermedia' here, both are implied in 'hypertext' and 'digital text'.

3.2.1 Overview of Hypertext Systems

The computer nodes that are linked in networks, which are then linked by Internet Technology, could each be regarded as repositories of records available in digital-text format. Taken together, all the internetworked nodes form a vast repository of every kind of record available in such formats. With appropriate publishing and displaying instructions, such records can be called upon as needed by those using Internet Technology at any one node (users). The Internet Infrastructure enables a user at any one node to reach, at least in principle, into the totality of this vast repository of all the nodes. This is possible because records produced for every conceivable purpose in different modalities and significative systems, across nodes with different capacities and specifications, are all stored in digital-text forms and are manoeuvrable through the interim space mentioned in Chap. 2. Further, by subscribing to certain instructions, any record can be associated with any other record according to a user's intent. This repository has several obvious characteristics: (a) it is accretive, in that such records are constantly added to it; (b) it is fluid, in that records that are on it are constantly open to modification or removal, copying, and adaptation; (c) it is self-contributory, in that its usage and processing as a repository is recorded and becomes part of the repository.

A hypertext system refers to a set of rules, methods, and processes through which Internet Technology users can engage with this extensive repository to fulfil their purposes. Naturally, such engagement is principally with the *content* of the records in the repository, which is used in the terms of actually existing societies (as written, performed, played, worked with, etc.). That these are all available in digital-text format renders them reachable and manipulable through Internet Technology; once availed, the content is used in ways that are meaningful in our social world. Engagement may incorporate a wide variety of usage. Some content, for instance, can be extrapolated and linked up to illuminate some theme or project (by being compared, combined, connected, etc.), some provide facilities for users to exchange views or carry out transactions, and some are called upon for users to entertain themselves or to play games. All such engagements are uses of the content that is reachable and utilizable in the vast repository. Hypertext systems provide ways for users to find and utilize this content through Internet Technology. These are quite specific ways: they were unorthodox when conceived but have gradually become habitual for internet users. To describe the peculiarities of hypertext systems, it is necessary to delineate the content of the repository more precisely.

3.2.2 *Content: Information and Knowledge*

Characterizing the content of this repository has in fact proved rather tricky. The challenging question is: what is this a repository of? What sort of content? The dominant term to characterize the content now is 'information'. 'Information' works as a catch-all word for whatever is recorded to be available in digital-text formats in that vast repository and is retrievable from there.

The use of 'information' here is a reorientation of the term from its erstwhile or older senses. In those received senses (the OED marks seven senses with various sub-senses), 'information' does not lend itself readily to describing something without being conditional to an active purpose—such as, describing facts or observations which *inform* some sort of search or intention. For example, a train timetable is information for those who intend to take trains, notes on the behaviour of ants are information for those studying wildlife, rules of a game are informative for those playing a game. Using 'information' to designate everything available in the vast repository irrespective of purposes seems to over-extend its received connotations. Much of the content in the repository is not for actively *informing* but purely for being *consumed* (e.g., listening to a song or playing games) or merely for *doing* something (e.g., making payments or exchanging messages). It is awkward to think of pleasurable consuming or pragmatically doing something as being an 'information'.

Moreover, the received term 'information' comes with certain normative nuances, as being meaningful and therefore helpful. Content which is erroneous, misdirected or merely context-providing or action-triggering seem to go outside the remit of 'information'. The content in the vast repository in question contains all that without prejudice. Nevertheless, it is now customary to use the term 'information' to characterize the content, and accordingly a specialist literature on 'information theory', 'information systems', 'information management' and the like has appeared. Here therefore, I will use the term in that way also, but with a distinction. I designate all the content that is available in digital-text format through Internet Technology as *I-information*, to distinguish it from the received purposive and normative senses of 'information'. I-information includes content that might be informing of something or for someone, but not exclusively or necessarily so. I-information also includes content which may be non-informatively consumed, acted upon, and even undermine or obviate informing.

With an eye on Internet Technology and hypertext, those who now use the term 'information' to mean I-information almost invariably consider that it has a relation to knowledge. The term 'knowledge' has been oft correlated to the received senses of 'information', and by a smooth slide I-information now appears to be coeval with knowledge. Given the distinction made, that is not quite the case. However, those who developed the concept and application of hypertext assumed automatically that they were doing something about knowledge—for reasons which I come to soon. And those who have dubbed I-information as simply 'information' have been drawn into the philosophical labyrinth of epistemology. It is therefore useful to pause on some common precepts about 'knowledge' here. In fact, to get to the core of my description of—and my larger argument about—hypertext here, this is necessary. A short digression on the term 'knowledge' follows, without delving the philosophical conundrums of epistemology. Its relevance to hypertext will become evident soon after.

As an abstract and uncountable noun-form of the verb 'know', 'knowledge' appears to refer to a very inclusive field: all that is known or knowable and expressed or expressible anywhere. That includes anything that is perceived/perceivable, recognized/recognizable, observed/observable, imagined/imaginable, formulated/formulable. That field of what is or can be known is the basis for knowledge: let me call this field the *known-base* (describing this has been a contentious philosophical preoccupation). Drawing upon that known-base, knowledge has usually been developed and presented in various expressive forms. Two such forms will serve to make my argument here: the *treatise* (any narrative with a systematic discussion of a subject) and the *encyclopaedia* (collected listings with elaborations of many subjects or dimensions of a subject area).

These two forms in fact incorporate somewhat different understandings of knowledge. Knowledge in the treatise involves weaving together relevant materials from the known-base into a coherent picture or system: let's call this *assimilated knowledge*. I struggled a bit to find an elegant way of delineating the process which the metaphor 'weaving together' captures. The philosophical divergences on this point are numerous and unresolved. For the area under discussion here, knowledge formation by *synthesis and analysis* seems to cover the process well (they are well-defined in mathematics, but again with various nuances—nineteen distinct approaches were discerned in Marco Panza and Michael Otte 1997: ix–xi). Gottfried Leibniz's general and formative definition still serves well to convey the gist of the process:

> Synthesis is achieved when we begin from principles and run through truths in good order, thus discovering certain progressions and setting up tables, or sometimes general formulas, in which the answers to emerging questions can later be discovered. Analysis goes back to the principles in order to solve the given problems only, just as if neither we nor others had discovered anything before. (Leibniz 1989 [1679]: 232)

From the assimilated knowledge perspective, knowledge follows from synthesis and analysis; the known-base is productive of knowledge insofar as processed by synthesis and analysis.

Knowledge in the encyclopaedia typically collects considered elaborations on various themes of the known-base and makes this collection available for convenient searching and for making connections between those facets: let's call this *consultable knowledge*. The encyclopaedia form offers a practical system for searching and connecting, but that system is not itself necessarily based on synthesis and analysis. Typically, the system has been an *index* which organizes the collected themes by naming them, usually in alphabetical or numerical order and with cross-links marked. Occasionally, maps of knowledge areas have also been used. From the consultable knowledge perspective, bringing together elaborations of themes from the known-base into a convenient order is a primary condition for understanding knowledge, more so than synthesis and analysis.

However, this precedence is not a straightforward matter. In the main, the encyclopaedia was conceived as choosing and presenting only those themes which have already been subjected to synthesis and analysis, even if there is no necessary coherence across themes. In brief, only themes in the known-base which are within the sphere of assimilated knowledge have been considered as worth incorporating in consultable knowledge. Put otherwise, the encyclopaedia focuses on presenting consultable knowledge after the fact of assimilated knowledge. Nor has it invariably been the case that collecting and ordering has been the primary focus in the encyclopaedia. Some of the most celebrated usages of the encyclopaedia form have in fact been as a vehicle for synthesis and analysis. As an obvious example, Denis Diderot and Jean d'Alembert's *Encyclopédie* (1751–1766) conceived of their indexed entries as presenting an overarching synthesis. Taking a different turn, G.W.F. Hegel's *Enzyklopädie* (1817) eschewed the indexical system in favour of an intellectual schema with keywords to access his assimilated knowledge (on the context for these, see Rajan 2007). Nevertheless, consultable knowledge with an index has been the mainstay of the prevailing understanding of knowledge in the encyclopaedia.

In sum, though there are different emphases in the understanding of knowledge in the treatise and encyclopaedia form—respectively on assimilated and consultable knowledge—they have been intricately co-dependent. They have fed each other by turns and constantly. A general conception of knowledge could be regarded as an aggregated version of assimilated and consultable knowledge.

Significantly, what I am calling the *known-base* in relation to knowledge is analogous to what I have dubbed *I-information* that is available through Internet Technology. These are analogous, which means they are also distinct and not the same. To emphasize the analogy: known-base is the total content that is availed for knowledge construction through treatises and encyclopaedias (and other such forms), and I-information is the total content of the digital-text records which Internet Technology makes available. My digression on information and knowledge was necessary to make this analogy.

Those who initially developed the idea and applications of hypertext system appear to have conflated the known-base with I-information and not distinguished them sufficiently. They conceptualized the latter as if it is the same as the former. Having the analogy laid out, and therefore the distinction foregrounded, allows me to track how those notions of information and knowledge played in the development of hypertext.

3.2.3 Conceiving Hypertext Systems

I now return to describing hypertext systems.

The following points guided the developers' approach to the hypertext system, which are the *why-do-it* considerations.

- It was taken for granted that I-information would be used to develop knowledge in the same way as the known-base. This was because hypertext was conceived within and for communities invested in specialist and professional pursuits, before networking and Internet Technology.

- With the notion that what is needed is a system for conveniently garnering I-information towards developing knowledge, the early developers framed their ideas in terms of the encyclopaedic form of consultable knowledge. They did not pause on the assimilative knowledge of the treatise format. Insofar as conceiving hypertext systems went, they did not feel processes of synthesis and analysis needed to be factored in. The communities they wished to facilitate already had a well-developed grasp of assimilated knowledge, so the developers could take users' ability to analyse and synthesize for granted. Their interest was in building upon what such users already do by getting I-information into something like an encyclopaedic format, as consultable knowledge.
- Effectively, they conceived of I-information content with a limited knowledge-forming scope, and simply disregarded other kinds of content, such as, I-information for pure consumption or for merely doing something. In other words, they considered only the sort of I-information content to be relevant that has already been subjected to or prepared for analysis and synthesis. In that sense, for them assimilated knowledge was both before the fact and after the fact of the system they wanted, and did not have to be within the system.
- The system for rendering I-information into something like consultable knowledge naturally brought up the encyclopaedia as the form to depart from. In fact, with assimilated knowledge put aside, the existing encyclopaedic form itself seemed somewhat clumsy. The encyclopaedia seemed too dependent on static systems for consultation, like alphabetical or numbered indexes, and too conditional on prior legitimation by syntheses and analyses. Thus, the form of the encyclopaedia was only considered useful as a point of departure, not for replication. The system they wanted should, they felt, enable collection and consultation in encyclopaedia-style but directly from the vast repository of I-information itself to bolster the syntheses and analyses users were already engaged in.

With these preconceptions in mind, the hypertext system that developers came up with had the following mechanics, effectively the *how-to-do-it* solutions.

- At the core, the hypertext system needs to consist of *applications for making exploratory consultations and contingent collections from I-information, by establishing or extending connections along fluid and expanding pathways rather than along trodden paths*. Such collections and consultations could be undertaken, then, according to the purpose of the user of I-information. Such users would then not have to depend on the indexes provided and selections made for encyclopaedias and treatises. In fact, encyclopaedias and treatises can now themselves be considered as content within the vast repository of I-information.
- As such, hypertext would then constitute a system for making content-based connections as one goes along ('*surfing*' has become the standard term for this), or as one sieves through the vast and accruing repository of I-information (*searching*). Hypertextual surfing and searching would replace the erstwhile recourse to consultable knowledge in the encyclopaedia form. In other words,

surfing and searching by making content-connections via *hypertext would become an open-ended and in-process way of consulting.* Limited (usually institutionalized) pockets of content amidst I-information could retain the encyclopaedia form, with ordered indexes and legitimized by prior synthesis and analysis.

To implement these solutions, two key technological features of hypertext emerged, which are the *how-to-do-it* applications.

- Producers of I-information records could mark or generate key-terms therein which are meaningful to the record's content. Each key-term could then be linked to other parts of the same record or to other I-information records which have a meaningful *association* with that content (a *hyperlink*). Searchers and surfers—i.e., users—could then start from any such record and connect via the hyperlinked key-terms to other records, and from them to yet others, and thus follow chains and webs of associated content through the repository of I-information. The paths of hyperlinkage users choose to follow would be according to their purposes or desires. Users could also enrich such linkage beyond what the producer had marked initially, e.g., by being given the facility to edit that record and introduce further hyperlinked key-terms.
- Further, instead of depending on producers to hyperlink key-terms in this manner, users could be offered *search engines*. Users could then enter their own choice of key-terms there, which they *associate* with their purposes and desires. Then a mechanical process of retrieving documents which contain those key-terms from the vast repository of I-information could follow, and the user presented with a list of resulting selections. The user could then either consult some of them as needed or start from one and follow the hyperlinks.
- These two technological features follow a common rationale: both work through users following *associative* links and connections that they primarily have in mind, and conditionally by prompts recommended by content producers. Importantly, to be able to build upon and develop such associative pathways over time, hypertext should include means for users to retrieve pathways and searches over single sittings for further use, at least for a while (such as, a *cache* facility).

To sum up: the *assimilated knowledge* that has conventionally been consulted involved searching indexes of encyclopaedias, treatises and the like, which were themselves formed by synthesis and analysis of the known-base. In contradistinction from that, the kind of knowledge that is actuated through hypertext consultation by tracking lines of associations directly through I-information could be called *associative knowledge*—if indeed knowledge is sought. Knowledge development aside, hypertext systems also undiscriminatingly enable individuals to follow *associative pathways* through I-information for the purpose of consuming or doing something, according to their desires.

3.2.4 A First Principle

Assimilated knowledge, whether in encyclopaedic or treatise (or other forms), are based on collective mediations and consensuses. The received understanding of knowledge is powerfully legitimized through assimilative processes, i.e., synthesis and analysis. Knowledge is understood as becoming such by at least some degree of assimilation of material from the known-base. Synthesis and analysis need to be demonstrated in the treatise form to present assimilated knowledge; synthesis and analysis legitimize what is rendered as consultable knowledge in the encyclopaedia form. This way of processing the known-base to develop knowledge is necessarily collectively underpinned. Each undertaking of synthesis and analysis is checked, tested, contested, evidenced, debated, etc. by others before the outcome can be acknowledged as being knowledge. So, knowledge has been understood as such through collective processing before being made available to individuals for consultation to fulfil their purposes.

Hypertext constitutes a technology for individuals to engage directly with I-information, i.e., with any content recorded in digital-data format that is available through Internet Technology. The primary entry point of hypertext into the vast repository of I-information is not necessarily mediated by synthesis and analysis; users plunge directly into the content of I-information and navigate their way through associations they themselves generated or which have been suggested by content providers. These associations may or may not be informed by synthesis and analysis, and the I-information they search and surf through may or may not be legitimized by collective processing. Users whose purposes are structured by assimilated processing could search and surf fruitfully through I-information for further knowledge generation. The developers of hypertext focalized this constituency. But equally, users whose purposes are not based on synthesis and analysis could also search and surf and, with their self-generated or chosen associations, follow pathways through I-information content. These pathways may or may not have any relation to assimilated knowledge, and indeed may or may not be knowledge at all. What they come up with may not even be information in the sense of being informing.

The point is that the technological features of hypertext privilege the individual user's associations for their direct engagement with content in I-information. Hypertext systems leave it to the user's individual proclivities and abilities to draw upon the collective basis of synthesis and analysis or to not do so. That is to say: *hypertext is designed for individual associations to precede collective mediations in engaging with I-information; collective mediations may or may not play at all, depending on the individual in question.* This is understood here as a *principle of precedent individuation* that is inbuilt in hypertext systems, and works as a social and political first principle insofar as an Internet Polity has formed on their basis.

3.2.5 *The Early Developers*

The political implications of precedent individuation were considered when the idea of centring associative thinking was first proposed by Vannevar Bush, and while being variously developed in the early stages by Bush, Theodor Nelson, and Douglas Engelbart. *Why-do-it* commitments were explicit in the conceptions of associative thinking for each of them; and, for each, the *how-to-do-it* applications remained unresolved. The *how-to-do-it* pathways that they tried out have been usefully discussed in Belinda Barnet's *Memory Machines* (2013), and elsewhere, and are not detailed here. In looking back to the early developers' ideas of hypertext, the focus here is on their *why-do-it* commitments. Those are discernible in terms of three issues: who and what their applications were for; what those attempted applications were meant to replace; what rhetorical expressions went into presenting them.

Quoting Vannevar Bush's succinct statement of associative thinking in his essay 'As We May Think' (1945) have become routine in writing about hypertext:

> Our ineptitude in getting at the record is largely caused by the artificiality of systems of indexing. When data of any sort are placed in storage, they are filed alphabetically or numerically, and information is found (when it is) by tracing it down from subclass to subclass. It can be in only one place, unless duplicates are used; one has to have rules as to which path will locate it, and the rules are cumbersome. Having found one item, moreover, one has to emerge from the system and re-enter on a new path.
>
> The human mind does not work that way. It operates by association. With one item in its grasp, it snaps instantly to the next that is suggested by the association of thoughts, in accordance with some intricate web of trails carried by the cells of the brain. It has other characteristics, of course; trails that are not frequently followed are prone to fade, items are not fully permanent, memory is transitory. Yet the speed of action, the intricacy of trails, the detail of mental pictures, is awe-inspiring beyond all else in nature. (Bush 1945)

Less noted are the specific uses and constituencies he had in mind in 1945. His essay was about how scientists could contribute to the public good by using scientific records: 'A record, if it is to be useful to science, must be continuously extended, it must be stored, and above all it must be consulted'. Scientists may be expected to have abilities to analyse and synthesize already, and the records they look for are already processed thus or are for such processing. So, the existing concept of the record that Bush sought to replace was in terms of an encyclopaedic form, with the kind of index and organization described earlier. In his words, 'Wholly new forms of encyclopaedias will appear, ready made with a mesh of associative trails running through them'. He evidently had in mind encyclopaedias of *assimilated scientific knowledge*, not quite I-information or the known-base. Interestingly, in thinking about replacing the conventional index by an associative mechanism, he glossed over assimilative processes of scientific knowledge (what scientists do) and resorted to an assertion about how 'the human mind' itself works (what everyone does). In this move, processes of scientific synthesis and analysis were swept aside in favour of a mechanism which can be used irrespective of analysis and synthesis:

> associative indexing, the basic idea of which is a provision whereby any item may be caused at will to select immediately and automatically another. This is the essential feature of the

> memex [the name he gave to a hypothetical knowledge management machine]. The process of tying two items together is the important thing. (Bush 1945)

His exemplification of the use of 'associative indexing' clearly suggests that he took assimilative processes for granted and therefore left them out of the MEMEX. He imagined that the MEMEX system would be available to any individual, who can use the device 'at will' to select and link from the record—the 'at will' emphasis marks the principle of precedent individuation. Of course, to Bush's mind the record is already of assimilated knowledge and the user (a scientist) whose will is exerted is already in possession of assimilative abilities; and yet, that tacitly slides into a system which is based on anyone's 'human mind' and an individual's 'will'. When he revisited the memex concept in 1965, with digital computing centred, he reiterated the second paragraph of the quotation above verbatim. At the same time, he widened his constituency from scientists in 1945 to users in other areas:

> This need holds true in science, in the law, in medicine, in economics, and, for that matter, in the broadest subjects of human relations. It is not just a problem for the libraries, although that is important. Rather, the problem is how creative men think, and what can be done to help them think. (Bush 1991 [1965]: 197)

In fact, the scientists were replaced by the vaguer 'creative men'. Scientists and users pursuing law, medicine, economics, etc. could all be taken as competent in consensually understood processes of assimilated knowledge. They abide by the collective norms of their disciplines, and much therein would be considered 'creative'. However, the term 'creative' is rather more catholic. It is difficult to argue that any individual human activity, however incommensurate with norms of assimilated processing, is not 'creative' in some sense.

Historians of hypertext have observed that the problems of such precedent individuation were noted and discussed very soon after Bush proposed the associative process (Nyce and Kahn 1991: 60–62; Bardini 2000: 38–41), and before the term 'hypertext' was coined by Theodor Nelson. Naturally, for Bush's readers too, the constituencies who were to be catered by this technological feature were scientists. The collective norms of knowledge assimilation were of considerable importance to them. Insofar as they were engaged in networking—by definition, a facility for collective work—associative linkage was of interest for directly facilitating assimilated knowledge. Various fusions of associative linkage with processes of synthesis and analysis were considered. For instance, J.C.R. Licklider's (1965) report on reconfiguring the consultable knowledge in libraries—conceived as an encyclopaedic accumulation—took its cue from Bush in the Preface but made only a tentative brush with associative chains for information retrieval (179–182). That was mainly in anticipating more work on defining 'the fundamental relatedness or relevance on which the "association" is based' (182). Contemplating the potential of computer networking, with a perspective that anticipates Internet Technology, Licklider and Robert Taylor (1968) focused strongly on 'cooperative modelling', 'on working on-line and interactively with computers' (28). Insofar as the facilities of making associative links went, they envisaged the advantages as subsidiary to communication, with an informing function to facilitate cooperation:

> The computer system was a significant aid in exploring the depth and breadth of the material. More detailed information could be displayed when facts had to be pinpointed; more global information could be displayed to answer questions of relevance and interrelationship. A future version of this system will make it possible for each participant, on his own TV screen, to thumb through the speaker's files as the speaker talks -- and thus check out incidental questions without interrupting the presentation for substantiation. (Licklider and Taylor 1968: 25)

Focusing on communication among scientists (or broadly knowledge communities) as the primary condition for using associative links seemed to be regarded as a tempering of precedent individuation.

Douglas Engelbart's conception of hypertext, as one among other devices for what he called 'augmenting' the human intellect, was accordingly grounded in communication. In particular, he focused on the structures of natural language: 'A natural language provides its user with a ready-made structure of concepts that establishes a basic mental structure' (Engelbart 1962: 35). In a close study of Engelbart's contribution to computing, Thierry Bardini (2000) plausibly saw him as factoring in the constitutive structures of natural language to balance the precedent individuation involved in associative linking. In fact, Bardini regarded Bush's emphasis on association as leading merely to an information retrieval system for individuals. However, Engelbart also conceived of natural language—where the 'important [links] are already established in natural language' (40)—as actively pre-structuring associative linkage in the hypertext system. So, the conception of hypertext he came up with had no mechanism for synthesis and analysis either; he simply depended on users already being adept in assimilated knowledge. However, not every kind of usage of natural language involves synthesis and analysis. Natural language allows for everything, including irrational expression, errors, and nonsense.

That also turned out to be the case for Theodor Nelson's concept of hypertext, albeit in a different way. The term 'hypertext' is strongly associated with him because he coined it and variously tried to define it. Nelson took a somewhat different turn from Bush or Engelbart. He felt that synthesis and analysis were incorporated in a received system of 'literature' or in textual features that he thought of as 'literary'. His idea was to integrate the literary system with a hypertext system, effectively building in some assimilative knowledge structures within the hypertext system. To be clear, Nelson understood the term 'literary' and 'literature' thus:

> By the term 'literature' we are not necessarily talking about *belles lettres* or leather-bound books. We mean it in the same broad sense of 'the scientific literature,' or that graduate-school question, 'Have you looked at the literature?'
>
> A literature is *a system of interconnected writings.* (Nelson [version 87.1] 1987: 2/9)

Nelson's approach to hypertext predicated on 'literature' crystallized gradually as he worked through the possible applications in hypertext (from 1965 onwards, usefully traced through his selection of writing in Nelson 1965–1977, and passim in Nelson 1975). His concept (and coinage) of hypertext was solidly grounded in Bush's concept of associative thinking (Nelson 1965–1977: 50–52; 1987). But the emphasis on 'literature' imbued it with a collective underpinning akin to prior synthesis and analysis.

However, in line with his literary emphasis, his definitions and elaborations of hypertext invariably took the features and forms of the *written text* as paradigmatic. His preferred one-liner eventually was: 'by "hypertext" I mean *non-sequential writing*—text that branches and allows choices to the reader, best read at an interactive screen' (Nelson 1987: 0/2). The corresponding XANADU project was meant to integrate Bush's idea of associative linking with reference to all dimensions of the existing literary system in a usable or applicable computer-based infrastructure. Put otherwise, this was an attempt to replace the existing *literary system* by a working *hypertext system* which emulated—better yet, enhanced—the key normative features of the former. He understood the existing literary system as centred on, among other features, the following: reading and writing; methods of intra and intertextual usage (editing, comparing, juxtaposing, adapting, extracting, selecting from, etc.); the forms of print production (scroll or codex based, in sequential orders); the modes of organizing corpuses, archives, repositories (indexes etc.); the publication and intellectual-property regimes. Nelson touched on all of these, and he sought to put together a hypertext system which could coherently extend the flexibilities and connections between all of these via the resources of digital computing. In effect, it seems that he hoped to ensure that a hypertext system would retain something of the processes of assimilated knowledge that have been built into the literary system.

Unfortunately for Nelson, it has been and remains difficult to pin down the collective norms of the literary system simply in terms of textual features and regimes for managing texts. Those depend greatly on consensual and yet unwritten conventions, on informal agreements as well as institutional histories, which are loosely designed to accommodate changing social circumstances. The literary system appears to have a conversational mode of maintaining collective norms, many elements of which are not formalized or textualized but function in contingent ways for producing assimilated knowledge. Nelson seemingly did not grasp the depth of unwritten contingencies which underpin the literary system. He apprehended these processes sufficiently to want them integrated in his version of a hypertext system, via the mechanics of associative linking. But at the same time, he apprehended them insufficiently to be able to construct a functional hypertext system to replace it. He sought to stick to some fundamental norms of the literary system while transforming it into a hypertext system with a different mechanics: 'And this [hypertext] world, this new literature, will be built from the "document" as we have long known it, the "author" as we have long known him or her, and an extended form of "writing" as we have long done it and read it' (Nelson 1987: 1/10). Each of these terms in quotations marks, while functionally used and institutionalized, are subject to various contestations and irresolutions. Indeed, numerous levels of elisions and crossed-purposes are found in Nelson's searching mediations for the XANADU project: he thought of writing and reading interchangeably; he wanted both to maintain textual integrity and allow for fluid textuality; he wanted to liberate texts from publishing/archiving regimes and yet stand by gatekeeping/intellectual-property regimes; he wished for new kinds of writing/reading with old standards for doing those; he wanted to conceive a virtual screen culture which would subscribe to some conventions of print culture and so on. In short, by contemplating the literary system as his horizon for realizing hypertext systems, Nelson did try to integrate assimilated knowledge into his hypertext system, but he was ultimately unable to do so. The principle of precedent individuation stayed unshaken by his attempts to engineer hypertext systems.

For the early developers, each of the moves to substantiate a hypertext system was impelled by a *why-do-it* social commitment which negotiated, often by circumvention, with the principle of precedent individuation. These moves were conceived within communities of assimilated knowledge and yet sought extension to every individual. At times, the drive was articulated directly as a form of political utopianism. In that sense, the *why-do-it* sensibility of the developers was characteristic of the period in which they were engaging with the *how-to-do-it* conundrums. They appeared to be striving for a society of perfected individuals, or a perfected society of individuals, or possibly a perfected knowledge society. Various resonances with what are loosely thought of as concepts of 'liberal' freedom and individuality/collectivity were woven into their reckonings. Bush hoped that MEMEX would 'yet allow [humans] truly to encompass the great record and to grow in the wisdom of race experience' (Bush 1945); and Engelbart looked forward to an 'augmented' humanity. Nelson expected his XANADU project to both 'simplify our lives' and 'read from and write on screens with new freedom'; and he added with ironic virtuousness, 'Remember those ideals that made our country great, such as liberty and pluralism and the accessibility of ideas? Some of us still do' (Nelson 1987: 1/4). As Barnet (2013) summed it up:

> In the last century this word ['association'] has come to acquire a meaning quite different from its original formulation by Aristotle in 400 BC; it currently implies a personalized, rhizomic (or for 'first wave' hypertext theorists, even liberatory) technique opposed to strict sequence or cognitive control. In contemporary critical theory, 'association' is often counterposed to 'hierarchical' structures as though these were distinct entities – *nomos* versus *logos*. (7–8)

In these hypertextual aspirations, along the way, commitments to assimilated knowledge with their collective undergirding were not quite relegated but rendered a personal choice in line with the principle of precedent individuation.

3.2.6 World Wide Web

In turning to the World Wide Web (WWW or W3), launched in 1992–1993, as the dominant hypertext system and as a received feature of Internet Technology, I am obviously stepping beyond the Cold War historical context, with which I began here. In fact, similarly sketchy notes on the 1990s are given in the next Chap. 4. WWW appeared as the internet opened up to mass uptake and commercialization after the Cold War. Its significance in grounding precedent individuation in the formation of the Internet Polity is such that it is best considered here, extending lines of *why-do-it* considerations from the early developments of hypertext.

WWW was more pragmatic and functional than earlier attempts at a universal hypertext system, and less tempered by implicit subscription to assimilated knowledge. Though developed in the scholarly environs of CERN, WWW was not designed particularly for or in the terms of communities engaged in synthesis and analysis. It was developed for the convenient management of I-information. At least through the 1990s, when it quickly became the dominant hypertext system of the internet, it appeared without ambitions to augment humans or replace the literary system or other such transformative agendas. The various explanations that came from the developers of WWW when it was launched (1992–1993), offered few *why-do-it* thoughts and focused on clarifying the *how-to-do-it* solutions. Terms like 'information' and 'knowledge', 'texts' and 'media' and 'documents' were taken as commonly used, without attempting definitions or honing their senses. Vannevar Bush's (1945) idea of associative thinking was accepted as the obvious core of hypertext and self-evidently true and was translated into practical terms:

> Computers give us two practical techniques for human-knowledge interface. One is hypertext, in which links between pieces of text (or other media) mimic human association of ideas. The other is text retrieval, which allows associations to be deduced from the content of text. In the first case, the reader's operation is typically to click with a mouse (or type in a reference number). In the second case, it is to supply some words representing that which he desires. The W3 ideal world allows both operations and provides access from any browsing platform. (Berners-Lee et al. 1992a, b: 33)

The mention of 'human association of ideas' came with a reference to Bush's article. Tim Berners-Lee's retrospection on developing WWW echoed Bush's notion that associative thinking is coterminous with how the brain works: 'There are billions of neurons in our brains, but what are neurons? Just cells. The brain has no knowledge until connections are made between neurons' (Berners-Lee and Fischetti 1999: 12). The developers were keen not to overegg the idea of hypertext beyond technical pragmatics:

> Most data on the web is plain text, accessed by automatically generated hypertext links (following for example the directory tree in which the files are stored) or an automatic indexing system. The prospective information provider need not be frightened by the term 'hypertext'. (Berners-Lee et al. 1992a: 456)

This untrammelled approach to hypertext meant going along with analysis and synthesis occurring, if at all, either before or after the fact of what WWW does. So, the WWW system was confined to maximizing searching and surfing functions by making associative links directly within I-information. Since it was developed upon the TCP/IP suite (and easily integrated as a feature of Internet Technology), it came with a clear apprehension of the scale and diversity of I-information. As its naming and the early explanations showed, WWW was designed for a global scope. Its objective was maximum reach in I-information, amenable to continuous scaling-up; consequently, its design minimized any narrow conception of how I-information should be used. In brief, WWW simply sidestepped any complex preconception of assimilated knowledge and thereby integrated precedent individuation as a structural principle. The result was a hypertext system which seemed disposed for precedent individuality as a first principle as the Internet Polity converged upon and very significantly collectivized through it.

The *how-to-do-it* considerations for WWW were succinctly outlined in historicist accounts by the developers: especially Berners-Lee (1999), and also James Gilliers and Robert Cailliau (2000). As is well known, the *how-to-do-it* areas consisted in developing the following, which gradually settled into the protocol in use till 2022 (HTTP 1.1, Fielding et al. 1999):

- An addressing system with Unique Resource Identifiers (URI), divided at times with Universal Resource Locators (URL) and Universal Resource Numbers (URN);
- Specifications for a Hypertext Markup Language (HTML) which could facilitate linking the content of coded text-data in the American Standard Code for Information Interchange (ASCII), and enable the transfer of content thus disposed across the internet by using the Simple Mail Transport Protocol (SMTP)—later the Multipurpose Internet Mail Extensions (MIME) enabled non-ASCII texts to be handled too;
- Specifications for a Hypertext Transfer Protocol (HTTP) which enable servers which have adopted it to transfer texts, menus, etc.

These constituent elements of WWW were premised on the existence of the TCP/IP suite (Gillies and Cailliau 2000: Chap. 2 began their account with a detailed history of TCP/IP and its spread to Europe). ASCII was adopted for the development of Internet Technology, and SMTP was developed within Internet Technology, before the WWW hypertext system. These were obviously grounded in HTTP, as the developers observed in their early explanations:

> HTTP is an Internet protocol. It is similar in its readable, text-based style to the File Transfer (FTP) and Network News (NNTP) Protocols that have been used to transfer files and news on the Internet for many years. Unlike those protocols, however, HTTP is stateless. (That is, it runs over a TCP connection that is held only for the duration of one operation.) The stateless model is efficient when a link from one object may lead equally well to an object stored on the same server, or to another distant server. The purpose of a reference such as a URI is that it should always refer to the 'same' (in some sense) object. This also makes a stateless protocol appropriate, as it returns results based on the URI but irrelevant of any previous operations performed by the client. (Berners-Lee et al. 1994: 78)

What is called the 'stateless model' here is particularly noteworthy because it is a design feature which puts a precedent emphasis on associative hyperlinking and downplays assimilative factors like synthesis and analysis. The latter could come into play in the WWW system only after that statelessness is first given play (e.g., by caching). Associations could be foregrounded in terms of the *sameness* of 'objects' that are linkable in an ongoing way. Along with the existence of the TCP/IP suite, the WWW hypertext system was also premised on the emerging condition of the Internet Infrastructure, especially the rapid development of personal computers (which Gillies and Cailliau 2000: Chap. 3 tied in with the development of hypertext prior to WWW). Given the growth of personal computing and the uptake of the TCP/IP suite, with the development of URI, HTTP, and HTML, a global system for associative linking across the internet was in place and quickly became a feature of Internet Technology. For users, engaging with I-information in all its diversity and scale involved making links by request/response moves, by extending individual searching and surfing via associations along keywords or hyperlinks. Effectively, the principle of precedent individuation was unproblematically designed into and taken up in using the WWW system.

Developers of the WWW hypertext system, principally Tim Berners-Lee, have generally given explanatory as well as historicist accounts with a strong *how-to-do-it* sense of the project. In these accounts, beyond maximizing associative linking and therefore, implicitly, precedent individuation, not much was added to the conceptual possibilities of hypertext. In Berners-Lee et al. (1994: 81–82), the authors included some pointers towards future developments which showed certain *why-do-it* concerns. They were evidently aware of the technological structuring of precedent individuation into the WWW system and were anticipating ways of facilitating collectively legitimized work or 'collaboration' within the hypertext system—in fact, considering how synthesis and analysis may be incorporated within WWW's mediations between users and I-information. That 'collaboration' should be concomitant with hypertext was, as observed earlier, taken for granted by the early developers. Indeed, that had been the premise on which computer networking had itself been envisaged, to recall Licklider and Taylor's (1968: 22–25) interest in 'cooperative modelling'.

In looking forward to facilitating collaborative possibilities, Berners-Lee et al. (1994) anticipated additional software for editing, conferencing, etc. A more intriguing anticipation was: 'Evolution of objects from being principally human-readable documents to contain more machine-oriented semantic information, allowing more sophisticated processing' (82). That this has a bearing on 'collaboration' might not have seemed self-evident then. It became much more so in Berners-Lee's (1999) wide-ranging reflections on the development of the WWW system. Here, interestingly, he noted that precedent individuation did not lead into 'collaboration' because of *how-to-do-it* limitations, such as facilities for editing hypertext, but also because of social proclivities:

> Without a hypertext editor, people would not have the tools to really use the Web as an intimate collaborative medium. Browsers would let them find and share information, but they could not work together intuitively. Part of the reason, I guessed, was that collaboration required much more of a social change in how people worked. And part of it was that editors were more difficult to write. (57)

In this observation, the appearance of a larger *why-do-it* ambition is apparent: WWW should not just serve individuals to manoeuvre through I-information as they wish but also to do the collective work that is in the province of assimilated knowledge. More importantly, Berners-Lee also anticipated—perhaps more accurately, envisioned—future possibilities for collaboration which gave a significant conceptual turn to hypertext.

Berners-Lee (1999) anticipated that the WWW system would become more adapted to greater collaboration between people (the 'first part of his dream', as he put it), and thereafter, more importantly:

> In the second part of the dream, collaborations extend to computers. Machines become capable of analyzing all the data on the Web – the content, links, and transactions between people and computers. A 'semantic Web,' which should make this possible, has yet to emerge, but when it does, the day-to-day mechanisms of trade, bureaucracy, and our daily lives will be handled by machines talking to machines, leaving humans to provide the inspiration and intuition. The intelligent 'agents' people have touted for ages will finally materialize. (158)

After outlining some tools which were under development in this direction, he observed:

> Real life is and must be full of all kinds of social constraint – the very processes from which 'society' arises. Computers help if we use them to create abstract social machines on the Web: processes in which the people do the creative work and the machine does the administration. Many social processes can be better run by machine, because the machine is always available, it is free from bias, and no one likes to administer these kinds of systems anyway. (172)

Here we have an explicit and distinctive *why-do-it* statement building upon the WWW hypertext system. The idea appears to push collaboration towards machine-learning processes, which would be integrated in layers within or upon the WWW protocol. Human users would continue working with associative links and follow primarily individuated paths through I-information via the WWW hypertext system, and automated systems integrated into WWW would do the work of assimilated knowledge development or of synthesis and analysis. In other words, the WWW system would effectively structure a sort of division of labour between humans and machine. In this division of labour, the machine is seemingly allocated the task of producing assimilated knowledge autonomously. This could only follow from machine-learning components of WWW conducting synthesis and analysis of data emerging continuously from humans using the information management components of WWW in line with the principle of precedent individuation.

To sell the idea of such a WWW division of labour, in the quotation above Berners-Lee employed a rhetorical strategy, i.e., a series of binary oppositions. The machine-learning side of the envisaged system was pegged as dull, 'administration', as opposed to the individuated human engagement side of the system, which was characterized as 'creative work'. A series of syntagmatic associations and oppositions was offered: collaborative assimilated knowledge ('analysing all the data') as syntagm for 'administration', opposed to individuated associative linking as syntagm for 'creativity', 'inspiration and intuition'. The rhetorical ploy was used to persuade that creativity and assimilative processes are independent of each other, and that the former is exciting and the latter boring. Moreover, the phrasing suggested that the exciting stuff can be enhanced for humans by surrendering assimilative processing to learning machines. Putting the rhetoric aside, the issue really is: what are the underpinning *why-do-it* considerations for that direction? An answer is suggested in the above quotation too, in what 'administration' consists in: 'the day-to-day mechanisms of trade, bureaucracy, and our daily lives'. That impetus appears to take away much self-possession from users in the name of freeing them. Arguably the *why-do-it* thrust of Berners-Lee's vision was to capture assimilated knowledge for control and capitalization by commercial and governmental entities without too much oversight and interference by users—putatively, for their benefit.

Perhaps that is making too much of a small extract from Berners-Lee's many visionary statements since. Irrespective of his convictions since, the general direction indicated there has been pursued energetically. The immediate idea of the Semantic Web involved evolving an information management system for the rational organization of data on top of the WWW information management system for individuated negotiations with I-information. In 2003, a volume of essays (Fensel et al. 2003) fleshing out the possibilities of this Semantic Web appeared, with a foreword from Berners-Lee. The essays were devoted to re-calibrating the WWW protocols and their constituent languages (hence 'semantic') for the purpose of knowledge management, business-to-business and business-to-consumer activity by organizing data for machine processing. Indicatively, here the deliberations were consistently focused on 'knowledge' being produced rather than 'information' being processed via the Semantic Web. The realization of the Semantic Web since is tracked in a stage-by-stage manner through the terms 'Web 2.0' and then 'Web 3.0' (which is now taken as coterminous with the Semantic Web). The WWW hypertext transmission protocol has been upgraded too (Fielding et al. 2022). The Semantic Web or Web 3.0 is work in progress. This has involved building metadata system tools. These are not conceived as devised for programming (where algorithms are purposed for users to do things that generate data), but as instilling logical reasoning functions to dispose the data for different kinds of 'declarative' employment (e.g., to feed algorithms for automated processing). Ongoing developments in the formal methods for doing this (laid out authoritatively in Szeredi et al. 2016) are effectively tracked on the W3C website.

Those developments are beyond the scope of the current focus on the political first principles underpinning the formation of an Internet Polity. I return to this conceptual thrust in the semantic web apropos of the Internet Polity in Chap. 6.

I turn now to another political first principle of the Internet Polity that is grounded in Internet Technology.

3.3 Targeted Collective Regulation and Security Controls

Thus far I have argued that the developers of Internet Technology resolved *how-to-do-it* questions in terms of certain *why-do-it* norms, which have effectively been grounded as social and political first principles for the Internet Polity formed through internet usage. With a historicist perspective, I have discussed two of these so far. One concerns the TCP/IP suite, which developed with and was adapted through usage as a principle of minimal-gradual-mechanical standardization; the other concerns hypertext systems, which crystallized a principle of precedent individuation in engaging with I-information. On the whole, these two principles seem to cohere well. Both appear to work jointly for a social condition where the scope of reasonable individual interests is maximized, and collectivity is rendered corollary.

Complementing and, to some degree, tempering the design of minimal-gradual-mechanical standardization and precedent individuation, a principle of targeted collective regulation through security controls was also integrated by degrees into Internet Technology and adapted as a first principle too for the Internet Polity. Security controls are not easily identifiable as *one* discrete feature of Internet Technology. In fact, they are distributed across various levels in and nodes of Internet Technology, and often work through the broader apparatus of Internet Infrastructure. They cohere as a technological area in being purposed for 'security'. The impetus for them usually came from and were implemented at the behest of institutional authorities according to their policies and practices, rather than in terms of technology developers' convictions and circumstances. These authorities may be characterized as state or non-state agencies or businesses enterprises. The specific tools variously designed to enable local to wider policing and restrictions—which I call 'security controls' for brevity—are attached to Internet Technology and cannot be considered built in as features thereof. However, such security controls have exploited the features discussed above, and become elements woven around and into them. This has occurred so pervasively and intricately that they are now inextricable from Internet Technology and Infrastructure.

To reiterate, the security controls are too diverse to be characterized as *a feature*. They constitute rather a collection of purpose-led features, which are being continuously incorporated or layered into Internet Technology. Their coherence and place in the structuring of the Internet Polity is dependent on how *security* is understood. In terms of policy making where the internet is squarely in view, the 2013 glossary of US National Institute of Standards and Technology's (NIST) Computer Security Resource Centre (CSRC) gave the following definition:

> A condition that results from the establishment and maintenance of protective measures that enable an organization to perform its mission or critical functions despite risks posed by threats to its use of systems. Protective measures may involve a combination of deterrence, avoidance, prevention, detection, recovery, and correction that should form part of the organization's risk management approach. (Kissel 2013: 173)

This definition placed 'security' in relation to the boundaries of organizations. The preventive measures named a range (deterrence, avoidance, prevention, detection, recovery, and correction) that could be understood in relation to such boundaries: i.e., they apply in terms of both what is inside the boundaries and what is outside. NIST-CSRC (Paulsen and Byers 2019) replaced this glossary by a website-based one, where, alongside this definition, eight further definitions were added from different policy sources (NIST-CSRC glossary 2019: entry for 'security'). Two of these nine definitions maintain the boundary reference to 'organization' and 'enterprise'. However, the other six shift the onus of the definition to the maintenance and legitimate use of 'information' or, in our terms, I-information (in terms of integrity, confidentiality, access) without reference to boundaries. Effectively, the reach of security considerations became unbound by these definitions. Such considerations could be extended to any context, with or without reference to boundaries. These could include: individual users and providers of I-information, organizations directly or indirectly transacting or holding I-information, and individual or collective entities featuring in I-information. In definitional terms, the 'condition' (as the above quotation has it) that comes under the purview of security extends in a fine-grained way to all dimensions of the Internet Polity and indeed to its actually existing contexts. In other words, security controls extend to potentially regulating the collectivity that is the Internet Polity itself, as well as the actually existing polities its participants live in. This comprehensive and extensive embrace of security controls naturally grounds itself as a social and political first principle of the Internet Polity, which I call a principle of *targeted collective regulation.*

The expansion in definitions of the policy reach of computer 'security' in the NIST-CSRC glossaries between 2013 and 2019 reflects a larger and earlier debate about the reach of security considerations. Conventionally, the concept of security centred on states of exception (situations considered not normal) and applied within institutional, geopolitical, or regional boundaries (especially, political state boundaries). It was regarded as the province of military and police prerogatives. During the 1990s, that approach was questioned as being too narrow and unfit for the post-Cold War world, influentially by the Copenhagen School of security studies. The Cold War arguably centred security concerns at an inter-state level (international), and civil unrest, such as the student movements discussed earlier, were considered intra-state (domestic) security issues. The Copenhagen School recommended thinking of security in terms of more fine-grained levels from individuals to trans-state organizations, and effectively extended the scope of security concerns beyond military/police prerogatives and exceptional circumstances. In fact, where security concerns could be anticipated and addressed appeared now to be conceived in a fluid manner, based on contextual assessments rather than objective criteria:

> The impossibility of applying objective standards of securityness relates to a trivial but rarely noticed feature of security arguments: They are about the future, about alternative futures – always hypothetical – and about counterfactuals. A security argument always involves two predictions: What will happen if we do not take 'security action' (the threat), and what will happen if we do (How is the submitted security policy supposed to work?). A security theory that could tell politicians and citizens what actually constitute security problems and what do not would demand that such predictions should be possible to make on a scientific basis, which means society would have to be a closed, mechanical, and deterministic system. Even this condition, however, would not be enough, because a second complication is that securityness is not only a matter of degree – 'how threatening' – but is also a qualitative question: Do we choose to attach the security label with its ensuing effects? Actors can choose to handle a major challenge in other ways and thus not securitize it. The use of a specific conceptualization is always a choice – it is politics, it is not possible to decide by investigating the threat scientifically. (Buzan et al. 1998: 32)

In fact, it is difficult to see why the fact that security relates to future possibilities, counterfactuals, and qualitative questions should preclude applying some objective limits to its scope of application (in terms of what is 'securitized'). But the effect of thinking that objective limits should not apply is clearly stated: security extends to wherever it is chosen to be attached, and the choice is inevitably a political one. Moreover, it becomes possible for anything considered a political matter to also be considered a security matter. Security becomes coterminous with politics, and regulatory practice for security becomes politics itself, being inevitably implicated in the existence of any polity. The problems of this position have been discussed intermittently since (thoughtfully in Neal 2019: Chap. 2, who recommends thinking of security in terms of 'problematizing').

Insofar as the internet goes, the elements inside and outside Internet Technology that can be regarded as security controls form a constantly expanding list. That also means that the political import of security is in an ongoing process of being honed and weighed. Every security control that is formed at any political juncture extends the targeting of collective regulation. Here, the main distinction to be borne in mind is where those security controls are enjoined by extrinsic political agencies apropos of the Internet Polity and where they are layered onto Internet Technology and become engrained in the Internet Polity. The former incorporates a raft of legislation and concordant policing and surveillance systems, organizational codes and policies, cybersecurity experts and firms scanning for vulnerabilities, ethics watchdogs and consumer ombudsmen and activist users and the like. Such parties and provisions determine what to securitize and what not to, and why. As Barry Buzan et al. (1998) put it, 'it is politics' and not something that Internet Technology was formatively based upon. The security controls as technological features are usually developed responsively and implemented according to those determinations. The process of their development and implementation is naturally integrated with the other features of Internet Technology, the internet protocols and hypertext systems, and must negotiate with the other first principles of the Internet Polity, minimal-gradual-mechanical standardization and precedent individuation. Arguably, the greater the density of security controls bolstering targeted collective regulation in synch with those first principles, the more those controls become integral to Internet Technology and habitual for the Internet Polity.

The essential concepts of security controls for the internet were put in place while networking and internetworking were still mainly for academic and governmental activities and predominantly publicly funded. In the earlier form of NIST in the USA, the National Bureau of Standards (NBS), for instance, published a framework for network security which extended to internetworking of the time (Cole and Branstad 1978; Heinrich 1978). The main security issues involved:

- the identification and authentication of users;
- control of user access to network resources;
- ensuring that users' requests and the responses match up and no unintended or inadvertent exposures or consequences occur;
- protecting transmitted data from modification or disclosure, whether deliberate or unintentional.

Each of those issues both recognized and anticipated clusters of security vulnerabilities, some known and others yet to emerge. These could arise due to numerous causes (e.g., maleficent actors, human errors and accidents, technological glitches, unforeseen social circumstances) and be evinced through various means (e.g., worm, virus and other attacks; unauthorized usage of data; data manipulation for undesirable ends). The main notion at the time was that all of these would need to be identified and gauged as security matters across networks by some responsible authority. Each of those issues could also correspondingly be understood as calling for clusters of security controls:

- obviously by encryption, but also
- by enacting organizational policies and laws;
- appointing policing and adjudicating authorities;
- developing technological checks and barriers, debugging patches and fixes, surveillance and recording systems, etc.

At that stage, a combination of Network Security Centres (NSCs), with oversight of specific networks/regions, and of Intelligent Cryptographic Devices (ICDs), focusing principally on protecting transmitted data, were accordingly proposed. Insofar as these reports envisaged security in relation to 'internetting', their understanding was that:

> This internet level provides to higher levels the appearance of a single large virtual network. The internet level translates the protocols of the virtual network into the protocols required by the local networks. (Heinrich 1978: 15–16)

Given that, no significant problems with scaling-up the security recourses of NSCs and ICDs were anticipated in the NBS reports.

That this was over-optimistic was demonstrated soon and well before the internet and WWW moved towards pervasive personal and organizational use in the 1990s. On 2 November 1988, the Morris Worm (named after the person who designed and released it, Robert Tappan Morris) infected networks using versions of the Berkeley Software Distribution UNIX operating systems. It reportedly infected and clogged up around 6000 computers before its advance was halted and a patch found within a few days. Nevertheless, it was the largest attack across networks known then, and brought the security implications of Internet Technology to widespread media and public attention. It also attracted governmental attention, leading to a Congressional hearing (see US Government 1989). It was, as a US General Accounting Office report on the incident noted, different from earlier computer viruses:

> First, previous viruses were almost always limited to personal computers (PCS), whereas the Internet virus infected larger systems, such as minicomputers, workstations, and mainframes. In addition, the Internet virus was the first to spread over a network automatically (i.e., without requiring other programs or user intervention to transmit it). (GAO 1989: 13)

In fact, technical analyses showed several limitations in the Morris Worm, which also suggested that its capacity for causing damage could have been greater. It was designed with a pointed albeit partially exploited grasp of Internet Technology's addressing protocols (detailed in Spafford 1988). In the discussions that followed, the need for some centralized monitoring of the decentralized internet, updating of legal and regulatory provisions, educating on ethical responsibilities, bolstering communications among technicians, and developing robust operating systems were raised. The 1978 NBS framework for NSCs looked well dated already.

However, the essential structure of security issues set out in that NBS framework has held thereafter, even as Internet Technology exploded in private and collective uptake with the 1990s. What occurred was a burgeoning of complexity and diversity around each of those issues and recourses. The role envisaged for NSCs became distributed in layers across every sort of organization—regional, national, and multinational, whether governmental, commercial, or other—and their legal and policy frameworks. Correspondingly, the normative codes and mandatory rules arising from these frameworks have been enjoined across all those organizations and down through formal and informal collectives to individual users, consumers, and citizens. As a structure of cybersecurity outside but bearing upon Internet Technology, these kinds of security controls reflect and increasingly constitute actually existing social relations. Insofar as Internet Technology goes, what is considered its decentralized formation is, as we have seen, largely grounded in its collective usage—in terms of the principles of minimal-gradual-mechanical standardization and of precedent individuation. These are premised on Internet Technology's core operations being self-consistent without being centrally administered across its global user base, hence decentralized.

Interestingly, extending targeted collective regulation across Internet Technology and the Internet Infrastructure, which suggests centralizations of authority and power, has involved less direct intervention in the core and a great proliferation and diversification of authorities and regimes working upon the core. Their diversity and numerousness are given some coherence by the relative stability of the core and seem thereby to not contradict the principles of minimal-gradual-mechanical standardization and precedent individuation. At the same time, from their multiple directions they work precisely towards imposing strong or even coercive standards against the spirit of minimal-gradual-mechanical standardization and precedent individuation. To this end, the enormous diversity of authorities and regimes instilling security controls exploit every possibility that the core of Internet Technology allows without quite compromising it. As observed in the previous chapter, the layering structure of the Internet Protocol allows for higher security layers to be introduced, differentiated according to applications and user cohorts. Domain naming and addressing—and related features—enable the introduction of authorities which can intervene in data transmissions in specific precincts. The dominant hypertext system encourages interoperability of applications, which also means the continuous recording of a great mass of linkable data which is open to security-driven analysis (e.g., for surveillance and gauging effects of security controls). Since engagements with I-information are as much for informing as for doing (buying and selling, communicating, gaming, etc.), such security provisions can be garnered to interventions in everyday activities.

Perhaps the most important consequence of the decentredness at the core of Internet Technology and the diversity of tendentiously centralizing security actors and regimes is that security controls is an area of competition and cooperation. They have become co-extensive with the politics and economies of our societies. Madeline Carr (2021) puts it well in concluding a brief history of cybersecurity:

> The problems of cyber security are not simply technological. Rather, they are embedded in the ways that we choose to integrate that technology into a whole range of social, legal, economic, military, and political practices and processes. They are shaped by us and shape us. (Carr 2021, 63)

Security controls are an ever-burgeoning commercial sector, with both technological and non-technological products catering to consumers across all levels. They define and mediate between political alignments on the internet, mirroring or enhancing or constituting social relations which are effective pervasively. In the space of security controls, in fact, the political and the commercial have become increasingly indistinguishable. More effectively, in being continuously integrated in Internet Technology, this space of security controls directly interlaces with the collective life of the Internet Polity, and effectively mediates between it and actually existing polities.

3.4 Towards Part II

In these chapters of Part I, I have argued that the developers of Internet Technology followed certain norms according to their contexts and circumstances in designing the technological structure. These norms could be thought of as being grounded in Internet Technology, which means they have then been adapted and become habitual through internet usage. In other words, they have become social and political first principles through collective engagement with the internet as a facility and space. They are, I have suggested, the basis on which the Internet Polity has assumed an organized and internet-oriented character. Thereby, the Internet Polity manifests the characteristics of a global polity in the sense presented in Chap. 1, i.e., in the terms used by Olaf Corry (2013). In Chaps. 2 and 3 (Part I) I have focused on three broad features of Internet Technology and the norms—the *why-do-it* considerations—that fed their development: the internet protocols, hypertext systems, and security controls. The norms guiding the development of these technological features realized three corresponding first principles of the Internet Polity: minimal-gradual-mechanical standardization, precedent individuation, and targeted collective regulation. Part I has been devoted to articulating the grounding of these through Internet Technology and emergence in the formation of the Internet Polity.

However, the mere description of the organizing first principles of the Internet Polity does little for conveying the breadth of its formative process and fleshing out its collective life. Those are addressed in Part II of this study. The main argument there is that a developing discourse of the Internet Polity has built upon those principles to evolve collectivized practices of communication and interaction. The focus on the next part is on this discourse, principally traced through the words and phrases which have spread to give congruence to collectivity. In other words, the following chapters focus on words which have emerged from and quickly become characteristic of engaging with the internet—which have, so to speak, caught on. How these accrued into a distinctive vocabulary for collectivizing is tracked, as are the various stages in the career of the Internet Polity.

References

April Third Movement reunion website (1970–1971) University of Stanford. http://www.a3mreunion.org/archive/1970-1971/70-71_laos_computer/1970-1971_laos_computer.html

Bardini T (2000) Bootstrapping: Douglas Engelbart, coevolution, and the origins of personal computing. Stanford University Press, Stanford CA

Barnet B (2013) Memory machines: the evolution of hypertext. Anthem, London

Berners-Lee T, Fischetti M (1999) Weaving the web: the original design and ultimate destiny of the world wide web by its inventor. HarperCollins, New York

Berners-Lee TJ, Cailliau R, Groff J-F (1992a) The world-wide web. Comp Netw ISDN Syst 25:454–459. https://doi.org/10.1016/0169-7552(92)90039-S

Berners-Lee T, Cailliau R, Groff J-F, Pollermann B (1992b) World-wide web: the information universe. Electron Netw Appl Policy 2(1):52–58. https://doi.org/10.1108/10662241011059471/full/html

Berners-Lee T, Cailliau R, Luotenen A, Nielesen HF, Secret A (1994) The world-wide web. Commun ACM 37(8):76–82. https://doi.org/10.1145/179606.179671

Bush V (1945) As we may think. The Atlantic, July. https://www.theatlantic.com/magazine/archive/1945/07/as-we-may-think/303881/

Bush V (1991 [1965]) Memex revisited. In Nyce and Kahn, pp 197–216

Buzan B, Wæver O, de Wilde J (1998) Security: a new framework for analysis. Lynne Rienner, London

Carr M (2021) A political history of cyberspace. In: Cornish P (ed) The oxford handbook of cyber security. Oxford University Press, Oxford, pp 49–65

Cole GD, Branstad DK (1978) Computer science and technology: design alternatives for computer network security. Institute for Computer Sciences and Technology, National Bureau of Standards, Washington DC

Corry O (2013) Constructing a global polity: theory, discourse and governance. Palgrave Macmillan, Basingstoke

Debord G (1964) Correspondance avec un cybernéticien. Internationale situationniste 9:44–48. http://debordiana.chez.com/francais/is9.htm#correspondance

Diderot D, d'Alembert's J Encyclopédie (1751–1766) The encyclopedia of Diderot and d'Alembert: collaborative translation project, directors Dena Goodman et al. University of Michigan. https://quod.lib.umich.edu/d/did/

Edwards PN (1996) The closed world: computers and the politics of discourse in Cold War America. MIT Press, Cambridge, Mass.

Engelbart DC (1962) Augmenting human intellect: a conceptual framework. SRI summary report AFOSR-3223, October. https://www.dougengelbart.org/pubs/augment-3906.html#6

Fensel D, Hendlet J, Lieberman H, Wahlster W (2003) Spinning the semantic web: bringing the world wide web to its full potential. MIT Press, Cambridge MA

Fielding R, Gettys J, Mogul JC, Frystyk H, Masinter L, Leach P, Berners-Lee T (1999) Hypertext transfer protocol—HTTP 1.1. Network Working Group RFC 2616. https://www.w3.org/Protocols/rfc2616/rfc2616.html

Fielding R, Nottingham M, Reschke J (2022) HTTP semantics. Internet Engineering Task Force RFC 9110. https://www.rfc-editor.org/rfc/rfc9110.html

GAO (General Accounting Office, US) (1989) Computer security: virus highlights need for improved internet management (GAO/IMTEC-89-57). Information Management and Technology Division, Washington

Gerovitch S (2002) From newspeak to cyberspeak: a history of soviet cybernetics. MIT Press, Cambridge MA

Gillies JM, Cailliau R (2000) How the web was born: the story of the world wide web. Oxford University Press, Oxford

Hafner K, Lyon M (1996) Where wizards stay up late: the origins of the internet. Simon and Schuster, New York

Harrison DF (1988) Computers, electronic data, and the Vietnam war. Archivaria; 26, Summer, pp 18–32. https://archivaria.ca/index.php/archivaria/article/view/11490

Hauben M, Hauben R (1997) Netizens: on the history and impact of Usenet and the internet. IEEE Computer Society Press, Los Alamitos CA. Online at http://www.columbia.edu/~hauben/book-pdf/

Hegel GWF (1817) Enzyklopädie der philosophischen Wissenschaften im Grundrisse. Facsimile print of the original Heidelberg 1817 version with a foreword by Hermann Glockner. Sämtliche Werke, vol 6. Frommann, Stuttgart 1927

Heinrich F (1978) The network security center: a system level approach to computer network security. Institute of Computer Sciences and Technology, National Bureau of Standards, Washington DC

Horkheimer M (1974 [1947]) Eclipse of reason. Continuum, London

Kissel R (ed) (2013) Glossary of key information security terms (NIST Interagency or Internal Report 7298 Rev. 2). National Institute of Standards and Technology, Gaithersburh MD

Kline RR (2015) The cybernetics moment: or why we call our age the information age. Johns Hopkins University Press, Baltimore MD

Leibniz GW (1989 [1679]) On universal synthesis and analysis, or the art of discovery and judgment. In: Philosophical papers and letters (ed. and trans: Loemker LE). Kluwer Academic, Dordrecht, pp 229–234

Leslie S (1993) The cold war and American science: the military-industrial-academic complex at MIT and Stanford. Columbia University Press, New York

Lidlicker JCR (1965) Libraries of the future. MIT Press, Cambridge MA

Licklider JCR, Taylor RW (1968) The computer as a communication device. Sci Technol 76:21–38

Medina E (2014) Cybernetic revolutionaries: technology and politics in Allende's Chile. MIT Press, Cambridge MA

Members of the Situationist International and Students of the University of Strassbourg (2000 [1966]) On the poverty of student life. Red and Black, Detroit

Moles AA (1964) Correspondance avec un cybernéticien. Internationale situationniste 9:44–48. http://debordiana.chez.com/francais/is9.htm#correspondance

Neal AW (2019) Security as politics: beyond the state of exception. Edinburgh University Press, Edinburgh

Nelson TH (1965–1977) Selected papers. Online at https://archive.org/details/SelectedPapers1977

Nelson TH (1987 [version 87.1]) Literary machines. Online at https://archive.org/details/literarymachines00nels/mode/2up

NIST (National Institute of Standards and Technology)-CSRC (Computer Security Resource Center) glossary (2019) website: https://csrc.nist.gov/glossary

Norberg AL, O'Neill JE, Freedman KJ (1996) Transforming computer technology: information processing for the pentagon, 1962–1986. Johns Hopkins University Press, Baltimore MD

Nyce JM, Kahn P (1991) From Memex to hypertext: Vannevar Bush and the mind's machine. Academic Press, London

Panza M, Otte M (1997) Introduction. In: Panza and Otte (eds) Analysis and synthesis in mathematics: history and philosophy. Kluwer, Dordrecht, pp ix–xiii

Paulsen C, Byers R (eds) (2019) Glossary of key information security terms (NISTIR 7298, revision 3). National Institute of Standards and Technology, Gaithersburg MD. https://doi.org/10.6028/NIST.IR.7298r3

Peters B (2016) How not to network a nation: the uneasy history of the Soviet internet. MIT Press, Cambridge MA

Rajan T (2007) The encyclopedia and the university of theory: idealism and the organization of knowledge. Textual Practice 21(2):335–358. https://doi.org/10.1080/09502360701264519

Rid T (2016) Rise of the machines: a cybernetic history. W.W. Norton, New York

Rosenzweig R (1998) Wizards, bureaucrats, warriors, and hackers: writing the history of the internet. Am Hist Rev 103(5):1530–1552. http://www.jstor.org/stable/2649970?origin=JSTOR-pdf

Spafford EH (1988) The internet worm program: an analysis. Purdue University. https://spaf.cerias.purdue.edu/tech-reps/823.pdf

Szeredi P, Lukácsy G, Benkő T (2016) The semantic web explained: the technology and mathematics behind Web 3.0. Cambridge University Press, Cambridge

Turner F (2010) From counterculture to cyberculture: Stewart Brand, the whole earth network, and the rise of digital utopianism. University of Chicago Press, Chicago IL

US Government (1989) Computer viruses: hearing before the subcommittee on telecommunications and finance of the committee on energy and commerce, house of representatives, one hundred first congress, July 20, Serial No. 101-71. US Government Printing Office, Washington DC

Vallance TR (1969) Classified research and related issues in science communication. AAUP Bull 55(3):360–365. https://doi.org/10.2307/40223835

Weizenbaum J (1976) Computer power and human reason. W.H. Freeman, New York

Wiener N (1961 [1948]) Cybernetics, or control and communication in the animal and the machine. MIT Press, Cambridge MA

Wisniowski M (2003) Inside "the system": engineers, scientists, and the boundaries of social protest in the Long 1960s. Hist Technol 19(4):313–333. https://doi.org/10.1080/0734151032000181077

Part II
The Formation of Internet Discourse

Chapter 4
Privatization Policies, 'Information Superhighway' and 'Cyberspace'

Abstract Notes on the relationship between the two Parts of this study, and of the methods employed in this Part, introduce the chapter. An explanation follows of how catchwords/phrases serve to illuminate discourse features at specific junctures. A section then outlines global regime-changes in favour of privatization and deregulation in the 1990s and the concurrent commercialization and opening-up of Internet Technology. Two further sections describe how perceptions of the internet were powerfully shaped by the two title catchwords of this chapter. 'Information superhighway' presented a top-down perspective of the internet. It referred to the internet as a policy and strategy area of principally the USA government and relevant corporations. 'Cyberspace' offered a kind of bottom-up perspective for internet developers and users. The term evoked a new world to take into possession, which could be designed and structured in original and unprecedented ways, where aspirations that extend upon and go beyond real-world practices could be pursued.

This study gives a systematic account of the advent of social life within and apropos of the internet, from two directions. Part I describes the *why-do-it* norms that were grounded in Internet Technology and were evinced as social and political first principles for the formation of the Internet Polity; and Part II concordantly describes how a distinctive discourse, with a characteristic vocabulary, evolved to actualise the life of the Internet Polity. This discourse could be understood as constitutive of the Internet Polity's social dynamics, which grew upon what it found—the facilities and space of the internet—rather than being programmatically brought about by Internet Technology. A straightforwardly deterministic relationship between Internet Technology and the Internet Polity is not suggested here. The construction of the former spurred the appearance of the latter; at the same time, the latter was formed by its own momentum upon the former. Features of this discourse are not inferred rigorously from the first principles in question, and yet these features are variously predicated upon those principles. Where relevant, the relationship between principles and discourse are noted in this Part.

In the following chapters, describing the discourse of the Internet Polity frequently involves tracking the careers of certain catchwords. Catchwords are a useful anchor

S. Gupta, *Collective Principles and the Formation of the Internet*, Springer Series on Cultural Computing, https://doi.org/10.1007/978-3-031-90470-7_4

for considering the Internet Polity's discourse and its characteristic vocabulary. So, to begin with, I give some methodological notes on what catchwords are and how they are approached here. That is followed by a brief section on how the internet was structured, so to speak, from above in the 1980s and early 1990s. Details of how an Internet Polity discourse was formed from this period to around 2010 occupy the remainder of this and the subsequent two chapters.

4.1 Catchwords and Discourse Formation

The defining feature of catchwords (and catchphrases, where used as fixed units) is that they are taken up quickly and become widely used. The main reason for attending to them is the rising frequency of their usage over significant periods of time in specific contexts. That does not mean that catchwords are therefore intrinsically culturally or socially significant. In fact, to many they might appear to be lightweight and trivial. They are not what Raymond Williams (1983) had influentially described as 'keywords', which offer general insights into culture and society. Of interest here is the fact that catchwords have caught on within some scope and this fact is indicative of social developments. Attempts to explain why they catch on make for mappings of shifts within prevailing discourse formations. Such words are variously and rapidly adapted, reoriented, or redefined across multiple registers and domains of usage, or through various modes of transmission. So, catchwords do not have an innate *keyness* (cultural significance, explanatory power, representativeness, etc.); they are conceptually accommodative signifiers which may be filled in with connotation according to contexts of usage. The behaviour and spread of catchwords are helpful for understanding the anatomy of discourse formations and their social contexts.

The connotations with which catchwords start catching on can usually be traced to a specific social juncture (an 'origin'). The initiation of catching on is likely to involve the following:

- An existing word or phrase acquires a new sense at a social juncture within a context (a distinct discourse area, linguistic domain, social group), which then leads to it catching on in a significant manner over a subsequent time-period. In standard dictionaries, word-senses are enumerated separately and new word-senses added as they settle.
- A neologism or new phrase-form appears at a social juncture within a specific context and then catches on in a significant manner over a subsequent time-period. Such a neologism is more than a coinage for occasional use (a 'nonce' word).

When the usage frequency of such words stop rising or diminishes, they cease to be catchwords. That could indicate that the word has entered a stable level of everyday usage, or has become idiomatic or a cliché, or has simply become outmoded. The rising or diminishing usage of a word can be measured if an appropriate corpus of sufficient scale is available. Below, where possible, I call upon the Google Book

Corpus and Google Ngrams to give an indicative sense of the growing frequencies of internet catchwords. As a rule of thumb, I take it that words and phrases which, starting from some usage frequency over zero, show steady growth in usage by a multiple of two or more in or in less than a ten-year period is a catchword. This rule of thumb is applied below by giving Google Ngrams for the catchwords in question, with the beginning and ending usage-frequencies over a 10-year period marked (for an elaboration of methods for studying catchwords generally, see Gupta and Gupta 2025; and on using catchwords to understand contemporary history, see Gupta 2022).

The most significant aspect of catchwords—i.e., significant growth in usage-frequency—is an index of collective uptake. For this study, the process of catchwords catching on is indicative of the genesis of an internet-based collectivity. Insofar as these internet catchwords widen their purchase in different registers and work through their syntactical and associative relationships with other words, they form a distinctive vocabulary that articulates the many dimensions of *Internet Polity discourse.* To a not insignificant degree, these catchwords adapt technological terms used to construct and designate features of Internet Technology, giving those a social character. To trace these processes, later in this chapter I focus by turn on two particularly influential catchwords in the development of the Internet Polity discourse: 'information superhighway' and 'cyberspace'. In the subsequent Chap. 5, I first move on to observations on 'internet' as a catchword, and relatedly terms with 'e-' and 'cyber-' prefixes and compounds with 'digital'. A broader discussion of how an Internet Polity vocabulary came about follows, drawing upon glossaries and dictionaries of computing and internet terms. A section in Chap. 5 also picks up concepts of Internet Culture and Internet Studies, and the changing significations of the catchword 'hacker'. Finally, Chap. 6 draws the discussion of the Internet Polity discourse into the twenty-first century. Here an account of the catchphrases 'Internet of Things' and 'social networking' (and related terms) suggest that the Internet Polity is now being variously contained in its scope while also being continuously scaled up.

I turn now to developments in the 1980s and early 1990s when this discourse picked up and became widespread. That occurred as the internet was programmatically commercialized and promoted by governments and businesses in synch with changing balances of power and economic restructuring, so, from above rather than from the base of the Internet Polity.

4.2 Late 1980s—Early 1990s

From a technological point of view, 'internet' became a popular catchword through the 1990s because of material developments in Internet Infrastructure. The coverage of cable and satellite networks widened, and the volume and speed of information transfers increased. Personal computers constantly became more affordable, with ever greater portability and capacities. Commercially packaged software focused on user-friendliness, so that even the modestly adept could access and work with internet services. Convergence on international standards in operating systems and programming languages brought together wider spans of usage and diverse users. Habituation to digital affordances increased dramatically through that decade—which also meant that digital divides, reflecting real-world inequalities, became a significant social concern. Of course, these developments reflected large-scale political and economic moves in actually existing societies, internationally. Business firms, governmental and non-governmental agencies worked in a broadly aligned direction through Internet Technology, sometimes in collaboration and sometimes in competition. In a fine-grained way, enthusiasts and sceptics played their part in enlivening the space cum facility connoted by the 'internet'.

The late 1980s and early 1990s were a momentous period. This was so much so that it appeared at the time that the descriptors of contemporary politics themselves needed to be renewed and reconceived. Numerous academic and media publications were devoted to delineating new political horizons and emerging social forces. Catchwords proliferated to capture the emerging 'new world order' or 'post-Cold War world/era' or 'age of globalization', at the 'end of history', amidst 'post-socialist transitions', characterizing a 'risk society', portending a 'clash of civilisations', presenting a 'unipolar world'. Several of these came to be associated with the growing reach and penetration of the internet. Academic catchwords of the period centred the internet as a society-defining formation: e.g., pre-emptively 'wired society' (Martin 1978), more immediately 'information society' (Masuda 1981; Rosenberg 1986; Lyon 1988, Katz 1988 and onwards), or 'network society' (van Djik 1999 [1991]; Castells 1996 and onwards). Such terms captured diverse conceptual negotiations with what was, at the time, a dizzying new development. Any attempt to comprehend the political context of the early1990s should dwell upon these, but that would be an overreach for this study. Instead, I take a limited view by focussing on one dimension of the period, and sketchily at that.

Perhaps the most consistent characteristic of the period was a policy convergence in economic regimes across numerous political states, despite diverse ideological foundations and vastly different histories. The main interlinked regime adjustments in this direction involved:

1. encouraging foreign investment and enterprise in domestic spheres by reducing import and licencing tariffs, making regulatory processes easier to manoeuvre, adjusting employment protections to enable knowledge and skills transfers, etc.;
2. governments reducing or removing direct management of public-sector industries/services while retaining ownership or share-holding and regulatory oversight, cutting public spending;
3. concomitantly enabling domestic and international private-sector organizations to enter public-sector industries/services as managers and shareholders, usually by offering fiscal and infrastructural incentives supported by public budgets;
4. moving towards aligning such moves with standards set by a range of international organizations (IMF, WTO, etc.) and regional agreements.

These moves are variously captured by terms like 'liberalization', 'deregulation and privatization', 'structural adjustment', 'neoliberalism'—with somewhat different normative thrusts. 'Privatization' seems to come closest to the nub of the matter, albeit somewhat misleadingly in that it suggests straightforward transfers from existing public to existing private sectors, whereas what it typically involved was a systematic reconfiguration of both sectors. In any case, the scale of this convergence is easily grasped through studies comparing privatization moves in a range of countries and across sectors from the 1990s onwards (for helpfully wide-ranging views, Ramanadham 1993; Clarke and Pitelis 1993; Bortolotti and Siniscalo 2004; Singham 2023). The immediate effects of such moves were as often deleterious as crisis-averting or unevenly enriching. The longer term and unfolding effects continue to be passionately debated by critics and champions. Though contentious, the single-minded drift towards and convergence on them suggest that political and corporate elites across the world have found them advantageous.

In brief, through this period governmental agencies and large businesses increasingly found that they could cooperatively draw upon and play upon an international field that seemed to be humming from the same hymn sheet. It was nevertheless a hymn sheet containing the discordant notes of internecine conflicts in various parts of the world (especially Eastern Europe, the Middle East, and Sub-Saharan Africa), the stirrings of new or renewed ethnic nationalisms and religious frictions around the world, with a decisive turn towards the politics of embodied identity both in line with and against those trends. The processes through which the internet, and 'internet' as a popular catchword, rose into the foreground in this period were woven intricately with these developments. The following sketchy overview of touchstone technological and policy moves to bring about the internet as we know it should be understood against this backdrop of global privatizations.

Through the 1980s, Internet Technology moved towards instilling the means for widespread and standardized adaptation, actualizing the first principles of a nascent Internet Polity (as discussed in Part I). By the late 1970s, a number of networks were linked to ARPANET, such as SATNET (Atlantic Packet Satellite Network) and PRNET (Packet Radio Network). Other networks connecting universities emerged, especially BITNET from 1981, which gradually took in university networks from other countries. Networks allowing more informal levels of communications and information exchange proliferated, such as USENET from 1980 onwards. In 1983, defence communications were separated out of ARPANET in the MILNET, and in 1986 the National Science Foundation (NSF) set up NSFNET principally for research centres, which was to become the backbone of the internet. ARPANET was decommissioned in 1990. UNIX computer operating systems, developed by AT&T Corporation, became the system of choice among programmers in the 1980s; it was the basis for the family of standards specified as the Portable Operating System Interface (POSIX) from the late 1980s. Of proprietary operating systems, Microsoft Windows 1.0 was launched in 1985 and was to become the most popular for personal computers through subsequent versions, especially Windows 95 (1995). Moves towards the standardization of Ethernet technologies for Local Area Networks (LAN) was initiated in 1981. The appearance of the IBM Personal Computer in 1981 and Apple Macintosh (Mac) in 1984 moved microcomputers beyond the sphere of techno-enthusiasts and specialists into the larger market. By the later 1980s, the big news in telecommunications was the beginning of largescale replacement of telephone cables by fibre-optic networks with much higher capacities.

Woven through these rapid and expeditiously upgraded developments, from the mid-1980s onwards the TCP/IP suite came to be adopted across governmental, commercial, and academic network systems and grounded in Internet Technology, winning out eventually over the OSI (Open Standard Interconnection) protocols. The World Wide Web (WWW) specifications, premised on TCP/IP, were launched in 1991 and the source code was openly released in 1993. After removing e-trade barriers in 1991, from 1993 to 1995 the NSF set up commissions for modifying Internet Technology to enable rapid commercialization. In 1995, as noted in Chap. 1, the Federal Networking Council influentially defined the internet as centred on the TCP/IP suite and the global IP addressing system. In 1995 it was estimated that there were 16 million internet users worldwide, around 0.4% of the world population (Internet World Stats), of whom around 12 million were in the USA (Pew Research Centre 1995). The burgeoning figures have been tracked zealously since, globally and country-by-country—in 2022 it was estimated that the figure was 5544 million (69% of the world population), with around 311.3 million in the USA (Petrosyan 2023).

The global 'privatization' or 'liberalization' adjustments in economic regimes mentioned above can be found in relation to Internet Technology and its social uptake. This was a matter of renegotiating the relationship between public and private investments, which is to say of commercial and governmental prerogatives, with mutually modifying effect. A much studied 'privatization' of the internet unfolded in this period, moving from reasonably strong governmental control to a modestly regulated 'self-governing' zone that facilitates commercial activity (e.g., Greenstein 2015; Smyrnaios 2018; Radu 2019). One way of trying to track the mutual modification is through legislative moves in the USA, variously echoed in other countries later, to establish the legal boundaries of governmental regulation and investment. These effectively determined the scope of deregulation and disinvestment. In the 1980s, these boundaries were mostly defined by US governmental control of national and individual protections (security and privacy) in relation to Internet Infrastructure—such as the Computer Fraud and Abuse Act (1986), Electronic Communications Privacy Act (1986), Computer Security Act (1987), Computer Matching and Privacy Act (1988) and onwards. By way of active developmental investment in and market encouragement of Internet Infrastructure, the High Performance Computing Act (1991), introduced by Senator Al Gore, famously paved the way for a structured business-government co-dependency. That is to say, it designedly blurred the boundaries of public and private investments so as to enable commercial capitalisation of Internet Infrastructure.

Focusing on such legislation, however, leads to an excessive emphasis on the governmental perspective. More indicative of the mutual modification of government and business vis-à-vis the internet were actual confrontations between them, where government tried to limit the activities of corporations by legal recourse. This was mainly in terms of anti-trust lawsuits brought against the monopolistic practices of corporations. Two significant and long-drawn antitrust proceedings were settled in 1982. One was against the AT&T Corporation, which had a monopoly through ownership of the Bell Telephone system for providing telephone services. This led to an agreement to break AT&T up into seven independent regional companies. Another long running antitrust suit against IBM's monopolistic hold on the computer market was dropped without concessions, effectively a capitulation by government. In fact, both antitrust suits ended on the same day, 8 January 1982, which led *New York Times* reporter Andrew Pollack (1985) to consider their implications together. He noted that until this time the two companies had not really infringed on each other's markets, but these agreements left both free of governmental interference in competing or converging for the emerging scenario, where: 'The communications network [...] becomes an information superhighway, able to handle voice and computer data and, in some cases, video as well' (Pollack 1985). These seemed to anticipate the antitrust suit brought against the Microsoft Corporation in the later 1990s. Though the initial judgement recommended the breakup of the company, on appeal the ruling was overturned in 2001. Evidently, the government's regulatory and protective initiative against largescale market domination was reconfigured through the 1980s and 1990s for the area of Internet Infrastructure. In the process, the governmental attitude to the internet as a commercial area was formed, with a vocal hands-on attitude and a pragmatic feathery touch. Also in the process, a popular conception of the internet—and the term 'internet'—surfaced.

The shift in the US governmental thinking about Internet Infrastructure and usage of the term 'internet' were neatly captured in two reports around that 1990 juncture. In 1988, the report *Toward a National Research Network* appeared, produced by four government bodies (National Research Network Review Committee [NRNRC]; Computer Science and Technology Board [CSTB]; Commission on Physical Sciences, Mathematics, and Resources [CPSMR]; National Research Council [NRC]). In 1994, a new report, *Realizing the Information Future: The Internet and Beyond*, was produced by the same bodies (NRNRC was now named the NRENAISSANCE Committee). Both were chaired by Leonard Kleinrock.

The 1988 report proposed establishing a National Research Network (NRN) linking mainframe computers used for research across and beyond the USA with government backing. It focussed on facilitating research across institutions, disciplines, and regions, especially by enabling 'person-to-computer remote access and computer-to-computer remote access' (NRNRC et al. 1988: 14). Various facets of the project and costs were considered. Notably, it was proposed that this should be built upon existing and emerging commercial network facilities rather than as a stand-alone facility. But this was on the understanding that: 'The basic architecture and technology issues should be settled by the network of researchers in cooperation with the potential user community, not the forces of the free market' (28). Reportedly, the report inspired Al Gore to prepare and present what became the High Performance Computing Act of 1991 (Leiner et al. 2009: 28), and led to the governmental National Information Infrastructure strategy. Though obviously all about consolidating Internet Technology for the benefit of research and development, the 1988 report did not actually use the term 'internet'. Instead, it conceived of three phases of 'internetwork' (25–28), with the situation at the time understood as a nascent phase 1, and the future phase 3 more or less in line with what 'internet' came to mean.

The 1994 report was a larger proposal for setting up an Open Data Network (ODN), which would be:

> - *Open to users*: It does not force users into closed groups or deny access to any sectors of society, but permits universal connectivity, as does the telephone system.
> - *Open to service providers*: It provides an open and accessible environment for competing commercial or intellectual interests. For example, it does not preclude competitive access for information providers.
> - *Open to network providers*: It makes it possible for any network provider to meet the necessary requirements to attach and become a part of the aggregate of interconnected networks.
> - *Open to change*: It permits the introduction of new applications and services over time. It is not limited to only one application, such as TV distribution. It also permits the introduction of new transmission, switching, and control technologies as these become available in the future. (NRENAISSANCE Committee et al. 1994, 3–4)

This was then, unlike the NRN of the 1988 report, more a strategy for managing networked information than a proposal for a material network. As opposed to facilitating and even protecting researchers' access, this foregrounded 'competing commercial or intellectual interests' and accepted 'competitive access'. Its goal was 'the successful commercialization of the Internet' (4). Though ODN was essentially a structured strategy, it was described in detail as a material network in line with Internet Technology; in fact, like Internet Technology, it was visualized as an hourglass model with four layers (53). Where the 1988 report advocated for expanded government support for researchers, the 1994 report proposed limiting government support to research and education, and areas like security, privacy, and copyright protections. Indicatively, in contrast to the 1988 report, the 1994 report took the internet as an existing rather than emerging formation, with a definition and scope:

> The Internet is a network of networks. Currently it consists of approximately 20,000 registered networks, some 2 million host computers, and 15 million users. Approximately half the networks are commercial (and this fraction is growing) and half noncommercial; about one-third of the hosts are associated with research or educational institutions. Most of the Internet connections are in the United States, but 149 countries or national entities have connections of one sort or another to international computer networks, with about 63 countries possessing direct connections to the Internet. (NRENAISSANCE Committee et al. 1994, 21)

Like most strategy documents, the 1994 report was replete with various visionary statements, including an 'Internet Vision'. This may well be the first significant governmental document headlined with the term 'internet' and foregrounding it in the free-floating way that characterizes a popular catchword.

The shift in the conception of the internet—and in the career of the term 'internet'–which took place in the late 1980s and early 1990s, so neatly expressed between the two reports, can be articulated through the underpinning political principles of Internet Technology. Establishing national and global standards was naturally critical to the commercialization of the internet as a 'self-governing' formation. Throughout the processes of establishing standards and upgrading Internet Infrastructure outlined above, it appeared that the principle of minimal-gradual-mechanical standardization was followed. Hardware and software standards seemed to emerge from gradual adoption by users instead of being imposed by design, and by garnering consensus before being mandated. Standard-setting was not presented as an act of authority exercised by established institutions or by committee, but as after-the-fact confirmation by such authorities Further, the regulation of such standards was mainly by setting mechanically operated policies with as little direct human intervention and hands-on monitoring as possible. Human intervention and monitoring were ostensibly concentrated on adopting and upgrading the emerging standards themselves, and thereafter on maintenance. In the process of opening up and commercializing Internet Infrastructure, the principle of minimal-gradual-mechanical standardization gelled with a philosophy of market testing. Public and private organizations seeking to garner consensus on their preferred standards could be regarded as competing to agree them—standards were a product. The competition could, it appeared, be won by the evidence of users' preferences, i.e., by market testing. In general, equivalence between the principle of minimal-gradual-mechanical standardization and the norms of market testing were regarded as given. However, as economist Leland Yaeger (1997)—an advocate of free markets with minimum regulation—had argued, there is good reason to be cautious about the notion. Market testing seems to justify attributing value according to majority tastes and holding majority decisions as arbitrators of truth. Underpinning both, there's what Yaeger calls 'secondhandism' (Yaeger 1997, 162–164): a tendency to base assessments in terms of irrelevant tangential indicators rather than directly relevant rationales.

The principle of precedent individuation settled down with the adoption of the World Wide Web (WWW) hypertext system as the dominant user and commercial standard. The commercialization of the internet, as the 1988 and 1994 reports discussed show, was a move from having the internet as a preserve of researchers and professionals to enabling the internet for all consumers and users. Where the former were generally accustomed to dealing with the plethora of I-information in terms of their existing analytical and synthetic frameworks—assimilating knowledge from I-information in well-developed ways—a great proportion of the latter had mainly their individual associations to work through I-information. Researchers and professionals could draw upon I-information with pre-determined objectives, honed by systematic methods. Most consumers could be expected to look for what appeals to them personally in I-information, for their specific doings and desires. Those could include seeking to be entertained, to find out more, to buy something, etc. in terms of individual associations and convictions. Their associations could be anticipated and guided by online product pushers. The commercialization of the internet was facilitated by a WWW architecture, based on the principle of precedent individuation. The hypertext system enhanced both the potential for generating confirmation biases and dogmatic polarization as well as for enhancing rational debate and assimilated knowledge for all. Arguably, precedent individuation via WWW for most users could well be accountable for such troubling later phenomena as 'disinformation' and 'filter bubbles' (catchwords of the present). These provide deeper grounding for such phenomena than the information targeting algorithms that are often held accountable.

The principles of minimal-gradual-mechanical standardization and of precedent individuation worked quietly across and became habitually adopted by users through that late 1980s/early 1990s shift. They were inculcated in the emerging Internet Polity as a received way of operating on the internet, understood as apolitical and functionally pragmatic. Distinct from those, public negotiations were explicitly concentrated on the principle of targeted collective regulation through security controls, albeit threaded intricately through both minimal-gradual-mechanical standardization and precedent individuation. In general, security controls were mandated through governmental legislation or corporate policy. This became the aspect of Internet Technology where the principles of minimal-gradual-mechanical standardization and of precedent individuation could be consensually contravened or suspended. Focalizing security controls made it appear that the internet is, at any given time, subject to the play of real politicking and ideological contests. Having already appeared at the forefront of internet related legislation in the 1980s (as noted earlier), security controls became increasingly salient through the 1990s, and, as the twenty-first century unrolled, ever more centrally the focus of political as well as commercial strategies. These moves are unpacked further in considering the catchwords 'information superhighway' and 'cyberspace' below.

With hindsight, the late 1980s/early 1990s shifts of the internet seem to cohere with explicitly formulated policy strategies and juridical moves. But the shifts in question worked in a more dispersed and widely penetrating fashion through nudges in and manoeuvres around specific words and phrases. These became repositories of popular subscriptions and constituted the vocabulary of Internet Polity discourse. As it happened, at the late 1980s/early 1990s juncture, two seemingly independent catchwords were considered coterminous with 'internet' and played a significant part in grounding the Internet Polity discourse: 'information superhighway' and 'cyberspace'. They had somewhat different thrusts.

'Information superhighway' presented a top-down perspective of the internet. It referred principally to the internet as a strategic policy area of the real-world polity represented by the USA government and relevant corporations. The phrase captured issues such as building the Internet Infrastructure to maximize access, determining processes of funding or defunding, defining areas of public interest, nudging Internet Technology to support facilities and markets, maintaining coherence across private sector operations and investments, legislating on security and policing. The energies of the phrase diminished by the late 1990s and usage plummeted after 2000. Through much of the 1990s, 'cyberspace' offered a kind of bottom-up perspective for internet developers and users. The term evoked a new world to take into possession, which could be designed and structured in original and unprecedented ways, where purposes that extend upon and go beyond real-world aspirations could be pursued. This potential was conceived as alternative to and yet synthesizable with the political economies, organizational modes, and simply individual and collective ways of living that exist. The word acquired quite different connotations after the 1990s, as a kind of descriptor of Internet Infrastructure (as noted in Chap. 1), especially in

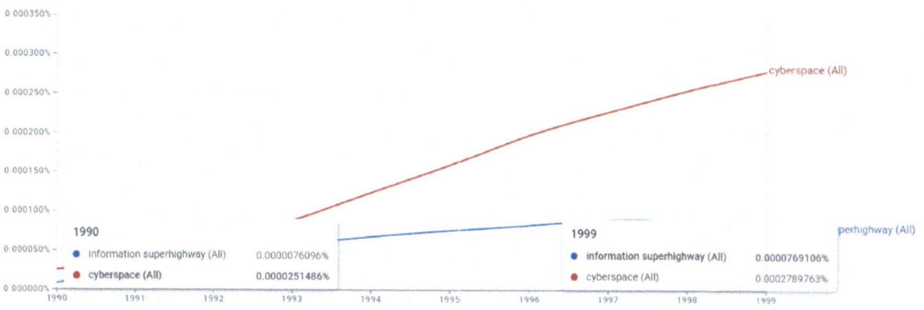

Graph 4.1 Google Ngram Viewer graph for 'information superhighway' and 'cyberspace', 1990–1999, showing a ten-fold increase in usage frequency for both terms over the decade

cybersecurity circles. In a way, the two terms seemed to articulate horizons in relation to which an Internet Polity could be consolidated, and an Internet Policy discourse could be fostered.

I consider these by turn in the next two sections of this chapter (Graph 4.1).

4.3 'Information Superhighway'

Through the 1980s, the metaphor of the transport highway—as in 'data highway' or 'information superhighway'—appeared intermittently in news media and governmental reports. Usually, it referred to what I have dubbed the Internet Infrastructure here. Of course, at the time this would not have been specifically related to the internet; it would have been thought of as the telecommunications infrastructure. The phrase 'information superhighway' was used, for instance, in the *New York Times* article by Pollack (1985, quoted earlier), about the antitrust suits against AT&T and IBM. In that instance, it gestured towards a future in which such companies could collaborate or compete and make hay. Elsewhere, the term referred specifically to developing fibre-optic cable networks. The first moves to connect domestic households by fibre-optic cables were hailed as the advent of the 'information superhighway', with the materiality of the cables metaphorically associated with that of transport roads. The term was aired in governmental policy circles as such, appearing in the House of Representatives hearing of the Committee on Science, Space and Technology in March 1988. This came with a policy recommendation:

> We should set a national goal of creating a billion byte-per-second national information superhighway of optical fibres within the next ten years. This national network would provide a foundation for the information economy of the next few decades in the same way that the interstate highways system did for the United States economy of the 1960's-1980's. (US Government, NSF Authorization 1989)

Several news reports had it in the same sense. For instance, a *USA Today* article of 1989 observed: 'Fibre optics already are widely used to transmit phone calls. [...]

But this information superhighway has almost no access roads—fibre-optic cables branching out of homes. So homeowners couldn't drive on it—until today' (Hillkirk 1989). The 'information superhighway' was regarded as a material structure in the making, of the present, on the cusp of realizing an imminent facility.

Starting from 1990, the phrase acquired a somewhat different nuance. More than designating the material fibre-optic network to facilitate communications, it seemed to become an abstract metaphoric pathway from the present towards a future social condition. It referred, in the same breath, to the cabled pathways connecting communication devices and to the metaphoric pathway leading from a technological present to a superior technological future. The latter emphasis came with a strong sense of activating salutary social transformation. This emphasis was upped, understandably, as the commercialization of the internet became *fait accompli* and emerged as one of the central planks of political campaigning and policy making. 'Information superhighway' acquired its catchword drive through the impetus of policy speak very expeditiously. In beckoning towards a technologically superior future, it also served to propel the term 'internet' into popular usage—imbued with the sense of being a facility and yet also much more than a facility, a basis for transforming social life.

In this sense, Al Gore made a strong claim to the phrase in 1990, while pushing for what was to become the High Performance Computing Act (1991). Thereafter it became a feature of Bill Clinton's presidential campaign, with Gore as his running mate, from 1992. It turned into a policy and media catchword for much of the 1990s when Clinton won the presidency in 1993, and Gore became Vice President. As a campaigning term in manifesto-like and publicity pronouncements, it served to set a current agenda of material investments and a vision of future society. As a policy term which had to be seen as guiding implementations, its connotations were constantly debated and interrogated, with as much scepticism as confirmatory zeal. A couple of articles in 1990 by Gore set the tone for the campaigning slogan, one in the *Washington Post* in July (reprinted in 1992) and another in *ComputerWorld* in September. In the former he claimed to have first proposed, 11 years earlier (so, 1979), 'a nationwide network of fibre-optic "data highways" to link supercomputers and digital libraries throughout our nation' (Gore 1992 [1990]: 144). He also elaborated on his vision of the future there. In both articles, the 'information superhighway', with the transport metaphor foregrounded, was recruited as a governmental prerogative that would work in concert with private interests. In his words:

> We didn't expect a turnpike company to build the interstate highway system, and we can't expect a private company to build the information superhighway. But, like the interstate system, once the information superhighway is complete, the demand for its use will skyrocket. And, as user fees are collected, private operation will be feasible. (Gore 1990: 21)

With the passing of the High Performance Computing Act (1991) such a governmental design seemed set to be implemented, but in fact the actual role of government—apart from producing enabling legislation and publicity—remained unclear. As the Presidential election of 1992 drew up, in Clinton's campaign the gist of the governmental design remained on the agenda. In the manifesto publication

Putting People First (Clinton and Gore 1992), there were occasional promises to build a 'national information network', but the slogan 'information superhighway' was eschewed—perhaps to distance its association with the George H. W. Bush era passage of the 1991 Act. On taking over the administration in 1993, however, Clinton and Gore took charge of the phrase again, and now it really became a catchphrase. In a report of September 1993, Gore proposed to build a 'National Information Infrastructure' (NII) by way of realizing the 'Information Superhighway' (Smith 1994: CRS-1). Both 'National Information Infrastructure' and 'information superhighway' became terms for bureaucrats, business managers, and journalists to conjure with. Immediately after assuming office, news reports noted that the governmental prerogative in building the 'information superhighway' seemed to be contested by business leaders (e.g., Markoff 1993). Nevertheless, the catchphrase purchase of 'information superhighway' was now variously confirmed. 'The Info Highway' featured on the cover of *Time* magazine in April 1993, along with two leading articles (Zoglin 1993; Elmer-Dewitt 1993) on the 'electronic superhighway'. These however mainly spoke of the advantage that the fibre-optic cable network would bring for access to entertainment products. The development of the material Internet Infrastructure in fact proceeded mainly at the behest of private companies, with some broad policy directions from governmental bodies (like the 1994 *Realizing the Information Future* report discussed in Chap. 4).

In terms of input, governmental prerogatives in the area were exercised mainly through the independent judicial apparatus, usually in the form of security strictures. The executive wing of the Clinton-Gore administration gradually confined its activities and claims mainly to publicly funded education and research, with particular emphasis on publicly funded schools and libraries and as a funding provider in some areas of advanced research. As such, the claims made through the burgeoning catchphrase 'information superhighway' in the early 1990s increasingly seemed more rhetorical than substantial, part of a policy and media jargon with nebulous content. The catchphrase, along with 'National Information Infrastructure', drew attention to its own sloganistic employment, and *that* became the point of interest. A 1993 report from the organization Computer Professionals for Social Responsibility (CPSR) observed:

> The very word 'infrastructure,' which has been mocked by the press and by conservatives as a kind of 'new age' term of Clinton era jargon, implies a sort of bedrock imperative, something essential to the function of society and the economy. Vice President Gore has popularized the phrase 'digital highways' [...]. The 'highway' metaphor gives the national information infrastructure a concreteness, to employ a pun, that otherwise escapes many technologically unsophisticated listeners when they hear about a multi-billion dollar public investment in computer networks. No one can imagine American life without the superhighways that the nation was known for in the 1960s, and which today are viewed as a basic element 'infrastructure' of the economy. The phrase 'infrastructure' and the metaphor of a new national highway system are attached to new telecommunications technologies to impart a sense of inevitability, of national compulsion, to something that most citizens don't understand or are only dimly aware of. It also lends the lustre of the public interest to a huge public investment that will handsomely reward very specific industries and which may tend to reinforce disparities in economic status. (Chapman and Rotenberg 1993)

The Congressional Research Services report of 1994 (Smith 1994: 4–7) on *The Information Superhighway* included a section entitled 'superhighway or Superhypeway' to address such notes of scepticism in numerous news features. In the world of professional implementation of 'information superhighway' policies, especially the schools and libraries in the eye of policy makers, both optimism in the drive and scepticism about the rhetoric spread well beyond the USA. For instance, both notes were numerously struck by librarians and library systems managers from various countries at an international conference in Essen, Germany (Helal and Weiss 1995). On the wider media background, one noted:

> A recent count of selected U.S. newspapers showed that the information superhighway was referred to as much as 1,200 times a month. Unfortunately, perhaps more than any other technological development, much of the coverage is not flattering. Critics focus on garbage littering the highway, road repairs, traffic accidents, speedbumps, toll booths, and highjackers. One critic goes so far as to say 'warning: when you travel the information superhighway, don't stop; keep your windows rolled up and your hand on your wallet.'
>
> Two of the most striking references are to 'Internot' or the 'Information superhypeway'. Authors are referring to the stark contrast of future visions and current realities. (Torok 1994: 135)

As the later 1990s rolled in, and developments in the implementation and capitalization of Internet Technology speeded up across almost every professional sector and beyond, the catchphrase career of 'information superhighway' waned. The 'Internet'/ 'Net'/'Web' seemed to be released from the policy thrust of 'information superhighway' (a facility in the making) and refer to something larger (a social space that already obtains). This larger reference also had a catchword which pushed 'internet' along: 'Cyberspace'. To this I turn soon, but before that it is worth registering at least one systematic account of 'information superhighway' policies at the time.

This appeared before the Clinton and Gore administration stepped in. Bruce Egan's *Information Superhighways* (1991) focussed on the economic demands and policy environment for the development of communication networks at the turn of that momentous decade. Policy considerations usually draw a continuous line from short-term towards long-term consequences and outcomes. Egan invested the phrase 'information superhighway' with both the connotations of a material facility and of a metaphorical pathway noted earlier. The dual-sense employment of the catchphrase imbued these hard-headed policy observations with a certain tentativeness about short-term outcomes and uncertainty about long-term outcomes. The short-term outcomes were conceived as synthesizing moves towards universal broadband networks (UBNs), involving:

> the technological transition to networks featuring a combination of new fibre optic and digital technologies and existing analog-metallic ones, providing for an initial infrastructure investment capable of supporting two-way residential broadband service. (Egan 1991, 4)

The long-term outcomes were in terms of an integrated UBN:

> The purest vision is an integrated all-fibre, all-digital, two-way, high-speed network over one 'super-pipe' which provides for everything from *plain old telephone service* (POTS) to on-demand interactive video. This definition is quite futuristic and expensive, but continues to receive attention in trade press and research articles. (Egan 1991, 4)

Thus, Egan tactfully put the long-term prospects outside the horizon of realistic policy and economic considerations, in the realm of idealistic expectations, and focussed on the short-term. The internet was effectively construed as a partial facility in the present and the repository of visionary future-gazing. Various pros and cons for the realization of the short-term outcomes occupied the book, including standards, regulation, stakeholder prerogatives, costs and modes of their retrieval, etc. A cautious conclusion highlighted challenges arising from the numerous sectors and competing private players involved, making for a fragmented field of interests. That gelled with a larger concern about the extent to which government should itself direct UBN deployment by public investment and direct control, or to which UBNs should be left to private investments amidst government regulation and market forces. Egan's prognosis was of an indecisive policy juncture where a decision would need to be made, which really was a larger decision about political principles. Ultimately these were the principles that were confronted globally in the early 1990s, under the rubric of privatization and liberalization moves. In Egan's words, the 'information superhighway' seemed at the same crossroads as the world at large:

> Current policy is inherently unstable, and pits public and private needs against one another. We cannot enjoy the best of both worlds: a private market paradigm, in which communication networks develop according to the forces of supply and demand, and the public market paradigm, which emphasizes social costs and benefits. Public policy prescriptions for achieving these separate goals are quite different. If we continue the *status quo*, however, we risk languishing in a world of inefficient technology, in which public utilities, which enjoy monopoly status, 'compete' with unregulated entrants. The resulting tug-of-war between entrenched interests, and their political constituencies puts politics, rather than societal issues, at the forefront of the policy debate. (Egan 1991, 167)

That politics can be separated from 'societal issues' is always a doubtful claim, though a common bureaucratic notion. Egan made the policy choices sound like an either/or issue, either following public or private paradigms, whereas the appetite of the time was for mixing them up (or fudging them).

The Clinton and Gore administration proceeded to articulate policies headlining 'information superhighway' and 'national information infrastructure' precisely in the spirit of mixing (or fudging) public and private prerogatives. Along with high expectations and intensive publicity, as noted earlier, cynicism and confusion came to be attached to the catchphrases. Slipping definitions, contested claims on prerogatives, passionate advocacy and critique followed the growing perception that the private paradigm was not only winning but seemingly being disguised in the process as the public paradigm. The direction was settled eventually with the Telecommunications Act of 1996 (at the 104th Congress, USA). This was headlined as an Act:

> To promote competition and reduce regulation in order to secure lower prices and higher quality services for American telecommunications consumers and encourage the rapid deployment of new telecommunications technologies.

It also included some principles to extend universal access. It was received by a flurry of reckonings with 'information superhighway' policies and their vagaries, now seemingly resolved (Egan 1996 appeared as a follow-up of his 1991 observations).

A reasonably even-handed overview of the various ideologically led interpretations of 'information superhighway' policies, from the late 1980s to 1996, was offered by Donald Case (1998). In the main this described the discourse features of these debates. Case's own view of the emerging prospects of the 'national information infrastructure' (NII) was indicated succinctly in his conclusion, and was equivocal:

> The uncertainty of the market for information and communication services, along with sometimes conflicting demands placed on regulators and policy-makers, makes the future of the NII hard to predict. With such large amounts of money and power at stake, policy-making will not be completely principled and rational. At present policy statements appear to be exaggerating benefits or dangers in order to encourage social change. (Case 1998, 405)

After the 1996 Telecommunications Act, the verve of 'information superhighway' and 'national information infrastructure' as catchphrases diminished. By this time the internet appeared to be a rather more complex formation than policy discourses could contain, and the 'superhighway' metaphor seemed increasingly reductive. Over the same period, as observed earlier, the internet was also woven into a social arena with a broader thrust and a different catchword: 'cyberspace'.

4.4 'Cyberspace'

The prefix 'cyber-' was introduced in the late 1940s in naming an emerging field of research, 'cybernetics', developed by Arturo Rosenblueth, Norbert Weiner, and their colleagues. In his influential overview of this field, Weiner reported:

> We have decided to call the entire field of control and communication theory, whether in the machine or in the animal, by the name *Cybernetics*, which we form from the Greek *γυβερνήτης* or *steersman*. In choosing this term, we wish to recognize that the first significant paper on feedback mechanisms is an article on governors, which was published by Clerk Maxwell in 1868, and that *governor* is derived from a Latin corruption of *γυβερνήτης*. We also wish to refer to the fact that steering engines of a ship are indeed one of the earliest and best-developed forms of feedback mechanisms.
>
> Although the term *cybernetics* does not date further back than the summer of 1947, we shall find it convenient to use in referring to earlier epochs of the development of the field. (Weiner 1961 [1948], 11–12)

The field of research sought a ratiocinative unified theory of communication in the broadest sense, including sign-based and behavioural processes. It involved, in brief, inferring the underpinning principles of animal (especially human) communication from observations and testing them by mechanization, and, correlatively, using principles of mechanical functioning to replicate and extend upon those principles of communication. Since the investigative field thus named 'cybernetics' synthesized a number of existing disciplinary pursuits, the name did not itself highlight a centred object of enquiry. It mainly suggested an aspiration or a claim: of steering or controlling communication/knowledge of natural/mechanical functioning … so to speak, a theory of everything. In that respect, the inspiration it drew from J.C.

Maxwell's (1868) well-known paper on 'governors', distinguished from 'moderators', that control the speed of steam engines, was mainly metaphorical. An abstract idea of control via feedback loops was extrapolated for employment in computational and social engineering. In a less abstract vein, the field of cybernetics and the prefix '-cyber' became associated with extending human capacities by technological means and extending technological capacities towards (enhanced) humanlikeness, or towards bringing about a symbiotic human–machine functionality. From the 1950s cybernetics became a discipline-like label for quite diverse projects on, for instance, prosthetics and machine autonomy. Disciplinary precincts, institutional departments, and project groups were dubbed accordingly. 'Cybernetics' became a catchword veering between a general theory of everything and a range of specialized pursuits linked to human–machine symbiosis or machine autonomy and robotics (and much in between).

The prefix '-cyber', released from its nominative function for a very broad field of research, came to be associated particularly with persons, such as combined human–machine persons or persons who are adapted to computing systems. The coinage 'Cyborgs' (cyber organisms) thus appeared in 1960, defined as follows by Manfred Clynes and Nathan Kline (1960) in speculating on how humans can become equipped for living in space:

> What are some of the devices necessary for creating self-regulating man-machine systems? This self-regulation must function without the benefit of consciousness in order to cooperate with the body's own autonomous homeostatic controls. For the exogenously extended organizational complex functioning as an integrated homeostatic system unconsciously, we propose the term 'Cyborg.' The Cyborg deliberately incorporates exogenous components extending the self-regulatory control function of the organism in order to adapt it to new environments. (27)

In this definition, the prefix 'cyber-' appears to gesture towards the 'unconscious' autonomy of the human–machine body, where the machine is not a tool but integral to the human–machine person. That is the sense in which cyborg became a term to play with conceptually, portending a development towards superhumanity (Halacy 1965) or interrogating the preconceptions of bodily identity (Haraway 1985). It was exploited fictionally, in numerous fantasy narratives. The prefix found a new turn in the coinage of 'cyberpunk', first as the title of a story by Bruce Bethke (1983 [1980]). This described a group of teenagers with highly developed programming skills (the narrator is the cyberpunk of the title), who have formed a private 'Net' and are able to hack into a larger network of computers—'CityNet'—designed to maintain institutional records of transport, education, banking, etc. Their skills are employed mainly to disrupt such institutional operations, and the story describes a growing and dangerous generation gap between the computer-adept youth and their parents' generation (the 'Olders'). The generation gap rests clearly in the technological leap that was, at the time, the nascent Internet Technology. As the cyberpunk narrator observes:

> Olders will never understand. They still think a computer has got to be a brain in a single box. I can get the same results with opsys stored in a hundred places, once I tie them together.

> Nearly every computer has got a dataphone port, CityNet is a great linking system … (Bethke 1983 [1980], 97)

The prefix 'cyber-' had thus been extended to the emerging Internet Technology rather than to machine-human persons, but it still attached to persons who are almost instinctively at one with the technology. The term 'cyberpunk' soon encompassed a genre of fantasy fiction dealing broadly with human–machine integrations and habituations. It came to be strongly associated with William Gibson's novels of *The Sprawl Trilogy*, which depicted a 'real' world inhabited mostly by cyborgs (though that is not the term he used) and intersected by a virtual world of data flows. To name the latter he gave the prefix 'cyber-' a distinctive and influential turn, with the catchword of interest here: 'cyberspace'.

In the first two novels of the trilogy, Gibson offered brief occasional statements of the idea of 'cyberspace' and elaborated its rationale through the plot. In *Neuromancer* (1984), a fleetingly caught broadcast offers a description:

> 'The matrix has its roots in primitive arcade games,' said the voice-over, 'in early graphics programs and military experimentation with cranial jacks.' On the Sony, a two-dimensional space war faded behind a forest of mathematically generated ferns, demonstrating the special possibilities of logarithmic spirals; cold blue military footage burned through, lab animals wired into test systems, helmets feeding into fire control circuits of tanks and war planes. 'Cyberspace. A consensual hallucination experienced daily by billions of legitimate operators, in every nation, by children being taught mathematical concepts... A graphic representation of data abstracted from the banks of every computer in the human system. Unthinkable complexity. Lines of light ranged in the nonspace of the mind, clusters and constellations of data. Like city lights, receding...' (Gibson 1984, 51)

It was described in terms of visual images, as a 'consensual hallucination', elsewhere in the novel and in the next one, *Count Zero* (1986). These descriptions were, in fact, less suggestive of Internet Technology or of the internet as a facility than of a virtual reality (VR) gaming space with advanced graphics and interactiveness.

The terms 'artificial reality' and 'virtual reality' had themselves been recently introduced then, via cyberpunk fiction (Broderick 1984) and a distinct field of engineering focussed on developing tools to facilitate sensory immersion in 3D environments composed of data (as defined by Lanier 1992). Bethke's (1980) 'CityNet' was much more straightforwardly the internet than Gibson's 'cyberspace'. The latter was imagined as a hyperreal shared environment in which every person's projected self could live for various periods, sometimes years, and where their senses switch from real-world to virtual-world experience. This environment was also peopled by virtual personae, some of them artificial-intelligence (AI) constructs. In other words, cyberspace was conceived as parallel to the 'human sensorium' (Gibson 1984: 55). In the novels, in fact, both the virtual cyberspace personae and the real-world cyborgs seemed to follow related or overlapping gaming rationales. Cyberspace derived, as noted in the quotation, from both gaming and neuroscience. It represented a collective human–machine integration while cyborgs represented individual human–machine integration, and these seemed to gel and at times merge. The emerging Internet Technology of the time, and the direction of development envisaged for it, was a necessary substrate of 'cyberspace' in Gibson's sense, but not coterminous with 'cyberspace'. Cyberspace was most straightforwardly imagined as a VR world and habitus, a gaming structure which has become as free-standing and complex as the real world.

Insofar as the term 'cyberspace' goes, importantly the coinage delinked the prefix 'cyber-' from its strong association with imagined or real *persons* and shifted it to the designation of a *space* which persons may virtually occupy. This turn gave the term its initial and quite original impetus. The idea of a disembodied and habitable space seemed to throw a new light on familiarly real and inhabited spaces. At the same time, the idea that such a space is technologically realizable, and has already been realized to an extent, appeared to augur some transformation in actually existing spaces. The associations made between 'cyberspace' and the 'internet' depended on where the emphasis was put in those ideas. If the emphasis was put on 'cyberspace' as consisting in an emerging VR habitus, built on a substrate that is Internet Technology to feed hardware and software sensory-immersion tools, then the terms 'cyberspace' and 'internet' did not equate easily. If the emphasis was put on 'cyberspace' as composed of virtual communities/doings that are already out there, growing upon facilities provided by Internet Technology and to be consolidated further, then 'cyberspace' and 'internet' appeared to be coterminous, almost synonymous.

In the later 1980s, when used independently of discussing Gibson's novels—i.e., as a term that denotes a general idea rather than a fictional construct—'cyberspace' mainly equated to VR gaming products and was not specifically referred to Internet Technology. Somewhere between 1986 and 1991, some aficionados and researchers leaned towards the VR emphasis and others preferred an internet emphasis in the term 'cyberspace'. Either way, naming an inhabitable if unmaterial space unlocked by technological means, the term 'cyberspace' concentrated a burst of intellectual energy. Several book-length publications in 1991–1995 dug into the idea of cyberspace with one or the other emphasis.

Those interested in philosophy and social and cultural studies preferred the VR emphasis, and focussed on, among other issues, the architectural and design possibilities, the slippages between bodies/corporeality and identities/recognition in social formations, and the linguistic practices underpinning cyberspace. In this vein, Michael Benedikt's edited volume *Cyberspace: First Steps* (1991) offered upbeat theoretical analyses of the space, with the editor marking the emphasis and the technological underpinnings (mainly Internet Technology) of the term:

> With the advent of fast personal computers, digital television, and high bandwidth cable and radio-frequency networks, so-called post-industrial societies stand ready for a yet deeper voyage into the 'permanently ephemeral' (by which I mean, as the reader is well aware, cyberspace). As a number of chapters in this book observe, so-called on-line community, electronic mail, and information services (USENET, the Well, Compuserve, and scores of others) already form a technological and behavioural beginning. But the significance of this voyage is perhaps best gauged by the almost irrational enthusiasm that today surrounds the topic of *virtual reality*. (Benedikt 1991, 11)

Michel Heim's *The Metaphysics of Virtual Reality* (1993) took up many of the themes covered in Benedikt's volume and understood cyberspace in squarely VR terms: 'We inhabit cyberspace when we feel ourselves moving through the interface into a relatively independent world with its own dimensions and rules' (79). The term 'interface' was conceived as the transition point into cyberspace, and seemed to stand in for the internet as substrate for or portal into VR. Heim regarded 'cyberspace' and especially 'interface' as buzzwords/keywords, and might be among the first to note the constitutive role played by catchwords in the construction of Internet Technology and an emerging discourse:

> *Interface* is a buzzword. Buzzwords cue conversations, directing our attention momentarily. Occasionally a buzzword strikes a deeper resonance: the word buzzes, we push on it, and suddenly a magic door swings open to who we are and where we stand in history. Such buzzwords are keywords. Keywords are not just fuzzy metaphors or poetic symbols of an epoch, like 'the computer age' or 'the nuclear age.' Rather, keywords apply analogously across the entire spectrum of cultural life. They apply accurately and in detail to many aspects of our lives -- each aspect differently. Keywords cut across our whole cultural world, and *interface* is a keyword. (Heim 1993, 78)

In fact, Heim's hyped-up account of the word 'interface' to suggest a passage between 'internet' and 'cyberspace' (as VR) was well chosen. 'Interface' has a complex career as a catchword across numerous disciplinary and professional registers since the late nineteenth century, and notably in computer networking since the mid-1960s. Where 'internet' immediately suggests the technology of computer networks, 'interface' seems to draw that into a wider process of linking technologies, organizations, and persons. At the time, Jonathan Grudin—who was investigating human–computer interactions at organizational level—was particularly interested in the concept and term 'user interface', noting the vagaries of its usage (especially in Grudin 1993, but also in Grudin 1989, 1990).

In the same period, those interested in policy, politics, and jurisprudence were inclined to understand 'cyberspace' as more or less synonymous with the 'internet' or, more precisely, as encompassing the social relations emerging through engagement with Internet Technology. In this sense, 'cyberspace' was taken as referring to the integration of Internet Technology in real-world arrangements and to the spatial scope of a new kind of social collectivity—in our terms, the Internet Polity. The tone was set in David Ronfeldt's *Cyberocracy, Cyberspace, and Cyberology* (1991), the title itself presenting a nice play with the prefix 'cyber-', often employed at the time (Ronfeldt claimed that 'cyberocracy was coined in a RAND memorandum in 1978 [iii]). Cyberocracy was understood at two levels of consequence from emerging information technologies, in terms of: a 'form of organization that supplants the traditional forms of bureaucracy and technocracy'; and a 'form of government that may redefine relations between state and society, and between the public sector and the private sector' (19). The spatial aspect of the term 'cyberspace' was deliberately recruited away from advocates of emphasizing VR (noting that that too is a new term) to encompassing existing spaces of information technology use: 'The term generally refers to the whole world, but it may be used to refer to a corporation, university, government, nation, region, or some other spatially limited environment' (31). The 'new domain of power and property' was described by listing a range of public, private, and community-based networks, precisely the domain of Internet

Technology. Similarly, Laurence Tribe's 'The Constitution of Cyberspace' (1991), carefully put aside the current sense of 'cyberspace' as VR and decided to use,

> the term 'cyberspace' much more broadly, as many have lately [taken it] encompass[es] the full array of computer-mediated audio and/or video interactions that are already widely dispersed in modern societies—from things as ubiquitous as the ordinary telephone, to things that are still coming on-line like computer bulletin boards and networks. (Tribe 1991)

Tribe proceeded to offer one of the earliest reflections on the conundrums opened for US constitutional law by the adoption of Internet Technology. Where, at the onset of the 1990s, cyberspace (as VR) aroused the unabashed enthusiasm of cultural studies and philosophy scholars looking to the future, those examining policy, politics, and the law were inclined to be circumspect about cyberspace (as internet) insofar as already at large.

Over 1990–1995 the catchwords 'cyberspace' and 'information superhighway' appeared coterminous, and the 'internet' emerged as a syntagmatic catchword on their backs, firmly enriched with both connotations of being a usable facility and an inhabited space. The Clinton and Gore presidential campaign and administration, the business opportunities opened by policy and legislation after the High Performance Computing Act 1991, the privatization moves with public backing that were consolidated with the Telecommunications Act 1996 … all these offered fertile ground for fervent techies and enthusiasts, entrepreneurs and lobbyists, bureaucrats and publicists to join forces and make 'cyberspace'/'information superhighway' the repository of hyperbolic proclamations. Manifestos and vision statements proliferated. Hackers and programmers came out of their niches into public media and awareness (on whom more in Chap. 5). A relentlessly optimistic politics of 'cyberspace' seemed to emerge as if from below by (often affluent) hackers, techies, entrepreneurs, and users, more or less in step with the upbeat policies of the 'information superhighway' from above. Through 'cyberspace', the prefix 'cyber-' seemed to explode into neologisms (elaborated in Chap. 5). In some respects, those hackers, techies, entrepreneurs appeared to take possession of 'cyberspace' as a kind of emancipatory counter-establishment subculture which needs to be defended from 'information superhighway' policies. But enthusiasm was the dominant note in any case and on all sides. John Barlow, Mitch Kapor, and John Gilmore founded the Electronic Frontier Foundation to defend cyberspace civil liberties in 1990 (its agenda and context were considered in Kapor 1991). Barlow's account of discovering the term 'cyberspace' caught the spirit of the time:

> Imagine discovering a continent so vast that it may have no end to its dimensions. Imagine a new world with more resources than all our future greed might exhaust, more opportunities than there will ever be entrepreneurs to exploit, and a peculiar kind of real estate that expands with development. […]
>
> Such a place actually exists, if *place* is the appropriate word. It consists of electron states, microwaves, magnetic fields, light pulses and thought itself—a wave in the web of our electronic processing and communication systems. I used to call it Datasphere until I read William Gibson's Neuromancer and discovered that he had already given it the evocative name of Cyberspace. (Barlow 1991: 19)

The Whole Earth 'Lectronic Link (WELL) online community, founded by Stewart Brand and Larry Brilliant in 1985, seemed to embody the idea of cyberspace. John Coate's influential essay 'Cyberspace Innkeeping' (1992, rev. 1998), divided cyberspace into the tangible aspect, 'the hardware and the software—the physical network', and the intangible aspect, 'as much defined and shaped by everyone's collective imagination as it is by the computers, discs and software tools', and focussed on the communal principles of the latter. Douglas Rushkoff's *Cyberia* (1991) gave a feeling description of the lives of some such community members. *Wired* magazine, launched in 1993 by Louis Rossetto, evinced this celebratory spirit in every issue and book it put out. In the early 1990s there were, in fact, few critiques of 'cyberspace', despite scepticism about the 'information superhighway'.

A series of publications around the turn into the 1990s by Arthur Kroker and his co-authors, under the New World Perspectives imprint, were one notable exception. Drawing upon a dense arsenal of postmodernist, post-Marxist, and media studies phraseology, these were a searching exploration of slippages between emerging technologies and received social norms. At precisely the point where 'cyberspace' enthusiasm and 'information superhighway' propaganda met, Kroker and Michael Weinstein's *Data Trash* (1994) reflected anxiously on that conjunction from the Canadian context. In their diffuse argument, an attempt at reconfiguring Marxist class analysis in cyberspace terms was a notable contribution. Cyberspace was producing, the book observed, a 'virtual class' or 'technological class' dealing in immaterial commodities at the intersection (interface?) of real world and cyberspace, replacing the industrial capitalist class:

> The *universal* interests of the recombinant commodity are carried forward by the *particular* interests of the technological class. Itself a virtual class because its historical interests are linked to hyperspace and its economic relations are (globally) coextensive with the world network of technocratic elites rather than bounded in local space, the technological class fuses with the high-speed backbone of the Net. Its expression as the emergent class of post-history is coterminous with the sovereignty of the recombinant commodity. (Kroker and Weinstein 1994, 77–78)

This widely dispersed virtual class has, the book argued, very real and comprehensive effects on the existing working class and its organizations (80).

Through the 1990s popular accounts, manifestos, professional and consumer guidebooks, and scholarly analyses headlining 'cyberspace' appeared prolifically while the fortunes of the phrase 'information superhighway' were relatively rocky throughout and started fading as the decade wound down. In almost all, 'cyberspace' was understood as grounded in the facilities of Internet Technology and synonymous with what was regarded broadly as the 'internet'. Or, perhaps, the connotations of 'internet' expanded by being woven through the imaginings and reimaginings of 'cyberspace'. As the decade progressed, the 'internet' gradually became the comparatively sedate replacement of the fervour-driven 'cyberspace' and also of the purpose-driven 'information superhighway'.

Through the first half of the 1990s, the communitarian buzz around cyberspace and the imaginary of a virtual territory—a 'continent' or 'new world', as Barlow had put it—seemed most straightforwardly to materialize the Internet Polity. This polity was described by a territory, by certain political principles concentrated on internet usage, and a distinctive vocabulary (taken up in the next chapter). At the time, insofar as ideologies were espoused amidst this collectivity, that tended to have a strong utopian character. However, the political principles considered were, as ever, such as could be brought to elucidating real-world arrangements and desires, to gel with or depart from real-world ideological registers. Put otherwise, the features of Internet Technology were not explicitly politically examined but were taken as being politically effective and implicitly politically formative.

In relation to actually existing social arrangements, the internet was promoted as a magical cure for contradictions—if not now, in the imminent future. Alternatively, Internet Technology was referred as a sticking tape for inconvenient fissures in policy and practice, often immediately implementable as a service or customizable facility. A celebratory mystique attached to the consolidatory or reparative powers of Internet Technology vis-à-vis existing social arrangements. Insofar as norms within the makeup of Internet Technology were tacitly invoked, that was predominantly by variously dressing up the principles of minimal-gradual-mechanical standardization (the core protocol) and of precedent individuation (hypertext systems). These were, however, understood as being co-extensive with specific social arrangements and ideological subscriptions. In the main, they gelled with libertarian aspirations (i.e., realizing a minimal state, maintaining the inviolability of individual self-interest, and maximizing market rationality, etc.) or some form of anarcho-capitalism (i.e., abolishing the state altogether for free-play of market rationality amidst localized self-determining communities). Encouraging adaptation instead of (or before) mandating standards by the minimal-gradual-mechanical standardization principle was understood as enabling free choice; the principle of precedent individuation was taken as securing necessary individual interests over collective determinations; and both seemed to gel with a minimally regulated and policed market arrangement. These are, of course, extremely condensed generalizations from what appeared to be a flowering of utopian idealisms at the time: crypto-anarchism, Californian Ideology, digital socialism, cyberdemocracy and the like (Coyne 1999; Ludlow 2001; Flichy 2007 [2001] gave helpful overviews soon after).

The utopianism that was firmly associated with the catchword 'cyberspace', which indeed made a catchword of 'cyberspace', took a hit by the 1996 Telecommunications Act. That the Act consolidated the privatization and corporate occupation of Internet Technology, anticipated in 'information superhighway' policies, was not in itself what troubled cyberspace enthusiasts. That this privatization was endorsed by an act of government, and moreover by setting out a modest regulatory framework and judicial oversight, seemed an overreach to the enthusiasts. It was received in some quarters as an attack on the civil liberties of cyberspace that the Electronic Frontier Foundation was founded to defend. With characteristic rhetorical flair, Barlow produced 'A Declaration of the Independence of Cyberspace' (1996), which announced:

> Governments derive their just powers from the consent of the governed. You have neither solicited nor received ours. We did not invite you. You do not know us, nor do you know our world. Cyberspace does not lie within your borders. Do not think that you can build it, as

> though it were a public construction project. You cannot. It is an act of nature and it grows itself through our collective actions. (Barlow 1996)

The claim of territorial occupation and speaking for the future naturally seemed overweening, and was taken to task (e.g., Jones 1996), but also often referred thereafter. But the consternation was shared widely enough among enthusiasts to suggest that the very term 'cyberspace' has been tainted. Reporting on the Sixth Conference on Computers, Freedom, and Privacy at MIT, March 1996, a *New York Times* report observed:

> Cyberspace is dead, many of its electronic pioneers said at a conference here this week.
>
> As the internet population has grown into the millions, what was once a small, self-regulating society of academics and computer wizards has been engulfed by mainstream culture. But in their efforts to preserve the libertarian spirit of the electronic frontier, the original members of the cyberspace community have emerged as a political and social force. (Lewis 1996)

Among other issues, the report observed that this force was evidenced in proposals to form 'an Internet Caucus in the Congress and a Senate bill to relax the Government's laws restricting the transmission of secrets over the global information network'. The report came with no ironic comment on the fact that cyberspace aficionados anxious about government regulation had a sufficient presence in governmental quarters to push for deregulation.

Despite the sagging energies of the term 'cyberspace', idealistic aspirations and freedoms continued to be pinned on it for a while to come. But three years later, law professor Lawrence Lessig raised the prospect of the 'death of cyberspace' again in a 1999 lecture, in view of the encroachment of intellectual property control by large corporations operating on the internet:

> Cyberspace *will* die, or at least the cyberspace that we know. It will be killed by these institutions that would recreate the 1970s in HTML. It will be killed by an institution that will disable once again the independent, unaffiliated, critical, questioning creativity that the Internet of the last ten years produced. (Lessig 2000: 347)

Lessig became one of the founders of Creative Commons in 2001. Not long afterwards, a less portentous 'end of cyberspace' was announced by Alex Soojung-Kim Pang, Research Director at the Institute for the Future in Silicon Valley. In January 2006 he wrote a blog declaring that such an end was nigh, because 'the idea of cyberspace as separate from the real world will collapse' (quoted in Thomas 2006: 389). Or, as phrased in its later version: 'As the Internet becomes more pervasive—as it moves off desktops and screen and becomes embedded in things, spaces, and minds—cyberspace will disappear' (Pang 2006). What he was getting at, it turned out in a co-authored *Wired* piece, was the need for a new term to replace 'Cyberspace': 'The Internet feels less like an alternate world that we "go to" and more like just another layer of life. Besides, doesn't *cyberspace* sound kind of played out? Clearly, we need a better word' (Pang and Pescovitz 2006). Of those they consulted, William Gibson dodged the question, and the others gave unsatisfactory answers.

As it happened, from around the mid-1990s the term 'cyberspace' was given a decisively governmental turn via another established employment of the 'cyber-'

prefix, in 'cybersecurity'. This in fact tendentiously took 'cyberspace' to the obverse of libertarian and anarcho-capitalist anti-governmental stances, towards what is now thought of as 'neoliberalism'. Briefly, the much discussed and contentious term suggests a partnership of government and businesses to control markets so as to favour rather than regulate the latter. The objective appeared as a subjection of public interests and resources to private interests and investments. From this perspective, instead of foregrounding principles of minimal-gradual-mechanical standardization and precedent individuation, those principles were gradually made firmly corollary to the principle of targeted collective regulation (security controls).

In 1996, a Subcommittee of Investigations of the US Congress held hearings on the theme *Security in Cyberspace* (US Government 1996), in which the vulnerabilities facing the country due to the development of Internet Infrastructure were discussed. Amongst the many witnesses who used the term 'cyberspace' knowledgeably, Robert Anderson of RAND Corporation offered a definition:

> By 'cyberspace,' I refer to the global collection of internetted computers and communication systems. The term originated, I believe, in the novel 'Neuromancer' by William Gibson in 1984. The public telephone network and the Internet provide the main backbone for cyberspace, but cyberspace also includes the computers that run many of the other control, communication and information systems.
>
> The key word in the definition is 'internetted,' [...]—the characteristic that makes it possible to access some systems from others perhaps half a world away. (111)

Defined thus and in that discursive context, 'cyberspace' was shorn of its ebullient spirit and seemed fraught. 'Control, communication and information systems' that were 'internetted' for exposure 'half a world away' seemed like exactly the sort of situation which needs reining in. All the other witnesses agreed and made recommendations accordingly. A quite different sort of 'cyberspace', tempered by 'cybersecurity', emerged. This governmental definition firmed up in steps after the Telecommunications Act 1996. In discussions surrounding the Uniform Electronic Transactions Act 1999 and Uniform Computer Information Transactions Act 1999 that followed (for a discussion of both see Weitzenboeck 2001), the term 'cyberspace' assumed a dry policy tone. On the one hand, policy and juridical definitions, and, on the other hand, dictionary definitions pulled 'Cyberspace' down to earth from utopian and communal aspirations. The no-nonsense tenor of these is best gauged by the influential definition offered in the US Army and Marine Corps (2013) joint policy document *Cyberspace Operations*, quoted already in Chap. 1:

> Cyberspace can be described in terms of three layers: physical network, logical network, and cyber-persona. The **physical network** layer of cyberspace is comprised of the geographic component and the physical network components. It is the medium where the data travel. The **logical network** layer consists of those elements of the network that are related to one another in a way that is abstracted from the physical network, i.e., the form or relationships are not tied to an individual, specific path, or node. A simple example is any Web site that is hosted on servers in multiple physical locations where all content can be accessed through a single uniform resource locator. The **cyber-persona** layer represents yet a higher level of abstraction of the logical network in cyberspace; it uses the rules that apply in the logical network layer to develop a digital representation of an individual or entity identity

> in cyberspace. The cyberpersona layer consists of the people actually on the network. (US Army and Marine Corps 2013, Executive Summary, v–vi)

As I had noted in Chap. 1, the term 'cyberspace', understood thus, could extend across what is understood as Internet Infrastructure here. In fact, the import of 'cyberspace' in cybersecurity terms after 1995 had a contrary thrust from what 'cyberspace' predominantly represented earlier. Where 'cyberspace' had earlier suggested a territory and collectivity that was separate from and yet woven into real-world polities, in cybersecurity terms 'cyberspace' was taken as simply an element of actually existing polities. It was seen as mappable territorially by countries and their citizenry, or as an addition to land, sea, air, and space where competitive national interests can be established. 'Cyberspace', so to speak, became part of the world to be secured. The layered way in which 'cyberspace' was now conceived became coextensive with a layered vision of all social arrangements (not unlike the Copenhagen School's conception discussed in Chap. 3). Security regimes could be understood as being layered upon all the layers in this continuous social *and* cyberspace stack; cybersecurity could be understood as undertaking such collective regulation across that stack. The latter involved establishing security controls within Internet Infrastructure, including Internet Technology, as well as all layers of actually existing society.

4.5 More Words

While focussing on two redolent catchwords of the 1990s throws some light on the emergence of the Internet Polity discourse, it also makes for an overly schematic account. 'Information superhighway' and 'cyberspace' suggested, as I observed earlier, conceptual horizons in terms of which this discourse came into its own. But within those horizons, the discourse consisted in an explosion of internet-based and internet-oriented exchanges with criss-crossing referents and concepts. This could be conceived as a rapid proliferation of catchwords referring to and circulating on the internet; or, more precisely, as a vocabulary catching on through the relationships between words in increasingly frequent usage. A vocabulary has conventionally been apprehended in terms of lexical listings, and the Internet Polity discourse in the 1990s was tracked frequently through such listings. In the process, the term 'internet' itself went through several connotative shifts, not so much in technical definition as in everyday-language usage. These turns are discussed in the next chapter.

References

Barlow JP (1991) Coming into the country. Commun ACM March 34(3):19–21

Barlow JP (1996) A declaration of the independence of cyberspace. Electronic Frontier Foundation. https://www.eff.org/cyberspace-independence

Benedikt M (ed) (1991) Cyberspace: first steps. MIT Press, Cambridge MA
Bethke B (1983 [1980]) Cyberpunk. Amazing Stories, November, 94–105
Bortolotti B, Siniscalo D (2004) The challenges of privatization an international analysis. Oxford University Press, Oxford
Broderick D (1984) The Judas Mandala. Timescape, New York
Case DO (1998) Enthusiasts, deregulators, guardians, and skeptics: contrasting policy viewpoints on the national information infrastructure. Libr Inf Sci Res 20(4):377–413. https://doi.org/10.1016/S0740-8188(98)90028-7
Castells M (1996) The Rise of the Network Society. Blackwell, Oxford
Chapman G, Rotenberg M (1993) The national information infrastructure: a public interest opportunity. CPSR Newsletter 11:2, Summer. http://cpsr.org/prevsite/publications/newsletters/old/1990s/Summer1993.txt/
Clarke T, Pitelis C (eds) (1993) The political economy of privatization. Routledge, Abingdon
Clinton B, Gore A (1992) Putting people first: how we can all change America. Times Books, New York
Clynes ME, Kline NS (1960) Cyborgs and space. Austronautics, September. 26-27/74-76. https://web.mit.edu/digitalapollo/Documents/Chapter1/cyborgs.pdf
Coate J (1998 [1992]) Cyberspace innkeeping: building online community. http://johncoate.com/Building%20Online%20Community.html
Coyne R (1999) Technoromanticism: digital narrative, holism, and the romance of the real. MIT Press, Cambridge MA
Egan B (1991) Information superhighways: the economics of advanced public communication networks. Artech House, Norwood MA
Egan BL (1996) Information superhighways revisited: the economics of multimedia. Artech House, Norwood MA
Elmer-Dewitt P (1993) Take a trip into the future on the electronic superhighway. Time, April 12. https://content.time.com/time/subscriber/article/0,33009,978216,00.html
Flichy P (2007 [2001]) The internet imaginaire. MIT Press, Cambridge MA
Gibson W (1984) Neuromancer. Ace Books (Penguin), New York
Gibson W (1986) Count zero. HarperCollins, London
Gore A (1990) Superhighways for computing. Computer World, 3 September, 24(36):21
Gore A (1992 [1990]) Networking the future: we need a national "superhighway" for computer information. In: Tinker RF, Kapisovsky PM (eds) Prospects for educational telecomputing. Technical Education Research Centre, Cambridge MA, pp 141–146
Greenstein S (2015) How the internet became commercial: innovation, privatization, and the birth of a new network. Princeton University Press, Princeton NJ
Grudin J (1989) The case against user interface consistency. Commun ACM 32(10, October):1164–1173. https://doi.org/10.1145/67933.67934
Grudin J (1990) The computer reaches out: the historical continuity of interface design. In: CHI '90: proceedings of the SIGCHI conference on human factors in computing systems, March 1990, pp 261–268. https://doi.org/10.1145/97243.97284
Grudin J (1993) Interface: an evolving concept. Commun ACM 36(4 April):110–119. https://doi.org/10.1145/255950.153585
Gupta S (2022) Political catchphrases and contemporary history: a critique of new normals. Oxford University Press, Oxford
Gupta A-Y, Gupta S (2025) Catchwords: an essay on research methods. Key Words: J Culture Mater (22):2024
Halacy DS (1965) Cyborg: evolution of the superman. Harper & Row, New York
Haraway D (1985) A cyborg manifesto: science, technology, and socialist-feminism in the late twentieth century. Socialist Rev 80:65–108
Heim M (1993) The metaphysics of virtual reality. Oxford University Press, Oxford
Helal AH, Weiss JW (eds) (1995) Information superhighway: the role of librarians, information scientists, and intermediaries. Universitatsbibliothek Essen, Essen

Hillkirk J (1989) Fiber optics bring fantasies to life. USA Today, July 18, 'Money' section. 5B
Jones R (1996) A critique of Barlow's "A declaration of the independence of cyberspace". Extropy#17 8(2):27–32. https://www.reillyjones.com/critique-of-barlow.html
Kapor M (1991) Civil liberties in cyberspace. Scient Am 265(3, Special Issue: Communications, Computers and Networks: How to Work, Play and Thrive in Cyberspace):158–165
Katz RL (1988) The information society: an international perspective. Greenwood, Westport CO
Kroker A, Weinstein M (1994) Data trash: the theory of the virtual class. New World Perspectives, Montreal
Lanier J (1992) Virtual reality: the promise of the future. Interact Learn Int 8(4):275–279
Leiner BM, Cerf VG, Clark DD et al (2009) A brief history of the internet. ACM SAGCOMM Comp Commun Rev 39(5):22–31. https://doi.org/10.1145/1629607.1629613
Lessig L (2000) The death of cyberspace. Washington Lee Law Rev 57(2/3):337–347. https://scholarlycommons.law.wlu.edu/wlulr/vol57/iss2/3/
Lewis PH (1996) Pioneers of cyberspace move into wider arena. New York Times, April 1. https://www.nytimes.com/1996/04/01/us/pioneers-of-cyberspace-move-into-wider-arena.html
Ludlow P (ed) (2001) Crypto anarchy, cyberstates and pirate utopias. MIT Press, Cambridge MA
Lyon D (1988) The information society: issues and illusions. Blackwell, Oxford
Markoff J (1993) Building the electronic superhighway. New York Times, January 24. https://www.nytimes.com/1993/01/24/business/building-the-electronic-superhighway.html
Martin J (1978) The wired society. Prentice-Hall, Englewood Cliffs NJ
Masuda Y (1981) The information society as post-industrial society. World Future Society, Bethesda MD
Maxwell JC (1868) On governors. Proc R Soc Lond 16(1867–1868):270–283. https://www.jstor.org/stable/112510
NRENAISSANCE Committee et al (1994) Realizing the information future: the internet and beyond. National Academy Press, Washington DC. https://nap.nationalacademies.org/catalog/4755/realizing-the-information-future-the-internet-and-beyond
NRNRC et al (1988) Toward a national research network. National Academy Press, Washington DC. https://nap.nationalacademies.org/catalog/10334/toward-a-national-research-network
Pang AS-K (2006) The end of cyberspace. http://www.endofcyberspace.com/
Pang AS-K, Pescovitz D (2006) "Cyberspace" is dead., Wired News, February 10. https://www.wired.com/2006/02/cyberspace-is-dead/
Petrosyan A (2023) Global number of internet users 2005–2022. https://www.statista.com/statistics/273018/number-of-internet-users-worldwide/
Pew Research Centre (1995) Americans going online…explosive growth, uncertain destinations: technology in the American household. October 16. https://www.pewresearch.org/politics/1995/10/16/americans-going-online-explosive-growth-uncertain-destinations/
Pollack A (1985) The battle of the titans: part 2. The New York Times, June 30, section 3. 1, column 2
Radu R (2019) Negotiating internet governance. Oxford University Press, Oxford
Ramanadham VV (ed) (1993) Privatization: a global perspective. Routledge, Abingdon
Ronfeldt D (1991) Cyberocracy, cyberspace, and cyberology: political effects of the information revolution. RAND, Santa Monica CA
Rosenberg RS (1986) Computers and the information society. John Wiley, New York
Rushkoff D (1991) Cyberia: life in the trenches of hyperspace. Harper, New York
Singham SA (2023) Market distortions in privatization processes. Routledge, Abingdon
Smith MS (1994) The information superhighway: status and issues. CRS report for congress 94-954 SPR. Congressional Research Service, Washington DC. https://www.everycrsreport.com/files/19941202_94-954_83b5f9ed7e299cdf31b614f3ae2d1cdd5c6f6a52.pdf
Smyrnaios N (2018) Internet oligopoly: the corporate takeover of our digital world. Bingley, Emerald
Thomas S (2006) The end of cyberspace and other surprises. Convergence: Int J Res New Media Technol 12(4):383–391. https://doi.org/10.1177/1354856506068316

Torok AG (1994) Technological speedtraps on the information superhighway. In: Helal and Weiss (eds), pp 134–148
Tribe LH (1991) The constitution in cyberspace: law and liberty beyond the electronic frontier. American Humanist Association, Washington DC. https://archive.epic.org/free_speech//tribe.html
US Government, NSF Authorization (1989) Hearings before the subcommittee on science, research and technology of the committee on science, space and technology, house of representatives, 100th congress, 22–24 March 1988, No 115. US Government, Washington
US Government (1996) Security in cyberspace: hearings before the permanent subcommittee on investigations of the committee on governmental affairs, United States senate, one hundred fourth congress, second session. U.S. Government Printing Office, Washington
US Army and Marine Corps (2013) Cyberspace operations, February 5. Joint Publication 3-12 (R). https://irp.fas.org/doddir/dod/jp3_12r.pdf
van Dijk J (1999 [1991]) The network society. Sage, London
Weiner N (1961 [1948]) Cybernetics: or control and communication in the animal and the machine. MIT Press, Cambridge MA
Weitzenboeck EM (2001) Electronic agents and the formation of contracts. Int J Law Inf Technol 9(3):204–234. https://doi.org/10.1093/ijlit/9.3.204
Williams R (1983) Keywords: a vocabulary of culture and society. Fontana, Glasgow
Yeager LB (1997) Austrian economics, neoclassicism, and the market test. J Econ Perspect 11(4):153–165. https://doi.org/10.1257/jep.11.4.153
Zoglin R (1993) When the revolution comes. Time, April 12. https://content.time.com/time/magazine/article/0,9171,978232,00.html

Chapter 5
The Vocabulary and Culture of Internet Collectivity

Abstract Taking a wider view, but still with a predominant focus on the 1990s, this chapter describes how a distinctive vocabulary for Internet Polity discourse developed and how cultural significance was attributed to collective activities on the internet. A brief discussion of the nodal term—'internet', and coterminously words with 'e-' and 'digital' prefixes—precedes that. An account of computing and internet dictionaries (and glossaries and word-listings) fleshes out the vocabulary that was consolidated as Internet Polity discourse. Several phases of dictionary making are covered: of computing terms for professionals, of computing terms for lay users, of hacker slang/jargon/techspeak, of internet terms in themselves, of internet slang and cyberlexicography. Turning next to attributions of cultural collectivity via Internet Technology, the overlaps and distinction between 'technoculture', 'cyberculture', and 'digital culture' are unpacked. After pausing on the rise of popular 'online communities', a final section delineates the normative and ideological shifts that took place around the term 'hacker'.

The vocabulary that came to characterize the Internet Polity discourse was propagated and taken up in a relatively short period, moving from specialist coteries to large constituencies of internet users and consumers. A constant and prolific production and redefinition of words and phrases occurred especially in the 1990s, many of which caught on widely at least for a while and some of which settled into stable everyday usage, often across diverse languages. These words and phrases conferred a distinctive character to the Internet Polity. More importantly, the speedy mechanics of their spread and mutual modifications themselves appeared to become a characteristic feature of Internet Polity discourse. The catchiness of catchwords or, more broadly, a fluidity in appointing and juxtaposing words became intrinsic to the Internet Polity discourse. This vocabulary has marked the life and character of the organized collectivity anchored to the internet, often designated by the accommodative term 'culture'. Accounts of 'digital culture' or 'online culture' were grounded in this vocabulary of the Internet Polity discourse.

The negotiations of minimal-gradual-mechanical standardization, precedent individuation, and targeted collective regulation as social and political first principles of

S. Gupta, *Collective Principles and the Formation of the Internet*, Springer Series on Cultural Computing, https://doi.org/10.1007/978-3-031-90470-7_5

the Internet Polity had a necessarily active relationship with rapid changes in Internet Technology and Internet Infrastructure. Constant modifications—fine-tunings, up-gradings, recalibrations—in protocol layers, hypertext systems, and security controls made for corresponding reconfigurations of the Internet Polity. Those were mostly activated by rapid developments in the material (hardware) dimension of the Internet Infrastructure, also entailing constant fine-tunings, up-gradings, recalibrations in designs and capacities. Devices continuously became more affordable and portable, greater degrees of interoperability and connectivity between populations and regions were achieved, larger volumes of I-information were processed and stored. Put otherwise, the Internet Polity evolved as quickly as its first principles were tested through the adjustments in Internet Technology and Internet Infrastructure. Amidst growing collective habituation, a certain mutability became engrained in the formation of the Internet Polity, which had the effect of consolidating it instead of dispersing it. That was reflected—or perhaps more precisely, performed—in the vocabulary of its discourse. The rise and fall of catchwords, with their intrinsic fluidity and cross-connections, are an endemic feature of the Internet Polity discourse and could be regarded as a cultural characteristic of this collective existence.

The career of the term 'internet' in the 1990s is a nodal catchword of many catchwords in this vocabulary. I have discussed its specific connotations for this study; here I pause on its larger career first. Then, I move to placing this nodal term amidst the larger vocabulary. The vocabulary is contemplated via relevant dictionaries, glossaries, and other word/phrase listings which sought to both legitimize and give order to the Internet Polity discourse at the time. The accounts of the social life and process of internet culture and online community, materializing the collective life of the Internet Polity, are explored in the final section of this chapter. The career of the catchword 'hacker', which says much about the development of internet culture, occupies a final sub-section there.

5.1 Nodal Catchwords/Prefixes

Alongside its close association with 'information superhighway' and 'cyberspace', the word 'internet' gained momentum in the 1990s by being implicated in numerous terms with the qualifier 'digital' and with 'cyber' and 'e' prefixes. These had applications predating Internet Technology, in the wider areas of cybernetics, electronic communications, and digital systems. In the 1990s these converged on an automatic implication of the 'internet'. The correspondence of the qualifier 'digital' and the prefix 'e-' with the travels of 'internet' in the 1990s is indicated in the Graph 5.1.

'Digital' was used contra 'analog' for computers since the 1940s and referred to various hardware and software products. It was defined before 'internet' in, for instance, the Oxford English Dictionary (OED) in 1989. In a note on its travels in the OED since, Richard Holden observed:

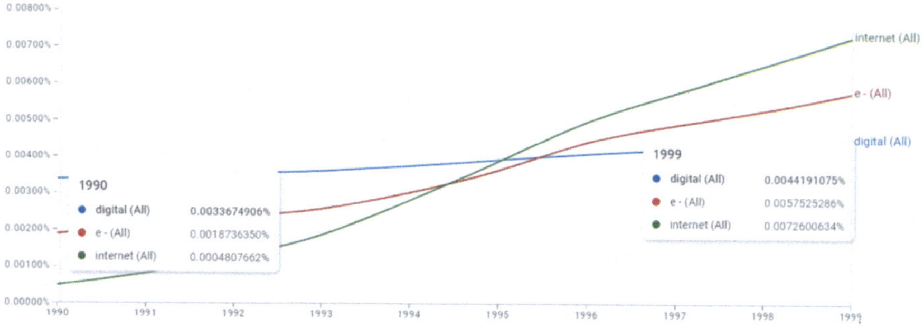

Graph 5.1 Google Ngram for 'internet', 'e-', 'digital', 1990–1999. 'Digital' shows a relatively small but steady 1.3-fold rise, but then it was already frequently used in 1990. 'Internet' showed a 15-fold rise. Words with 'e-' prefixes (only tracked here where hyphenated, also see Graph 5.3) showed a threefold rise

> as *digital* has gained greater significance, so senses with a looser meaning have begun to emerge. Terms such as digital art, digital economy, and digital money are now covered in the revised entry, along with a more general sense: 'involving or relating to digital or computer technology, esp. the Internet'. Similarly, another new sense—'designating a virtual, computer-mediated counterpart of an object that exists in the real world'—covers such entities as *digital negatives, digital shopping carts*, and *digital ink*. Whole organizations or countries can now be described as *digital*, when they are seen to adopt or embrace computer technology or the Internet. (Holden 2023)

As far as the 'cyber' prefix goes, it is difficult to track through the Google Ngram Viewer because this does not permit the use of a wildcard with an unhyphenated prefix, which, unlike 'e-', has usually been the case for 'cyber'. However, a breakdown of 'cyber', insofar as used as a qualifier word or as a hyphenated prefix, gives a reasonable albeit limited sense of its complicity with 'internet' in this period, see Graph 5.2.

A significant proliferation of the usage of 'cyber' as an unhyphenated prefix to effectively coin new words coincided precisely with the opening of Internet Technology to wider access and commercial services. A listing of 'new words' in 1994

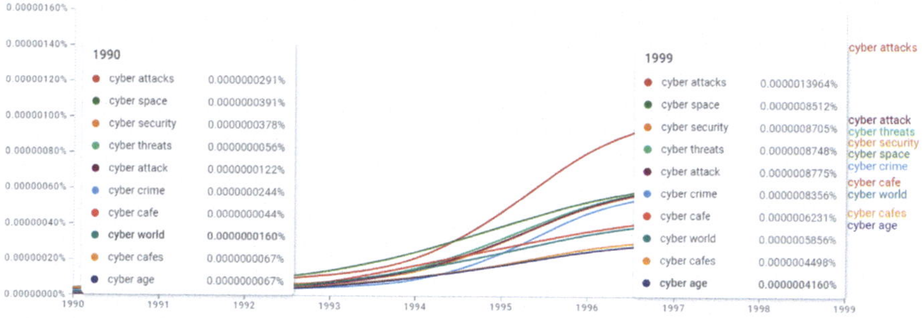

Graph 5.2 Google Ngram for 'cyber *', 1990–1999—the top 10 terms with 'cyber' prefixes with word spaces. Taken together, these 10 'cyber' prefixed words showed a 32-fold increase in usage

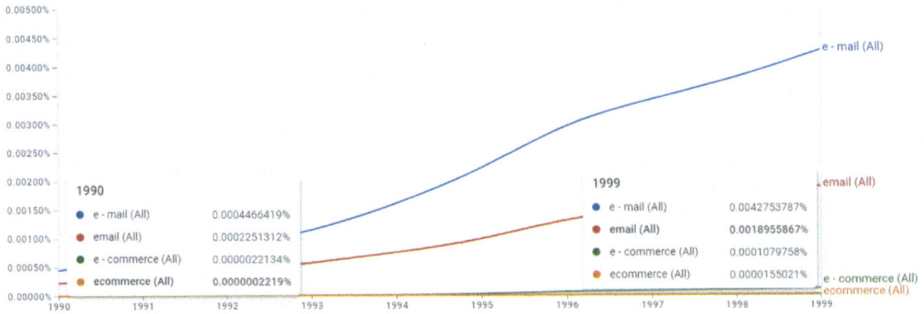

Graph 5.3 Google Ngram for 'e-mail', 'email, 'e-commerce', 'ecommerce' (case-insensitive), 1990–1999. Both 'email' and 'e-mail' showed nearabout tenfold increases in usage. Though considerably lower down the range, the next highest 'e' prefixed word, 'e-commerce'/'ecommerce' showed in the 2 forms respectively a 48-fold and 70-fold increase

observed that '*Cyber* is especially noteworthy as a voguish prefix' (Algeo and Algeo 1994b, 398) and listed an extraordinary 96 new usages between 1991 and 1994 (400-6). The use of the prefix 'e-'/'e', where *e* stands for 'electronic', became strongly associated with the internet through the burgeoning use of 'e-mail'/'email' and 'e-commerce'/'ecommerce', and with lower frequencies in 'e-business', 'e-book' and 'e-governance' and their unhyphenated forms. Prior to the 1990s it was rarely used in any term other than 'e-mail'/'email' (Graph 5.3).

The frequency of the use of prefixes like 'cyber' and 'e-'/'e' are, however, imperfectly gauged through published text corpora like Google Books. These were employed numerously in everyday usage with reference to some dimension of the internet, sometimes in neologisms which caught on and sometimes more transiently as nonce words (used in a context-specific manner, for an occasion). Thus, in a paper on 'e-' words, Lucinda MacDonald (2005) drew upon various lists and online sources to identity 152 'e-' words, of which only 29 had been included in standard dictionaries (the author regarded inclusion as 'institutionalization'). Written shortly after the dot-com crash of 2000, she found a change in attitude towards 'e-' words:

> At first, e-words are used enthusiastically as the benefits of doing business on the Internet are explored. Eventually, as the 'new economy' is revealed to be just a massive boom in the traditional boom bust cycle, our infatuation with the e-craze turns to frustration. (MacDonald 2005, 87)

Leaving aside the frequent usage of 'e-mail'/'email' (and their verb forms), the more frequently used 'e-' words have fared reasonably well after peaks of enthusiasm, and 'e-books' is going strong.

5.2 Lexicography

The vocabulary that accrued around the nodal word 'internet' (and its variants) in the 1990s can be examined via dictionaries, glossaries, and other word/phrase listings. This vocabulary lies at the heart of Internet Polity discourse, expressing both its collective spirit and sense of place. Turning to dictionaries means touching upon the weighty field of lexicography, i.e., the diverse scholarly approaches to making and studying word listings and definitions (usefully, Bergenholtz and Gouws 2012 have attempted a unified definition of 'lexicography'). Given the complexity of this field, it is prudent to delimit the scope of the following observations on dictionaries presenting this vocabulary; by doing so, I also foreground some of their distinctive features.

To begin with, there are some common lexicographical pursuits which are not covered here. First, no attempt is made to elaborate general linguistic concepts of words and word usage, or to formulate broad principles and methods for identifying, assembling, defining, and exemplifying relevant words. These occupy much lexicographical scholarship, but do not feature here. Second, I do not discuss the effect this vocabulary has had on everyday language usage at large, and on different social contexts and discourses. This is a particularly buzzy area of investigation, with numerous publications (Crystal 2001 and McCulloch 2019 gave popular overviews). Third, nor do I fully delve the sea-change that the internet and Internet Technology have brought to the principles and practices of dictionary making and usage. I do touch upon this in a cursory way, but much more has already been done on this (overviews are found in Fuertes-Olivera and Bergenholtz 2010; Granger and Paquot 2012; Fuertes-Olivera ed. 2018: Parts V and VI). Fourth, I do not detail the inclusion of specific terms from this vocabulary of Internet Polity discourse in standard general language dictionaries (of English, French, Russian, etc.). There is much that remains to be done in this area, but that is not for this study.

I turn instead to some observations on dictionaries insofar as squarely relevant to the internet and the formation of the Internet Polity discourse, in the Anglosphere and mainly within the 1990s. By and large, these are conventional listings in alphabetical order. In considering these, I draw upon two relatively marginal aspects of lexicography: first, the politics of the dictionary, specifically the concepts of authority which underpin the form; and second, some ideas of dictionary usage and users.

Since dictionaries have generally attempted to set standardized or authoritative definitions for word usage at given junctures, various kinds of authority are invested in it (unpicked at some length for British and American English in Wells 1973; in relation to a range of contexts in Kachru and Kahane 1995; succinctly in Seargeant 2010; and intermittently elsewhere). Most commonly, this authority is vested in the institutions that appoint or endorse the dictionary makers: governmental or official bodies representing nations and cultures; scholarly and professional bodies for disciplines or technical areas. These exercise the prerogatives of being standard setters as well as regulators/gatekeepers for general language dictionaries or specialist and professional dictionaries. Those prerogatives are undergirded by the content of the dictionary: for instance, by calling upon authority-bearing archives of texts/authors or legitimizing inferences from language corpora, and by following or building upon established systems for word definitions and dictionary organization. The dictionaries of internet terms discussed here, however, largely fell outside these norms, except those designed for pedagogic or professional usage by engineers and programmers. Insofar as this study is concerned with Internet Polity discourse, the latter are of less interest than those for wider markets, but I do consider them below. Popular dictionaries of internet terms often came from authors whose lexicographical authority was not formally sanctioned or officially endorsed. This is a distinctive feature of such dictionaries: *their purpose in this period was not so much to set standards for and regulate an established space (like the language of a nation or culture) as to constitute a discursive space (to bring about Internet Polity formation).* The main institutional backing that some such authors received after the fact was from commercial publishing houses.

Concordantly, such dictionaries were often designed to appeal to notional categories of users rather than meant for an existing community of language users. However, in this respect too, these dictionaries took a somewhat different line from the kind of dictionary usage that occupies mainstream lexicography. Research into ordinary usage has consisted mainly in gauging specific cohorts of readers through surveys (educators, translators, academics, etc.), and increasingly by tracking usage through internet domain records (in fact, internet-based dictionary production and general language usage have become mutually entwined). Linguists have occasionally pondered appropriate ways of using dictionaries (crystallized into a wishful ideal user in Crystal 2003: 325–326). These preoccupations extend indifferently for the dictionaries of internet terms discussed here, whose authors either presented themselves as model dictionary users or outlined what kind of usage they anticipated (had well-defined implied readers in mind). In brief, *such dictionaries seemed to be designed as much to draw in users as to define words/phrases; clarifying the vocabulary of Internet Polity discourse was conceived as a way of consolidating and expanding the Internet Polity.*

5.3 Word Listings

Dictionaries of specifically internet terms emerged from and drew upon various strands of lexicalizing computing terms. The strands that converged into dictionaries of internet terms reflected both the practices of existing adept users of those terms and anticipated would-be users entering this linguistic field. Seen thus, the following strands can be distinguished behind the 1990s emergence and lexicalizing of a vocabulary for Internet Polity discourse: dictionaries of computer terminology for professionals, computer terminology for laypersons, hacker slang/jargon/techspeak. These variously converged on the following: dictionaries of internet terms for various constituencies, and of internet slang (usually in cyberdictionary or online dictionary forms). I discuss these by turn, broadly in chronological sequence.

5.3.1 *Dictionaries of Computing Terms for Professionals*

In the area of computing, the obvious first strand involved standardizing words/phrases for professional and pedagogic purposes, when different sets of terms were being employed by variously located research groups. The initial moves from the early 1950s have been examined by Bernadette Longo (2021: Chaps. 6 and 7), who describes the professionalizing impetus as follows:

> Establishing [a] specialized language as a distinct body of professional knowledge is a process that rests on defining technical words. The people engaged in that work of defining terms are also defining boundaries around their fledgling profession, determining who will be admitted as one of these professionals and who will be outside this group. Thus, the people who were engaged in defining computer terminology were also determining who would become a computer scientist—with all the societal rewards that came along with that professional position—and who would not be in this newly forming professional community. (Longo 2021, 102)

Longo covered such glossary production from three sources in the period: Edmund Berkeley's more or less single-handed attempts to bring together such a glossary in the commercial journal *Computers and Automation*, and those of two professional bodies which produced glossaries for free uptake, the ACM (Association for Computer Machinery) Committee on Terminology and the IRE (Institute of Radio Engineers) Professional Group on Electronic Computers (IRE later merged into the Institute of Electrical and Electronics Engineers [IEEE]). The authorizations of the latter naturally prevailed over Berkeley's efforts. Of some interest here is that even in this most standard-setting of enterprises, a whiff of the minimal-gradual-mechanical standardization principle in the development of Internet Technology is prefigured. In acrimonious exchanges with critics of his definitions, Berkeley felt that the committees' approach was 'authoritarian' and that computer terms should be inclusively defined, by consulting and negotiating between existing nuances (Longo 2021: 104).

In any case, the standardization of computing terms in glossaries for professional purposes followed apace. Through the 1960s a number of dictionaries for students as well as professionals were produced (e.g., a pocket dictionary by Howard Sams and Co. 1962a alongside a 6-volume set entitled *Computer Basics*, 1962b; Breur 1966; Sippl 1966). Anthony Chandor et al. *A Dictionary of Computers* (1970), published by Penguin, targeted both professional and lay usage (Chandor had published a popular *Short Introduction to Computers* 1968). Dictionaries of computing from mainstream global publishers followed soon, in growing numbers and often with multiple subsequent editions over the following two decades (including Hyman 1976; Galland 1982; Illingworth 1983; Meadows 1984; Vollnhals 1984 [covering five languages]; Hipgrave 1985; Sinclair 1986; Longley and Shain 1986; Quentin 1987). Terms to do with Internet Technology naturally appeared in all the dictionaries of computing from the 1970s onwards. From the technical and engineering point of view, Internet Technology was a sub-section of the field, inextricably connected with other fields. With the authority of being the dominant professional body in the field, the IEEE Computer Dictionary Project started producing glossaries from the mid-1980s which set the standard, while noting that 'Use of an IEEE Standard is wholly voluntary'. The glossaries were brought together in the *IEEE Standard Computer Dictionary* (IEEE Computer Society 1990). This included terms that would be included in the *IEEE Standard Glossary for Computer Networking Technology* (IEEE Computer Society 1995), variously revised and rescinded thereafter. Gary Scott Malkin and T. LaQuey Parker produced an *Internet User's Glossary* from the Internet Working Group (1993, RFC 1392; updated Malkin 1996, RFC 1983). Within the framing authority of the group, this naturally seemed designed for specialist users; at the same time, the term 'internet user' had already extended beyond professional and pedagogic communities and had a much wider capture. About the term 'user' in relation to the internet at the time, Jonathan Grudin (1993) observed: 'Although "user" was a convenient identifier among engineers, its use has spread beyond the engineering environment, creating confusion in several ways' (112). The confusion was in seemingly including specialist as well as casual 'users' in the term, while at the same time retaining an 'engineering perspective' (112–114).

5.3.2 Dictionaries of Computing Terms for Lay Users

I noted in passing that Anthony Chandor et al.'s *A Dictionary of Computers* (1970) had already strayed outside the bounds of professional and pedagogic usage, claiming to cater to both specialists and laypersons. Some of the other dictionaries from the major publishing firms cited above followed suit. In fact, the assumption that laypersons would seek out computing dictionaries is worth a pause. Such dictionaries form the second strand in question here, with a notable bearing on the 1990s dictionaries of internet terms.

In a period when computing was only accessible to small coteries of the technically adept, Chandor et al.'s dictionary (1970) anticipated a wider interest by extending its address to both professional and lay readers. In fact, Chandor's dictionary set the format for such dictionaries to come. It provided both short definitions and explanations of technical terms and offered brief essays for lay readers to fill knowledge gaps. Something of an educationist's enthusiasm for raising awareness of their specific disciplines might have encouraged this move. Notably, the first computing dictionary exclusively for lay readers, *The Layman's Dictionary of Computer Terminology* (1973) was compiled by Norman E. Sondak and Eileen Sondak. Norman Sondak had played a prominent part in setting up pedagogic programmes in computing. But such an urge had not gripped educators in many other technical areas and had certainly not given rise to such an industry of dictionaries from mainstream publishers. Most likely, the vaunted commercial and political design in developing computing played an anticipatory role here: such dictionaries were both *forming* and *catering* to a general interest. The conflation of professional and lay interest in such dictionaries did arouse some comment at the time. A review of three computing dictionaries in 1986, found that the two addressed to well-defined users were worthwhile (Hipgrave 1985, for professional librarians, and Illingworth 1983, for computing students and teachers), while noting of the third edition of Chandor et al. in 1985 that, 'It is hardly possible to serve laymen and professionals in one booklet' (Bragt 1986: 388). Nevertheless, Chandor et al.'s dictionary became an oft-used model for dictionaries of internet terms when they started appearing in the 1990s, combining definitions of terms with explanatory essays.

5.3.3 Dictionaries of Hacker Slang/Jargon/Techspeak

Dictionaries of words used by self-professed 'hackers' had a strong influence on 1990s dictionaries of internet terms (on the term 'hacker', more later in this chapter). These differ significantly from the computer technology dictionaries considered above. Such listings consisted of in-group terms used by computing researchers in MIT, Stanford, etc. and other aficionados. The first such compilation was kept by Raphael Finkel at Stanford in 1975 (see Hacker's Dictionary website, 'Revision History'). It was maintained and updated initially in these groups' network as the Jargon File, and then went through various versions before appearing in print as *The Hacker's Dictionary* (Steele et al. 1983).

Shortly before its publication, Stan Kelly-Bootle's *The Devil's DP Dictionary* (1981) had already taken some terms from and credited the Jargon File, announcing itself ironically as a book that is 'aimed at the dearth of useful data processing glossaries' (ix). Its choice of terms and 'definitions' deliberately belied that lead-in. These were more often jocular than 'useful', had the breeziness of technically adept and rather clever friends joshing each other, and were attended by witty and anecdotal 'diatribes' in small print. The definition of 'artificial intelligence' gives a quick sense of its tone:

> **artificial intelligence** *n. abbrev.* **AI**: **1** The area researched by the artificial intelligentsia (attributed to Christopher Strachey 1916-1975). **2** The misguided search for a lower-unit-cost *Homo sapiens* at a time when the majority of the species remains critically underexploited [unemployed]. **3** The construction of algorithms for the blackleg assembly of wooden building-block motor cars. (Kelly-Bootle 1981, 14)

Much in this was distinctively in Kelly-Bootle's style, especially in the political satire, but the erudite and light-hearted approach was shared with the contributors to the Jargon File.

The Jargon File itself then appeared in printed book form as *The Hacker's Dictionary: A Guide to the Computer Underground* (Steele et al. 1983). An expanded print volume, *The New Hacker's Dictionary* (Raymond 1991) followed, with a second edition in 1993 and a third in 1996, and further online versions till 2001. Guy Steele et al.'s 1983 print edition stated succinctly what was distinctive about it:

> There are many dictionaries of computer buzzwords and jargon. This book is different. It is a dictionary of slang.
>
> Jargon consists of technical words that are needed for very precise communication in a specialized subject. Economists, truck drivers, chemists, and steelworkers will use a specialized vocabulary to convey technical meanings.

> Slang, on the other hand, is used for fun, for *human* communication rather than technical communication. Slang is often derived from jargon. When a bit of technical jargon is used in an extended or metaphoric way, it becomes slang.
>
> Many 'computer' words are making their way into everyday use. Thanks to the proliferation of home computers, many people have heard of bytes, RAM, memory banks, terminals, processors, and floppy discs.
>
> You won't find those words defined here. This, we warn you, is supposed to be a *fun* book. (Steele et al. 1983, 1)

In the preliminary materials, self-reflexive observations on the characteristics and usage of the chosen terms were included. Subsequent published versions and editions added to that, as well as refined and updated definitions and added new terms. As a dictionary of slang, it both fell into a long tradition and carved a distinctive direction. The tradition is charted in Julie Coleman's (2004–2010) magisterial four-volume *History of Cant and Slang Dictionaries*, covering the period 1567–1984, and is one of great diversity. Coleman understood 'slang' loosely:

> Slang is now typically used to delineate a level of language more informal than the standard, less domestic than the colloquial, and less official than jargon. Slang may be as geographically contained as dialect or as widespread as standard English, but its defining feature is its restriction to social subgroups, whether defined by age, shared interest, or social circle. Slang is often ephemeral, but many slang terms are surprisingly resilient, even though each individual user's contact with them may be temporary. Slang typically functions to establish and cement group membership, often by rejecting social norms. (Coleman 2009, 2)

In the fourth volume, Coleman (2010) included a discussion of technology-centred slang (Chap. 12), beginning with dictionaries of Citizen's Band Radio slang of the 1970s. She pegged *The Hacker's Dictionary* as a collection of terms by users who form a group identity and vocabulary by dint of communicating through new technologies. It was, however, rather more than that. With hindsight, some of the influential features of *The Hacker's Dictionary* and editions of *The New Hacker's Dictionary* were as follows.

Wider interest in an in-group vocabulary could arise from a dominant population's curiosity about marginalized or 'other' groups or among those who discover a consumable interest in some group's lifestyle and occupations. *The Hacker's Dictionary* (1983) was in the latter category. In fact, it was designed to not merely describe a group's lifestyle and occupations, but to publicize and promote those. This group identified itself as composed of 'hackers' in the sense defined in this dictionary as, first and foremost: 'A person who enjoys learning the details of computer systems and how to stretch their capabilities—as opposed to most users of computers, who prefer to learn only the minimum amount necessary' (70). Five other senses enumerated programming abilities, and only one sense gave an inkling of the illegal activities that dominate in current connotations of the term. A brief essay by Steele in the preliminary pages, 'Confessions of a Happy Hacker', announced this lifestyle as that of the 'hacker community'. *The New Hacker's Dictionary* (Raymond 1991) added a further essay, 'Hacker in a Strange Land'. The preliminary materials expatiated on 'hacker culture' and 'hacker style' as consisting of much more than professional or academic concerns—as articulating a distinctive way of life for an intellectual elite structured around computing. With 'hacker culture' thus wedded to computing, the path towards more democratic cultural investments in computing seemed possible and imminent. An in-depth discussion of the term 'hacker' appears later in this chapter.

Along with the promotion of hacker culture and style, came a light-hearted informal tone (*fun*, as Steele et al. 'warned') which was emulated often in the dictionaries of Internet terms to come. Unusually for a technical area, the tone was reminiscent of satirical or parodic dictionaries like Gustave Flaubert's *Dictionary of Accepted Ideas* (1968, compiled in the 1870s) or Ambrose Bierce's *The Devil's Dictionary* (2011 [1906]), which obviously inspired Kelly-Bootle's *The Devil's DP Dictionary* (1981). But *The Hacker's Dictionary* was neither satirical nor parodic; it was celebratory, and the definitions, while interspersed with anecdotes and jibes, were exultantly savvy and informative. In a curious way, this tone undergirded a distinct kind of lexicographical authority: that of hackers as a collective. The tone was of persons at ease with computing, living rather than using programming, somewhat more than professionally expert, indeed casually habituated. In other words, this voice appeared so much at ease that information or knowledge of computing was taken for granted. Basic technical terms, Steele et al. observed blithely, do not even need defining here, they are too common for elucidation.

Interestingly, the word 'Internet' only appeared with a separate entry in the third edition of *The New Hacker's Dictionary* (1996), when it had become unavoidably ubiquitous. The entry opened with the epithet, 'The mother of all networks', and gave a brief history of its development. The final paragraph of the entry observed:

> That year, 1994, was also the year the mainstream culture discovered the Internet. Once again, the **killer app** was not the anticipated one—rather, what caught the public imagination was the hypertext and multimedia features of the World Wide Web. [...] It is now a commonplace even in mainstream media to predict that a globally extended Internet will become the key unifying communications technology of the next century. (Raymond 1996 [3rd edition])

There is a slight hacker-like dismissiveness there about the public preoccupation with merely, so to speak, the user surface that is the hypertext system (World Wide Web) and indifference towards the underlying networking protocols. As it happened, the year before 'Internet' was admitted into *The New Hacker's Dictionary* (1996), Stan Kelly-Bootle came up with a second edition of *The Devil's DP Dictionary* (1981), now entitled *The Computer Contradictionary* (1995). This too included a definition of 'Internet' with a matriarchal metaphor: 'The anarchic mother of all networked networks'—with a scoffing 'diatribe' explaining: '"Mother" is to be taken here in the Black-American elliptical sense. Apart from a few O'Reilly & Associates authors, nobody really understands or needs to know how Internet works' (101).

To begin with, *The Hacker's Dictionary* (1983) went in precisely the opposite direction of the computer technology dictionaries outlined earlier. Those were designed to standardize terms for rigorous and consistent usage in the emerging discipline; in other words, they sought to still the fluidity of words for well-defined technical usage. *The Hacker's Dictionary* embraced the fluidity of words in relation to computing, charting the accumulation of neologisms, and highlighting lexical play. Standardized terms were for a formal register, while such fluidly used words were slang. By and large, subsequent editions of *The New Hacker's Dictionary* stayed with that, but gradually allowed technical terms and more poker-faced definitions to creep in. In *The New Hacker's Dictionary* (1991), Eric Raymond made new distinctions between three kinds of terms:

- *slang*: informal language from mainstream English or non-technical subcultures (bikers, rock fans, surfers, etc.)
- *jargon*: without qualifier, denotes informal 'slangy' language peculiar to hackers—the subject of this lexicon
- *techspeak*: the formal vocabulary of programming, computer science, electronics, and other fields connected to hacking (Raymond 1991: 3)

He observed that these seem to slide into each other. What Steele et al. (1983) had characterized as 'slang', was now largely covered by 'jargon'; much of what Steele et al. regarded as 'jargon', was now pegged as 'techspeak'. The seething effervescence of neologisms seemed an especially noteworthy feature of the 'jargon'/ 'slang', apparently concentrating the relationship between cultural and linguistic change in computing.

For the savvy authorities of hackerdom, the distinction between 'jargon' and 'techspeak' made by Raymond (1991) might have seemed culturally meaningful; for those less habituated to computing, it all appeared to be 'jargon'. The advent of computing services for ordinary consumers (users) was *fait accompli* by the early 1990s, propelled by the development of affordable personal computers and the privatization and commercialization of the internet. Unsurprisingly, a dictionary for lay readers appeared at the time, entitled *Jargon: An Informal Dictionary of Computer Terms* (Williams 1993). This was unusual in being produced by claiming a sort of counter-authority: i.e., that of knowing what lay readers want because the author is one. As the author Robin Williams disarmingly put it:

> This book was not easy to write. I'm not a very technical person, and I had to struggle with many of these esoteric concepts. As I was writing this (and constantly complaining) many people would tell me (especially male technonerds) that no one wants to know this stuff anyway. But computers are becoming part of everyone's lives and we are all bumping into technical terms in magazines, catalogs, promotional literature, manuals, and so on. [...] I wrote this book because I was frustrated with every computer dictionary I own (which is 12, plus 2 on discs) and all the glossaries I had collected (which is about 20). [...] I realized that I had a personal obligation to write definitions that simple people like me and my mother would understand. (Williams 1993, viii)

This lexicographical counter-authority of the lay reader fits with the market authority of consumer demand—already exposed to computing products in magazines, catalogues, promotional literature, manuals. The dictionary also offered a pertinent counterpoint to hacker authority, at odds with it while also drawing upon it (getting something that 'technonerds' hold back). Its definition of 'hacker' was mildly dismissive without attaching moral doubts: 'a computer enthusiast, one who is willing to hack away tediously at understanding and programming computers' (253). Moreover, the Personal Note was nicely layered with stereotypical gendered binaries: the reticent 'technonerds' are *male* as opposed to the frustrated *female* consumers, 'me and my mother'. *Jargon* (1993) hailed the appearance of computing in the world of domestic shopping, traditionally a female preserve. The 'jargon' covered in this dictionary mostly consisted of what *The New Hacker's Dictionary* (1991) had described as 'techspeak'.

5.3.4 Dictionaries of Internet Terms

Dictionaries defining and forming a distinctive vocabulary for Internet Polity discourse, woven out from those three strands of dictionary making, started appearing from 1994.

But there's a bypath in this direction to consider first.

New media designers Bob Cotton and Richard Oliver's *The Cyberspace Lexicon* (1994) exemplifies this bypath admirably. It was neither specifically a dictionary of specialist computing terms, nor of hacker jargon/slang, and nor of internet terms for users—yet, to some degree it was a dictionary of all those. Its address was not quite to computer engineers or programmers and nor to domestic shoppers, but to savvy users in between those sorts. These included: designers, artists, and 'creative-industry' workers who use computer programmes and internet services; aficionados who are drawn to hacker slang and lifestyles; digital gamers and game-producers; enthusiasts of cyberpunk and virtual reality; researchers in the recently invigorated disciplines of Media and Culture Studies; etc. The book had the gloss and proportions of a coffee-table art or lifestyle volume, typical of its publisher Phaidon's volumes.

Following the model set by Chandor et al. (1970), the entries were in two formats: short definitions and explanations for technical terms, including acronyms and brand names; brief essays in coloured boxes on broader conceptual terms or marketing phenomena. The essays were entitled both with an alphabetically ordered term and with a sloganistic phrase: for example, under 'C', 'Cyberspace' with an phrase 'The new world game'; under 'D', 'Data Superhighways: Roads to the future'; under 'F', 'Fibre Optics: high-bandwidth gossamer' and so on. Readers were courted with the relentlessly upbeat essay logos, not unlike advertisement slogans. Unlike Chandor et al. (1970), both levels of entries—short definitions/explanations and brief essays—were directed to the same savvy reader, not differentiated by being lay and professional. A few hundred images were interspersed to press home its appeal to this savvy reader.

The lexicographical authority at work here seemed to be grounded in the shared sensibility of the designer-authors and the readers they anticipate, i.e., those looking for, in their words, a

> referential map of these 'trendings'—a guide through the maze of new and emerging technologies. [...] As media and telecommunications converge with computing and with consumer electronics to create the cyberspace infrastructure, as concepts collide and catalyse, so the vocabulary needed to deal with this phenomenon becomes polyglot, even pidgin. (Cotton and Oliver 1994, 8)

The 'pidgin' here comes close to the 'slang' of *The Hacker's Dictionary*. The lexicographical authority of this shared sensibility was crystallized further in the various publications of the *Wired Magazine*. A couple of years later *Wired* came up with an analogous dictionary for the savvy user, *Wired Style: Principles of English Usage in the Digital Age* (Hale 1996). Here, the alphabetic entries of terms were clustered under—made secondary to—a set of logos: i.e., each section was entitled with a sloganistic phrase and introduced with a short essay, and the terms relevant to each sloganistic phrase were listed alphabetically in that section. The list of leading sloganistic phrases gives a reasonable sense of the shared sensibility uniting the *Wired* editors and the readers: 'Voice is Paramount', 'Be Elite', 'Transcend the Technical', 'Capture the Colloquial', 'Anticipate the Future', 'screw the Rules' and so on. The 'voice' was understood as capturing 'the quirky individualist spirit of the Net' (5). 'Net' was defined as: 'The world of cyberspace. The abbreviation for the Internet' (74). Soon after Andy Ihnatko made a last-ditch effort in *Cyberspeak: An Online Dictionary* (1997) to adopt the voice of a scoffing and yet high-priestly techie, reminiscent of *The Hacker's Dictionary*, talking down to common consuming folk. This stuck to a small selection of uncommon terms that the cognoscente use, classifying them as 'technical term', 'online jargon', 'product', and 'online entity' without troubling with defining the classifications. But the pioneering spirit captured by *The Cyberspace Lexicon* and *Wired Style*, and the savvy users associated with it, were already widely dispersed—Ihnatko's 'elitist' techie tone in courting them seemed rather anachronistic.

The shared sensibility such dictionaries captured and appealed to was thought of as that of being 'cool'. Through much of the 1990s, terms associated with media and culture gurus, hackers, cyberpunks, and other cyberspace aficionados were strongly evocative of being 'cool'. Alan Liu's *The Laws of Cool* (2004) saw this as a systematically promoted way of characterizing a collectivity for atomised 'knowledge workers' plying digital systems amidst incessant information flows:

> Strip away all the colourful metaphors of information seas, webs, highways, portals, windows, and the rest (like picture calendars tacked to the wall), and what comes to view is only the stark cubicle of the knowledge worker. Yet precisely in this cold space of nonidentity, cool appears as the cultural face—perhaps not the best or truest face, but the interface by which it knows itself—of knowledge work. (Liu 2004, 76)

The irony, as Liu saw it, was that this aspect of knowledge work is itself an erasure or refusal of knowledge:

> Cool is the aporia of information. In whatever form and on whatever scale (excessive graphics, egregious animation, precious slang, surplus hypertext, and so on), cool is *information designed to resist information*—not so much noise in the information theory sense as information fed back into its own signal to create a standing interference pattern, a paradox pattern. Structured as information designed to resist information, cool is the paradoxical 'gesture' by which an ethos of the unknown struggles to arise in the midst of knowledge work. (Liu 2004, 179)

That might seem a bit dismissive but, in this context, these are suggestive observations and offer a useful frame for the fragmented, platitudinous, and upbeat listings in dictionaries like *The Cyberspace Lexicon* and *Wired Style*. The 'stark cubicle of the knowledge worker' is a downbeat restatement of the *Wired* editors' upbeat 'quirky individualist spirit of the Net' mentioned earlier (Hale 1996: 5). 'Cool' could be thought of as the glue that sticks and yet separates the already individuated pathways of surfing, searching, participating, and doing things on the internet.

Tom Fahey's *net-speak: The Internet Dictionary* (1994) could be regarded as the first to list and define a set of terms specifically for internet users who are not technologically adept or adapted: i.e., those who might wonder 'what's the difference between a bridger and a router' rather than those who listen to 'Internet authority figures babble about the Simple Network Management Protocol' (ix). It covered 'words, terms, slang, and catch phrases you hear the computer jocks spewing every time you hang around your company's dot matrix printers for more than three minutes' (ix). Throughout, the dictionary had something of the dismissively self-regarding tone of a cognoscente speaking to his brethren while being chummy to the uninitiated (Fahey announced his credentials before the Introduction). The book also came with short essays with 'amusing stories and anecdotes' addressed to 'you', the fumbling would-be user, and various 'tips'. The uninitiated this was meant for were, however, somewhat different from the lay persons addressed earlier by Chandor et al. (1970), Sondak and Sondak (1973) and other such. Fahey's anticipated readers were closer to 'users' in that ambiguous sense that Grudin (1993) had noted, mentioned above. And yet, these were not addressed meaningfully as 'users' of personal computers and the internet. Fahey's dictionary did not elaborate on the specific kinds of usage that the internet could be put to. Readers were conceived more as entrants into the facility cum space that is the internet than as functionally users. They were effectively being invited to find their place alongside the 'computer jocks'. It was assumed that such readers would largely be based in some company and their interest would be for some professional purpose. But the entries encompassed more leisurely doings as well.

In a similar mould, Christian Crumlish's *The Internet Dictionary* (1995) followed soon after: 'not a technical manual' but 'a huge list of the most common Internet terms, explained in plain English' (ix). Bryan Pfaffenberger and David Wall's *Que's Computer and Internet Dictionary* (1995) gave clearer directions about the kinds of general usage it was designed for, capitalizing on market offerings at the time: 'buying your computer system', 'understanding application program capabilities', 'reading computer manuals', 'using the Internet', 'Using Microsoft Windows 95' (viii). The circuit of consumption and utility indicated thus was centred broadly on middle-class consumers and white-collar workers. There were relatively few dictionaries for specific professional sectors at that stage, with the early exception of George Machovec's *Telecommunications, Networking and Internet Glossary* (1993) targeting librarians. Interestingly, as the decade progressed, dictionaries that had previously been devoted to explaining technical 'computer terms' for general readers now became dictionaries of 'computer *and* internet' terms. Thus, *Que's Computer and Internet Dictionary* (Pfaffenberger and Wall 1995) was preceded by *Que's Computer User's Dictionary* (Pfaffenberger 1990); Barron's *Dictionary of Computer Terms* (Covington and Downing 1986) became, in its 6th edition, Barron's *Dictionary of Computer and Internet Terms* (Downing et al. 1996); where earlier one might have referred to *Collins Dictionary of Personal Computing* (Sinclair 1988), now one could turn to *Dictionary of Personal Computing and the Internet* (Collin 1997). Dictionaries of 'computer and internet' appeared to allocate to the internet a separate and equally weighty territory as to computing, though in a technical sense the 'internet' was obviously contained within the umbrella term 'computing'. And yet, the separated construction was meaningful. For the users that such dictionaries were courting, the internet was something more than 'computing', something that had spiralled out of there and occupied a space and functionalities of its own.

The appearance of new words in or from the internet was a constantly highlighted feature of these dictionaries Generally, the coinage of neologisms in specific circles—cultural coteries or professional collectives—which then move into ordinary usage has ever been a dimension of language change. These have usually been tracked through updated and expanded editions of general-language dictionaries in most domains. Inclusion of such words in general-language dictionaries is regarded as recognition of their having caught on too widely to be overlooked, and as giving licence for usage in an authorized and standardized manner. The journal *American Speech* (of the American Dialect Society) had maintained a helpful listing of new words from 1941, initiated by Dwight Bolinger, following the format of the Oxford English Dictionary (i.e., offering a definition and giving examples of usage). Looking back to this record, the editor of this section from 1987, John Algeo, pegged a 'new word' as having 'a form or the use of a form not recorded in general dictionaries', and included single and compound words as well as idiomatic phrases. Newness encompassed the following:

> The form of the word itself may be novel, a shape that has not before been seen or heard in English [...], or the newness may lie in the novel use of an existing form. In the latter case, the novelty may be in what the word refers to [...], the word's grammar [...], or even its relationship to those who use it [...]. (Algeo 1991: 2)

This was a flexible and accommodative description of the newness of new words in 1991.

The steady appearance of distinctively internet terms amidst new words, following Algeo's (1991) definition, became apparent in 'Among the New Words' sections of *American Speech* in 1994. In the Summer 1994 edition, the section (Algeo and Algeo 1994a) featured 'information superhighway' and noted that it was declared the 'New Word of 1993' by the American Dialect Society; it also noted the new word 'cybersex' as the 'Most Amazing'. The listing featured a significant number of internet terms, mainly clustered around almost-sex ('computer porn', 'computer sex', 'cybergasm'/'Cyborgasm', 'cybersex', 'virtual sex', 'virtual reality sex') and metaphorical highways ('data highway/superhighway', 'electronic highway/communications highway/superhighway', 'information superhighway' and variants thereof)—a selection conveying the heady mix of speed, desire, and fecundity that emanated from the internet at the time. The Winter 1994 section was entirely devoted to 'computer and network terms' related to the 'information superhighway' (with a nod to Raymond 1993 and Williams 1993, discussed earlier). 'Cyber' was 'especially noteworthy as a vogueish prefix'; and 'e-mail' was pegged as an 'almost new word', since it had not been included in standard dictionaries yet except for the *American Heritage*

College Dictionary (Algeo and Algeo 1994b: 398). Altogether 38 separate word entries were listed, of which one was the prefix 'cyber', which itself packed in 96 new words using it. The entry of internet terms, including these new words, into general-language dictionaries followed various and uneven pathways. For instance, the OED's second edition (Simpson and Weiner 1989) naturally had very few to do specifically with the internet (e.g., 'electronic mail' and 'electronic mailbox' made it as compounds under 'electronic'). New words to be included in the subsequent edition planned for 2000 were released in 3 volumes of the OED *Additions* series (Simpson and Weiner 1993, 2 volumes, and Proffitt 1997). It was only in the 1997 volume that internet terms appeared markedly in the OED sphere, including well established coinages like 'cyberspace'.

The appearance of neologisms in dictionaries of internet terms, however, brought an additional edge to familiar lexicographical assumptions. Here, the new words were not acknowledged by inclusion in established general-language dictionaries but nevertheless settled quickly through everyday usage. Within a concentrated period the constant introduction of new words itself became a feature of this emerging vocabulary. Thus, each dictionary of internet terms from 1994 onwards, in every subsequent edition, was especially promoted in terms of the addition of new words—usually from the generative fertility of slang and promotional or in-group usage or coinage. The growing number of new words marked the growing reach of the vocabulary of Internet Polity discourse and indeed the scope of the Internet Polity. But internet-related new words did not stay confined to dictionaries of internet terms; they also started appearing thick and fast in general dictionaries. As the Internet Polity was consolidated through its discourse, it also seemed to assume distinctive cultural practices overlapping with real-world cultures. Or, put otherwise, it was also integrating with and modifying general culture, so that the Internet Polity could be regarded as becoming co-extensive with real-world polities. Culture pinned on the internet speedily become part of 'mainstream culture' from 1994, as *The New Hacker's Dictionary* (3e) put it (Raymond 1996).

5.3.5 Cyberlexicography and Internet Slang

By the end of the 1990s the entire business of lexicography, and the specific enterprise of tracking internet terms, was beginning to shift *into* the internet. To some degree this move was via the use of large language corpora for dictionary making, drawing upon the methodological authority of quantitative analysis rather than of authoritative exemplification (for overviews, Ooi 1998 and Halliday et al. 2004). From there it was a small move towards both exploiting the gigantic corpora that the internet offers while, at the same time, exploiting the possibilities of having e-dictionaries online (useful overviews in collections like Fuertes-Olivera and Bergenholtz 2010, Granger and Paquot 2012), with the integration of machine-learning processes in the prospect. In fact, in this space the lexicographical authority of appointed specialists and sanctioned institutions themselves began to be mediated and, to some degree, challenged. Looking to the future of lexicography with current internet resources in view, Michael Carr (1997) anticipated developments that were nascent then. He consulted 91 'cyberdictionaries' from the Yahoo! subject index, of which 20 were computing dictionaries. Carr observed that what he considered 'bottom-up' lexicography 'may prove to be the most significant transformation of cyberlexicography' (215). He noted several prototypes that were continuously updated either by crowdsourcing (contributions by user availing of editing facilities) or by automatically mining internet sites (e.g., using bots). Shortly afterwards, in January 2000 the most successful general crowdsourced internet encyclopaedia (there were precursors) Wikipedia was launched (see 'History of Wikipedia' webpage). Two years later, using the base of Wikipedia, Wiktionary appeared as a lexicographical project; in 2002 also, using a similar model, OpenThesaurus appeared. By this time, the established 'top-down' dictionaries from mainstream publishers had also been made available on the internet.

An important element in Carr's (1997) early observations on 'cyberlexicography' has been little discussed. He noted in effect that the impetuses that take users to dictionaries are in fact consonant with the paths through which users already engage with the internet. There is an overlap in modes of accessing internet facilities (e.g., for conferences or for information searching) and ways of consulting dictionaries. Carr thus expected that, 'The user-friendly and user-reliant edges of the Internet will both simplify and complicate lexicography' (220). He was in fact pointing to the mechanics of associative linking that underpin hypertext systems. As discussed in Chap. 3, hyperlinked pathways are extended across I-information and render texts locatable and searchable by foregrounding words. Using search engines, surfing, and recourse to various internet services are inevitably ways of checking and honing word-sense and word usage. Acclimatization to keyword searching and surfing does not necessarily mean that the convenience of looking up word definitions via the conventional alphabetical index will diminish. But it does mean that, somewhere along the way, the habits of internet usage could overlap and converge with the habits of dictionary usage, perhaps in conjunction with the shifting balances of 'top-down' and 'bottom-up' lexicographical authority. The principle of precedent individuation that is grounded via hypertext systems could reconfigure both lexicographical authority and usage. It has occasionally been observed, for instance, that behaviour in using search engines influences behaviour in consulting online dictionaries (de Schryver et al. 2006; Lew and de Schryver 2014). A voluminous and growing literature on sophisticated ways of tracking dictionary usage and online behaviour has followed, drawing upon and feeding into Natural Language Processing and Machine Translation.

As regards dictionaries of internet terms, features of the vocabulary of the Internet Polity discourse were substantially ensconced by the end of the 1990s. In the conventional print-dictionary format (and their e-book counterparts), compiled by specialist editors or authors, definitions of internet terms gradually became brief, and exemplification of usage was largely dispensed with. Simply keeping up with the continuous proliferation, the rise and fall, of internet terms became the main thrust of such dictionaries. In this vein, it seemed to be assumed that knowing the word of the moment was what users seek; correspondingly, interest in etymology, connotation shifts, contextual nuances, etc. are irrelevant for most users. The lexicographical form assumed a constantly shifting and expanding synchronicity for the vocabulary of the Internet Polity discourse. Even where terms had obviously been re-oriented or become archaic (such as in erstwhile usage of 'hacker' or 'cyberspace'), it was only the vestigial nuance of current relevance that was retained—otherwise the term was expunged. Due to strong technical and business investments in this vocabulary, acronyms and abbreviations had come to be treated as a particularly numerous word-form here. Keeping track of the spiralling proliferation of these, and of the dizzying variety of wordplay in chatrooms and social networking exchanges, was a challenge for this lexicographical enterprise. The standard-setting authority of the dictionary seemed on the verge of buckling under the pressure of such lexical excess. The conventional form of the dictionary now appeared to be playing catchup with the standards-in-usage that were constantly resetting internet terms and the overall shape of the vocabulary. There was no time to track the histories and contexts of terms. The vocabulary of Internet Polity discourse seemed to become, so to speak, a shapeshifting, ahistorical, ever-of-the-moment plethora.

Nevertheless, valiant efforts at maintaining a semblance of lexicographical standardizing authority and oversight of this vocabulary were made. Oxford University Press's *A Dictionary of the Internet* (Ince 2001) is a good example of this. This focussed on terms associated with Web technology, commerce, Internet Infrastructure, distributed processing and systems, internet security, and, most ambitiously, jargon and abbreviations; it largely left out general computing terms and commercial brand names (vii-viii). However, even as that appeared, a flip in such dictionaries' centre of gravity was becoming evident in the Internet Polity discourse. Online sites collecting internet terms were already foregrounding a digital-to-print direction or simply settling for digital sites. The NetLingo website, established to collect and define internet terms by Erin Jansen in 1996, was evidently better equipped to keep up with this burgeoning and shifting vocabulary. Nevertheless, Jansen drew upon it to produce a series of (no doubt profitable) print dictionaries, beginning with *NetLingo: The Internet Dictionary* (Jansen and James 2002). Interestingly, in the Introduction Jansen echoed Robin Williams *Jargon* dictionary (1993), discussed above, in observing: 'As a woman who is publishing an Internet dictionary in a field that's dominated by men, I decided to keep it personal and explain the technical stuff as if I'm describing it to my mother' (Jansen and James 2002: 6). Shortly afterwards, NetLingo set up crowdsourcing facilities on the website.

Claims of the user's authority in this area came to be firmly set in crowdsourced dictionaries. Both the production of slang and the slanginess of the lexicographer's tone, pioneered in *The Hacker Dictionary* (1983), became the preserve of crowdsourced online dictionaries. In fact, as far as dictionary making goes, slang itself seemed to move out of the streets and in-groups that Julie Coleman's history (2004–2010) had carefully charted and become concentrated in the vocabulary of the Internet Polity discourse. The Urban Dictionary website, launched by Aaron Peckham in 1999, set the trend. Though not particularly devoted to internet terms, its accrual of words and phrases, often with idiosyncratic definitions and descriptions, sourced by individual users (with their internet handles, hyperlinks, user-approval indicators) seemed to be peculiarly *of* the internet. Nevertheless, Peckham drew upon it to publish a series of light-hearted (and no doubt profitable) print dictionaries, beginning with *Urban Dictionary: Fularious Street Slang Defined* (2005). In the Introduction he observed that 'The content of Urban Dictionary has become the irreverent calling card of a linguistic generation' (vii). Though it was to become the most popular and discussed, Urban Dictionary was preceded by the Online Slang Dictionary website (Walter Radar founded it in 1997, the site was registered in 2001). Since the early 2000s, websites focussing specifically on computing and internet terms, especially acronyms and abbreviations, have appeared regularly, such as the Foldoc website (registered in 2000), the Internet Slang website (registered in 2001), and the All Acronyms website (registered in 2002).

Through the 1990s, dictionaries and other word-listings brought together a vocabulary for the Internet Polity discourse and effectively enlarged the scope of the Internet Polity. In the process these also variously challenged and reoriented received lexicographical assumptions, especially about specialist authority and dictionary usage. Insofar as dictionaries have conventionally standardized word usage at the behest of official and professional authority, those took a backseat for dictionaries of internet terms. The standardizing drive was naturally germane to technical dictionaries of computing, including Internet Infrastructure, for professional and pedagogic purposes. However, the dictionary makers focusing on internet terms seldom came with professional assent or formal sanction. Arguably, in this vocabulary of the Internet Polity discourse the principle of minimal-gradual-mechanical standardization was performed in the flexible flow of standardizing, de-standardizing, re-standardizing, of setting and resetting and introducing terms, of accepting and generating slang and jargon and techspeak. Standards for usage in this area always appeared provisional and subject to adaptation, just as Internet Technology seemed to settle into common formats by adaptation before mandating. Further, the gradual division of lexicographical labour between users and authority-bearing specialists, eventually in favour of the former, seems to reflect the precedent individuation principle. In both the generation and definition of internet terms on crowdsourced and continuously updated online dictionaries, a range of individual associative pathways through internet vocabulary are negotiated and aggregated—untrammelled by the rigours of text-based or corpus-based evidence. The vocabulary that caught on so quickly through the 1990s, accruing and mutating through dictionaries and other listings, appeared as the living expression of the Internet Polity.

5.4 Culture

5.4.1 Culture Catchwords

As Internet Polity discourse spread and collective life formed upon those social and political first principles, the cultural practices therein were recorded and studied. These were both distinguished from and inserted into real-world cultures by employing a cluster of catchwords: in the 1990s, mainly, 'cyberculture', 'digital culture', 'technoculture', and occasionally 'internet culture'. A few notes on these terms follow, before pausing on the formation of internet communities, and then focussing on the constituency that presented a notable schism in this area, designated 'hackers' (a significant catchword in the period).

'Culture' is understood here as related to the following definitions in Branch III in the OED entry (as a noun), which are often sharply distinguished and more often conflated in scholarly accounts:

- 'The cultivation or development of the mind, faculties, manners, etc.; improvement by education and training' (5a);
- 'The devoting of attention to or the study of a subject or pursuit' (5c);
- 'Refinement of mind, taste, and manners; artistic and intellectual development. Hence: the arts and other manifestations of human intellectual achievement regarded collectively' (6);
- 'Chiefly as a count noun. The distinctive ideas, customs, social behaviour, products, or way of life of a particular nation, society, people, or period. Hence: a society or group characterized by such customs, etc.' (7a);
- 'With modifying noun: a way of life or social environment characterized by or associated with the specified quality or thing; a group of people subscribing or belonging to this' (7b);
- 'The philosophy, practices, and attitudes of an institution, business, or other organization' (7c).

A note in the OED on the etymological complexities behind these senses refers to Raymond Williams's account of 'culture' in *Keywords* (1983). There Williams had observed that '**Culture** is one of the two or three most complicated words in the English language' (Williams 1983, 87), and given some helpful direction for those using the term in a considered way:

> Faced by this complex and still active history of the word, it is easy to react by selecting one 'true' or 'proper' or 'scientific' sense and dismissing other senses as loose or confused. [...] It is clear that, within a discipline, conceptual usage has to be clarified. But in general it is the range and overlap of meanings that is significant. The complex of senses indicates a complex argument about the relations between general human development and a particular way of life, and between both and the works and practices of art and intelligence. (Williams 1983, 91)

This study of the Internet Polity is not strictly discipline-bound, so I have taken Williams's in-general approach to heart.

I am also, perhaps more emphatically, guided in my approach here by factors which are not covered by Williams's (or the OED's) sense of the complexity of this *keyword*. An inclusive approach is expedient because of the sheer proliferation of 'culture' as a catchword. Insofar as considered attention to 'culture' goes, its usage has constantly expanded over the late twentieth and early twenty-first centuries. By way of putting a scale on this, the British Library catalogue is usefully indicative—it has the advantage of indexing a legal-deposit library, with significant publications in most major global languages and nearly comprehensive in English. On consulting it in mid-2023, the number of published books and journals with the exact word 'culture' in the main title came up with the following breakdown:

	Books	Journals
1980 to 1989	4952	136
1990 to 1999	10,669	196
2000 to 2009	14,360	274
2009 to 2019	16,955	159

As far as article listings in the catalogue with 'culture' in the main titles go, for 1976–1990 there were 642 items, whereas for 1991–2006 there were 90,387 items. I am assuming that words in the main title are meant both to foreground the main themes of the publication and to appeal to a ready readership. Though only loosely indicative, a proliferation of thinking about 'culture' is suggested from around 1990.

With that proliferation, preoccupation with the term's fluid nuances have also been constant: in the British Library catalogue, 48 books and 467 articles are listed since 1985 with the exact phrase 'concept of culture'/'definition of culture'/'idea of culture' in the main title. These present various strategies for dealing with its prolific applications. Apart from the pragmatically limited disciplinary definitions that Williams (1983) mentioned, a manageable account of the word's general implications has occasionally been recommended. For instance, Terry Eagleton (2000) pushed for wider consensus on one description; more schematically, Martyn Hammersley (2019) narrowed senses down to four main meanings (7–8) and seven clarifications in terms of contrasting terms/concepts (61–8). Taking a different tack, there have been upbeat arguments about how 'culture' functions more to frame the (agency-conferring) production of meaning than as a carrier of meaning. This strategy was assumed by Kenneth Allan:

> My intent in the use of the term 'culture' is to emphasize its function as a symbolic reference system whereby humans manufacture and reproduce a meaningful, real world of action and interaction. This definition stresses human agency in the creation of meaning: it is my position that signs and symbols and discourses are cultural artifacts. They themselves do not produce meaning; humans produce meaning in concert with the cultural system. (Allan 1998, 4)

Some such conception of the term, variously expressed, is found in much writing on the political claims of different identity groupings.

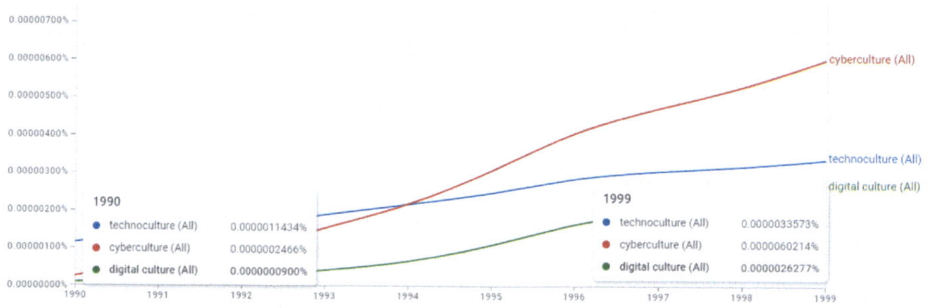

Graph 5.4 Google Ngram Viewer graph of 'technoculture', 'cyberculture', and 'digital culture', 1990–1999. The usage-frequency of 'technoculture' increased nearly threefold, that of 'digital culture' 29-fold, and 'cyberculture' 24-fold

I note these strategies not to adopt them but to add them to the 'complex of senses' (as Williams put it) that the term now has. In relation to the Internet Polity discourse of the 1990s, every dimension of the complex of senses was evoked. To a significant degree, the term 'culture' burgeoned in engagements with Internet Technology. With reference to the internet, three culture-centred catchwords found a firm purchase in various registers through the 1990s: 'cyberculture', 'technoculture', 'digital culture' (Graph 5.4).

'Technoculture' and 'cyberculture' refer to areas that are much larger than the internet: respectively, culture in relation to the use of technology in general and information systems at large. Those extend wherever technology and information exchanges are germane, so that it is difficult to say what is outside 'technoculture' or 'cyberculture'. 'Digital culture' concerns somewhat more contained domains, namely, the culture pertaining to digital forms and processes or manifested via Internet Technology. 'Digital culture' is commonly conceived as replacing or evinced alongside 'print culture' or 'analog culture'. That in the 1990s the three terms became aligned and caught on in concert has much to do with Internet Polity discourse, where the internet appeared to absorb the dimensions of 'cyberspace', concentrate digital processes and forms, and become representative of technological advance.

Of these 'cyberculture' was coined earliest, when cybernetics appeared as a potentially universal science with human–machine relations centred in the 1960s. Mary Alice Hilton set the tone for the term in several publications from 1964 onwards. Her views were presented succinctly and yet sufficiently in her paper, 'An Ethos for the Age of Cyberculture', with the brief explanation that 'Cyberculture is composed of "cybernetics', the science of control, and "culture", the way of life of a society' (Hilton 1964: 139). The term was meant to capture imminent wide-ranging changes—a 'cybercultural revolution [that] is comparable in magnitude to the agricultural revolution' (141)—due to technological developments, such as in nuclear science and particularly in automation and computing. The changes would involve, Hilton declared, a restructuring of work and leisure, of economic distributions and ethical norms, growing populations, etc. Much of the paper was devoted to making recommendations on how these changes should be prepared for and managed. More than the substance of the argument, its tone gave the coinage an immediate energy. The paper was composed of confidently visionary pronouncements, with sweeping observations on all human history, declared as a spokesperson for the inevitable and universal adoption of 'cyberculture'. It was with this future-gazing, what-is-to-be-done verve that the term circulated for a while from the 1960s to the 1980s, especially in ideologically charged debates on capitalism and automation (Simon 1965; Heilbroner 1966, and onwards). In this period, computer networks were abuzz with exchanges about issues touching on various interests and areas of life other than the professional and pedagogical, which were apt to be thought of as 'cultural'. A strong sense of this was conveyed in Theodor Nelson's *Computer Lib/Dream Machines* (1974).

Through the 1980s, those with access to internetworked systems like USENET and LISTSERV, experienced their textualized exchanges as being participant in a cultural collective which is coextensive with real-world culture. But these formed a relatively small constituency, and their activities and concerns did not quite have a name. By the 1990s, with the spatial emphasis of 'cyberspace' in hand, these diverse activities and concerns were dubbed 'cyberculture', in a somewhat different way from the future-gazing 'cyberculture' of Hilton in the 1960s. The term was described accordingly by Mark Dery (1992):

> The subversive use of technocommodities, often framed by radical body politics, lies at the gravitational centre of *cyberculture*, a far-flung, loosely knit complex of sublegitimate, alternative, and oppositional subculture. This psychogeography is divisible into several major territories: visionary technology, fringe science, avant-garde art, and pop culture (509).

Dery took this as a definition in the two books on 'cyberculture' that he went on to publish (Dery 1994, 1996), where the term encapsulated various in-group realizations of some aspect of William Gibson's fantasy 'cyberspace'. But as the decade progressed, 'cyberculture' came to be seen more soberly as all the kinds of activities and exchanges that were mediated by the internet. This was not so much as a *sub*-culture but as a mode of communicating, doing, and producing that is coterminous with and coeval with the internet. Existing principles of markets and commodities, entertainment and aesthetics, ideologies and ethics, identity formations and fluidities, physical and psychological experience seemed at the same time extraneous to as well as in implicated within 'cyberculture' (elaborated as such in Aronowitz et al. 1996, Lévy 2001 [1997], Calcutt 1999). Contemplating 'cyberculture' simply became a way of coming to grips with internet collectivity instead of the wider cyberspace. An institutional or disciplinary territory was carved out in academia for research into 'cyberculture', thus understood. It was formalized with professional affiliations, curricula and key theorists, scholarly journals, professional bodies and the like. Before long, histories of that academic territory were being put together, which is usually the last step in consolidating a new discipline. David Silver entitled a paper on this emerging discipline in 2004, 'Internet/cyberculture/digital culture/new media/fill-in-the-blank studies', beginning with the observation: 'For the time being, it appears as though the largest umbrella underneath which many of us would huddle is called internet studies' (Silver 2004, 55). Soon after, he co-edited *Critical Cyberculture Studies* (Silver and Massanari 2006). Meanwhile a sort of dictionary appeared, *Cyberculture: The Key Concepts* (Bell et al. 2004), offering a subset of the vocabulary of Internet Polity discourse, with an eye on 'new forms of human interaction [… heralding] the emergence of new cultural discourses' (vii).

In fact, the other 'culture' catchwords highlighted above—'technoculture' and 'digital culture'—were variously woven through the patterns captured by 'cyberculture'. The choice of these terms began with slightly different emphases to cover the internet as space cum facility. Initially both were used interchangeably to examine two kinds of areas (as in Hayward 1990; Penley and Ross 1991). Firstly, these explored the mechanics and effects of the new medium for producing and encountering various kinds of putatively 'cultural' expression: for script, for aural forms, for still and moving images, for multimodal packages or immersive VR constructs. Secondly, these examined the representations of 'cultural' forms, icons, and occupations in the new medium: of cyborgs, in cyberpunk, of online gender and sex, hacking, games, etc. Used thus, 'technoculture' and 'digital culture' seemed to be a bit different from, for instance, Dery's (1994) 'cyberculture'. 'Technoculture' and 'digital culture' were more attentive to the medium through which 'culture', variously defined, is sieved, while 'cyberculture' appeared more concerned with its positioning apropos of the actually existing mainstream culture (as sub-cultural, alternative, oppositional, edgy, etc.). But this is a rather fine distinction, largely obscured by the numerous shared focuses and themes.

In a relatively lowkey way (never quite a catchword), 'internet culture' or 'Net culture' also had a slightly different emphasis from all the other terms, but only very slightly. The term seemed to be predominantly employed to connote *community* formations based upon Internet Technology (emails, news groups, bulletin boards, chatrooms, game forums, etc.). The term was employed less often to examine and investigate such communities (Porter 1996 did that), and more to report from their midst, usually as an enthusiastic participant or impressed observer (as in Coate 1998 [1992]; Rheingold 1993; Rushkoff 1994; Moore 1995, and with a historicist turn Hauben and Hauben 1997 [online 1994]). Various catchy terms to name the communities emerged from these: 'online community', 'virtual community', 'netizens', etc. Later in the decade though, 'internet culture' became simply synonymous with or subsumed 'cyberculture', 'technoculture', and 'digital culture'. Perhaps the most notable nuancing of all these 'cultural' terms occurred not in their fluid general usages but in their growing density in academic usage. In various academic areas, especially in the institutional precincts of the Social Sciences and Humanities, these terms became weightier with concentrated 'critical' theorizing.

5.4.2 Internet Communities

For those with access to computing networks in the early 1990s, enthusiasm about the culture of internet 'communities' was of the moment. With the dawning of the so-called 'post-Cold War era', amidst many 'transitions', some uncertainty about and need for renegotiating received ideologies were widely felt. The fall of several communist regimes was attended by a general disenchantment with state ownership and centralized redistribution. At the same time, the concerted global turn towards privatization and market forces for public-interest sectors aroused misgivings. Of the various attempts to find a consensual line between state and market, private and public, individual and collective interests (it was an age of 'Third Ways'), one proposed a reinvention of or return to 'communitarianism'. Very briefly, the idea was to form (or consolidate) collective solidarities in terms of policy tenets and ethical norms somewhere between those polarities of state redistributions and market mechanisms. The idea was effectively to undergird market-based economic arrangements with beneficent state regulation. Communitarianism involved promoting solidarities within the remit of interpersonal, local, or customary collectives that accept nation-state jurisdictions, market-based operations, and abide by some universal democratic and ethical tenets (Kymlicka 1989; Selznick 1992; Etzioni 1993 were influential; for an overview, Etzioni 1998). This reassuring recourse for political anxieties of the time seemed to fit the community-building drives on the internet.

The enthusiasm with which internet communities were discussed was stoked by the peculiar fact that the individual community-members were physically distanced from each other. They were removed from the usual community-forming habits of mutual recognition, identification, and in-person interaction. As a physical circumstance, internet users ('participants' was often the preferred word) formed communities while being materially individuated, simply separate and separated persons before a networked computer. This meant that community forming seemed disinvested from material conditions and physical proximities. Such physically disinvested community building was regarded as a new opportunity to constitute communal norms from scratch, by making and declaring choices rather than by sharing cognitive environments and dealing with given physical and behavioural attributes. In other words, such internet communities could putatively come together without conceding to inevitable identity markers and received boundaries like nation, region, economic class, or institution. They appeared as a purified communitarian phenomenon, untroubling to market and state restrictions, untroubled by existing individual and collective real-world circumstances. They formed upon a base where a principle of precedent-individuation was a necessary material predicate, and the principle of minimal-gradual-material standardization bolstered community self-determinations. In numerous ways, these internet communities seemed to crystallize in their microcosms some of the tacit and habituated structures of the encompassing Internet Polity.

Notably, while culture seemed imbued in such internet communities in every sort of area, it did not really seep into business practices. Or rather, there was relatively little discussion of a distinctive internet 'business culture' or 'business community' at the time. This might seem counterintuitive since the process of opening-up and privatizing the internet was largely designed to facilitate business. The internet's emergence as such was marked with numerous texts on the business opportunities it presented, with serial publications like *The Internet Business Journal* (launched in 1993), and various general guidebooks (such as Resnick and Taylor 1994; Ellsworth and Ellsworth 1994; Heslop and Angell 1994). Insofar as businesses had communities and cultures, those remained described by their commercial principles and institutional character. In those existing business terms, the internet was perceived not so much as an inhabited space cum facility but as merely a very serviceable facility for extending business. The purposive use of Internet Technology in businesses was to consolidate businesses *as* businesses. Internet Technology was expected to make the existing cultures of business firms more productive by existing standards, and to expand the range of products and services that businesses could marketize. Nothing fundamentally changed in business cultures and communities, except that they became more of what they have always tried to be: productive, profitable, efficient, competitive, etc. These facets of the part that Internet Technology played were designated by their own distinct catchwords in the 1990s: 'e-commerce', 'e-business', and, in relation to the exchange of products and services, 'B2B' (business to business) and 'B2C' (business to customer). Businesses, we could say, grew and expanded on the back of the internet as facility without changing their functional principles and cultural norms. Instead, the internet served to disseminate those principles and norms outside business circles, so that those principles and norms seemed to become characteristic of general culture. Arguably, the Internet Polity was structured to work in synch with businesses without becoming integrated into them—in that sense, much like actually existing polities.

5.4.3 Hackers

To round off these observations on the attributions of 'culture' apropos of the Internet Polity in the 1990s, let me turn to the complex connotations of the term 'hacker' at the time. It had a special bearing on the ways in which 'culture' came to be attached to internet collectivity, drawing upon 'hacker culture' (or 'sub-culture') and the vocabulary of *The Hacker's Dictionary* (Steele et al. 1983). At the same time, even as 'internet' burgeoned as a popular 1990s catchword, 'hacker' signified an uncomfortable cultural fissure therein. In the popular imagination, 'hacker' appeared to be more akin to producers of the internet as space cum facility than those dry professional computing personnel who had their fingers squarely in Internet Technology—the scientists, engineers, programmers employed in governmental and corporate organizations. The hacker seemed to crystallize the more culturally redolent qualities away from the latter. And yet, they also began to represent the anti-social or anti-communitarian quotient amidst the buzz of internet communities. 'Hacker' was, in fact, possibly the most sustained of catchwords in this area through the 1980s and the 1990s. Close attention to its shifting connotations and adaptations say much about how cultural norms attached to the Internet Polity as it formed (Graph 5.5).

The origins of the term 'hacker' in computing have been traced from the 1950s, as student slang in elite US universities, especially in engineering circles (see Levy 1984: 10–11). More considered connotations of the term have been available from the 1970s, mainly from AI researchers. In his MIT thesis, Gerald Jay Sussman

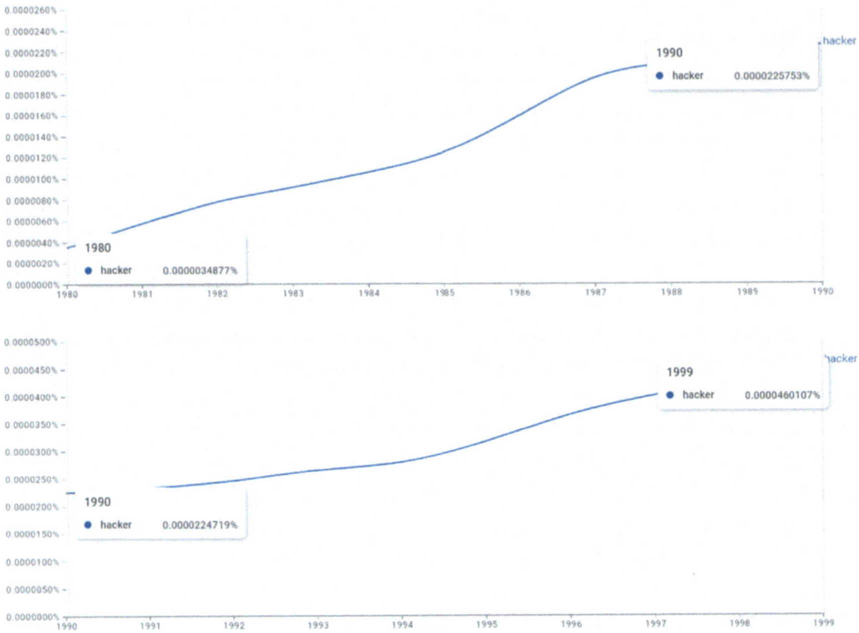

Graph 5.5 Google Ngram Viewer graphs of 'hacker', 1980–1990 and 1990–1999. Note that this is case-sensitive, with lower-case 'h', mainly to avoid overlap with the not uncommon proper name 'Hacker'. In the 1980s the term showed a higher than sixfold increase in usage-frequency, and in the 1990s a further twofold increase

(1973) had called his block-arranging problem-solver programme, with an automatic programmer component, 'HACKER'. The naming was probably indicative of what the term suggested for programmers at the time: someone with the ability to either identify an existing programme for the solution to a given computing problem or, in case one is not available, to produce such a programme for the solution and then make it available for future use. The term had to do with a narrow rationale of using programmes or programming to solve a target problem. It is this narrowness of application that Joseph Weizenbaum (1976) picked up in his description of 'hacker' as a 'compulsive programmer' with obsessively cultivated programming skills focused on short-term problem-solving:

> The compulsive programmer spends all the time he can working on one of his big projects. 'Working' is not the word he uses; he calls what he does 'hacking'. To hack is, according to the dictionary, 'to cut irregularly, without skill or definite purpose; to mangle by or as if by repeated strokes of a cutting instrument'. I have already said that the compulsive programmer, or hacker as he calls himself, is usually a superb technician. It seems therefore that he is not 'without skill' as the definition would have it. But the definition fits in the deeper sense that the hacker is 'without definite purpose': he cannot set before himself a clearly defined long-term goal and a plan for achieving it, for he has only technique, not knowledge. He has nothing he can analyse or synthesize; in short, he has nothing to form theories about. His skill is therefore aimless, even disembodied. It is simply not connected with anything other than

> the instrument in which it may be exercised. His skill is like that of a monastic copyist who, though illiterate, is a first-rate calligrapher. His grandiose projects must therefore necessarily have the quality of illusions, indeed, of illusions of grandeur. He will construct one grand system in which all other experts will soon write their systems. (118)

Weizenbaum parenthetically allowed that in its own terms it is ‘highly creative labour’, without which many advances in computing would not have occurred—useful, that is, insofar as garnered to productive ends. The somewhat slighting description makes a useful distinction between knowledge (rather like my description of assimilated knowledge in Chap. 3) and the intensely individualistic cultivator of a skill for its own sake.

Despite Weizenbaum, so long as ‘hackers’ were associated with productive enterprise, their celebration—often self-celebration—grew and peaked around the mid-1980s. Steven Levy came up with a eulogistic account of ‘hacker’ icons, unambiguously entitled *Hackers: Heroes of the Computer Revolution* (1984). It inspired the first Hackers Conference in California, November 1984, organized by Stewart Brand, and a documentary entitled *Hackers: Wizards of The Electronic Age* (Florin 1984). With these collectivizing activities, and the published appearance of *The Hacker’s Dictionary* (Steele et al. 1983), the shape of a cheery hacker vocabulary, community, and culture were well in place, with a committed membership. As the dictionary observed: ‘Hackers consider themselves somewhat of an elite, though one to which new members are gladly welcome. It is a meritocracy based on ability. There is a certain self-satisfaction in identifying yourself as a hacker’ (71). Nevertheless, this happy culture was underpinned, in Weizenbaum’s vein, by the image of the ‘hacker’ as a maverick and compulsive individual playing with programmes in self-absorbed and secluded isolation rather than as the soul of expansive communal bonhomie. In fact, even in *The Hacker’s Dictionary* a tiny ripple of a distinctly anti-social and anti-community connotation to the word was noted. Of the seven senses given for the term, six were about enjoying and being good at programming (or at anything in a specialist way), but the seventh was, ‘A malicious or inquisitive meddler who tries to discover information by poking around’, like trying to find other people’s passwords by ‘deceptive or illegal means’ or trying to learn about computer networks so as to ‘interfere’ rather than ‘improve’ it (71).

In fact, some ‘hackers’ were already embracing rather than eschewing that seventh sense and, moreover, offering arguments to justify doing so. Some had formed secretive fifth-estate groupings, with ominous sounding handles like the Legion of Doom and the Masters of Deception. From their midst appeared the brief document, ‘The Hacker’s Manifesto’ (Blankenship 1986), on the heels of the Computer Fraud and Abuse Act (1986) which did not quite name ‘hackers’ but unambiguously criminalized that seventh sense. The manifesto began with the sentence ‘Another one got caught today’, and observed:

> This is our world now... the world of the electron and the switch, the beauty of the baud. We make use of a service already existing without paying for what could be dirt-cheap if it wasn’t run by profiteering gluttons, and you call us criminals. We explore... and you call us criminals. We seek after knowledge... and you call us criminals. We exist without skin colour, without nationality, without religious bias... and you call us criminals. You build

> atomic bombs, you wage wars, you murder, cheat, and lie to us and try to make us believe it's for our own good, yet we're the criminals. Yes, I am a criminal. My crime is that of curiosity. My crime is that of judging people by what they say and think, not what they look like. My crime is that of outsmarting you, something that you will never forgive me for. I am a hacker, and this is my manifesto. You may stop this individual, but you can't stop us all... after all, we're all alike. (Blankenship 1986)

It was addressed to an establishment 'you' of governmental and corporate agencies which had launched a concerted drive to criminalize and counter such 'hacking'. Others embraced the seventh sense of 'hacker' (according to *The Hackers Dictionary*) by publicizing their methods for breaking through secured digital boundaries. To that end, using the pseudonym Emmanuel Goldstein, Eric Gordon Corley launched *2600: The Hacker Quarterly* in January 1984. The following year, Hugo Cornwall (real name Peter Sommer) published *The Hacker's Handbook* (1985) with the reassuring note: 'This book uses the word [hacker] in a more restricted sense: hacking is a recreational and educational sport. It consists in attempting to make unauthorized entry into computers and to explore what is there' (vii).

With the appearance of the Morris Worm in 1988 (discussed in Chap. 3), on the eve of the opening-up of Internet Technology, the dangers of this anti-social 'hacker' seemed to become magnified, threatening to subsume the other senses of the term. 'Hackers' continued to come under escalating attack from government agencies through the 1990s. Those who thought of themselves as, and felt they represented, 'hackers' put up a flailing resistance to this turn in the early 1990s. I have touched upon the activities of the Electronic Frontier Foundation in this vein earlier (in Chap. 4). Insofar as this turn in the connotations of the catchword 'hacker' went, the shifts in this period tracked the progress and failure of such resistance. Andrew Ross (1991) produced the most nuanced political analysis of the 'war on hackers' that was underway, with a perceptive comparison of metaphors used for computer viruses and for the AIDS epidemic at the time, summarizing critical accounts of hackers as offspring of a privileged class. Importantly, he put his finger precisely on the fissure that hackers presented from the establishment perspective, implicitly extending the account given by Weizenbaum earlier:

> 'Hacking' must then be designated as a strictly *amateur* practice; the tension, in hacking, between *interestedness* and *disinterestedness* is different from, and deficient in relation to, the proper balance demanded by professionalism. Alternatively, hacking can be seen as the amateur flip side of the professional ideal—a disinterested love in the service of interested parties and institutions. In either case, it serves as an example of professionalism gone wrong, but not very wrong. (118)

As an amateur practice it was close to the kind of interest that user-communities may cultivate or develop as a culture; at the same time, it was so close to (even indistinguishable from) professional abilities that it needed to be contained within existing institutional cultures and legal regimes (like those associated with businesses). Self-avowed hackers' attempts to disinvest from anti-social associations were bound to fail before this larger structuring conundrum. While upping the authority of being and celebrating 'hackers', Eric Raymond tried to deflect the unfortunate seventh sense in *The New Hacker's Dictionary* by packaging that into a straightforwardly anti-social word, 'cracker': '**cracker** n. One who breaks security on a system. Coined ca. 1985 by hackers in defence against journalistic misuse of **hacker**' (Raymond 1993: 110). Raymond variously insisted on the distinction, on keeping 'hackers' free of suspicion and 'crackers' culpable, over the following decade with indifferent success. In fact, it was not just journalistic misuse that was at stake; 'hacker' had entered the vocabulary of US government departments dealing with computer security as early as 1983 (as in the Report for the 98th Congress, US Government 1985: 58).

The pejorative sense of 'hacker' gained momentum in those governmental and corporate circles while the 1996 Telecommunications Act crept up. As enthusiasm about user- 'communities' grew, so did misgivings about 'hackers'. The bid to contain 'hackers' within a professional or establishment order in which the larger social restrictions of intellectual property, governmental and business confidentiality, legal regulation of privacy and security prevail, the anomalous position of 'hackers' (very much more than 'crackers') centred intensive scrutiny. To some degree this was scrutiny through the production of public information. Cyberpunk novelist Bruce Sterling's well-researched monograph *The Hacker Crackdown* (1992) covered all sides of the containment drive from 1990 onwards. In the process, it revealed a great deal about the extent to which this term and its proponents had already focussed attention in governmental and corporate circles. At the same time, it also stitched together a narrative which gave the term a decisive and, importantly, informed public emphasis. This was a deliberate and slightly reluctant move, introduced thus:

> [Law-abiding hackers], as a class, instinctively recognize that a public, politicized attack on hackers will eventually spread to them—that the term 'hacker,' once demonized, might be used to knock their hands off the levers of power and choke them out of existence. There are hackers today who fiercely and publicly resist any besmirching of the noble title of hacker. Naturally and understandably, they deeply resent the attack on their values implicit in using the word 'hacker' as a synonym for computer criminal.
>
> This book, sadly but in my opinion unavoidably, rather adds to the degradation of the term. It concerns itself mostly with hacking in its commonest latter-day definition, that is, intruding into computer systems by stealth and without permission. (55)

There is a shift performed there: first the constituency referred as 'hackers' is divided into law-abiding and criminal, and second it is decided that the term should attach to the latter. It was explained that the former have been 'corraled into governments, universities, or large multinational companies, and forced to follow rulebooks and wear suits and ties' (55), and thus have become professionals.

Indeed, through the 1990s a growing number of former self-professed 'hackers' were absorbed as *bona fide* professionals into computer security departments and institutional offices. By implication, the remaining hackers had preferred to be amateurs, and therefore remained 'hackers', named as such. The last line of Ross's book was: 'It is the End of the Amateurs' (313). There were several publications along these lines at the time, though few that were as informative. After Sterling's book, within governmental circles a process of identifying, mapping, charting, tracking, organizing information on 'hackers' as potential or real criminals followed. An Australian Intelligence Corps officer, Alan Nicholas Chantler, produced a careful ethnographic PhD thesis on *Risk: The Profile of the Computer Hacker* (1995) which, though unpublished, fed various governmental reports. Several years later, an extensive (and largely sympathetic) study of the psychological profiles of hackers appeared in *The Hacking of America* (Schell et al. 2002). Particularly informative of this knowledge-mapping of 'hackers' were the Subcommittee on Telecommunications and Finance Hearings of the 103rd Congress (US Government 1994), on the 'integrity of telecommunications transmissions and networks, including personal privacy, data, and network security, and electronic fraud' (1). This presented records of entertaining exchanges between captains of government and industry and 'hacker' experts like Emmanuel Goldstein (i.e., Corley, editor of *2600: The Hacker Quarterly*) and Bruce Sterling. After the Telecommunications Act 1996, and yet another amendment of the Computer Fraud and Prevention Act in 1996, Matt Devost came up with *A Hacker Primer* (1997) for the President's Commission on Critical Infrastructure Protection. This presented the mapping in a matured template, giving lists of communication mechanism that hackers use, the known groups, their targets, their tools and information sources and circuits.

Though the term 'hacker' thereafter came to be ensconced within cybersecurity circles and associated with the risks of and threats to internet-based services and systems, it retained a kind of contained glamour within those circles, harking back to the heyday of hackers. But moral qualifiers needed to be attached to the term. Techies working in cybersecurity organisations and firms still fancied themselves as 'hackers', but with desirable social values, whose moral fibre has led them to choose establishment stability and light—and yet not without some longing for the dark side (on this, see Hafner 2000). Such professionals designated themselves with terms like 'white hat hackers' as opposed to criminal 'black hat hackers', fighting against 'hack attacks'. A blog in 2000 by the pseudonymous 'Jude Thaddeus' (perhaps denoting a tongue-in-cheek guilt in betraying amateur hackers), then Head of Information Security Systems for the professional enclave of *Computerworld*, observed:

> This 'white hat' nomenclature confused me when I first heard it. White hat is a fairly common term for people who hack legitimately—security staff, researchers and so on. By contrast, black hat hackers hack maliciously. Basically, white hats are the good guys; black hats are the bad guys. […] I'm told the terms come from the early Western movies. Because the movies were filmed in black and white, the chase scenes tended to get a bit confusing, until someone decided to give the good guys white hats and the bad guys black hats. (Thaddeus 2000)

Similarly, the term 'ethical hacker' gained some momentum in these niches (see Palmer 2001).

Hacker conferences continued to be organized and came to be dominated mainly by such professionals; 'hacker' guidebooks continued to appear and were now for the information of cybersecurity professionals (it is a sellable catchword and headline numerous publications since 2000); and, of course, cybersecurity formed its discrete professional 'hacker' vocabulary, with dictionaries galore. Of the latter, one was entitled *Webster's New World Hacker Dictionary* (Schell and Martin 2006), with a curiously sympathetic attachment to the term 'hacker' amidst its cybersecurity-centred listing of terms. A detailed introduction went through the history of hacking, with no reference to the earlier *Hacker's Dictionary* or *New Hacker's Dictionary*, and the entries generally made no concessions to fun or wordplay. The definition of 'hacker' was confined to 'the positive sense of the word' as 'an individual who enjoys learning computer system details and how to capitalize on his or her capabilities' (145); all negative senses were directed towards the term 'crackers', described as:

> Black Hats who break into others' computer systems without authorization, dig into code to break a software's copy-protection provisions, flood Internet sites, deliberately deface Websites, and steal money or identities. (73)

However, outside the professional cognoscenti, 'cracker' has not caught on and 'hacker' is more strongly associated with those heinous activities. Of course, unauthorized and non-professional hackers and hacker-collectives continued to operate and multiply too. Since it was no longer possible to garner significant public sympathy for the designation 'hacker', they had to dissociate it from compulsive programming (now predominantly a business activity) or the blithely 'entertaining and educational sport' of unauthorized activities. Insofar as this kind of activity courted some degree of public sympathy, the term 'hacktivism' surfaced in the late 1990s (for a useful account, see Shantz and Tomblin 2014: Chaps. 2 and 3). 'Hacktivist' imbued the now largely tainted term 'hacker' with a social conscience and commitment, an 'activist' commitment. It fell under the umbrella of criminalization that attached to 'hackers', but with the public appeal of having a heroic and idealistic political stance and exercising a new and necessary mode of protest. In fact, the term 'hacktivist' also soon moved in the direction of being demonized (see Ludlow 2013 on what he calls the 'lexical warfare' around the term).

This brief account of the fate of the term 'hacker' takes me to the area of the next chapter, devoted to the mutations that Internet Polity discourse went through and how the Internet Polity fared after the 1990s. Where 'communities' of internet users flourished and multiplied and became encultured and expanded into 'social networks', a kind of de-culturation of 'hacker culture' followed, with its energies being assimilated into business culture and institutional functioning. Slippages in the attributions of culture to user 'communities' and 'hackers' in the 1990s say much about the boundaries that were being drawn into the space cum facility that is the internet. In various ways, the catchwords of the 2000s served to focalize and underscore those boundaries. More importantly, new boundaries were erected, and, as the next and final chapter argues, the Internet Polity came to be contained. The term 'hacking', associated with breaking such boundaries, was outweighed by catchwords and technological developments that explicitly foreground these new boundaries.

References

Algeo J (1991) Fifty years 'among the new words': a dictionary of neologisms, 1941–1991. Cambridge University Press, Cambridge

Algeo J, Algeo A (1994a) Among the new words. American Speech 69(2):177–186. https://www.jstor.org/stable/455701

Algeo J, Algeo A (1994b) Among the new words. American Speech 69(4):398–410. https://www.jstor.org/stable/455857
All Acronyms website: https://www.allacronyms.com/
Allan K (1998) The meaning of culture: moving the postmodern critique forward. Praeger, Westport CO
Aronowitz S, Martinsons B, Menser M (eds) (1996) Technoscience and cyberculture. Routledge, London
Bell D, Loader BD, Place N, Schuler D (2004) Cyberculture: the key concepts. Routledge, Abingdon
Bergenholtz H, Gouws RH (2012) What is lexicography? Lexikos 22:1. https://doi.org/10.5788/22-1-996
Bierce A (2011 [1906]) The devil's dictionary. Dover, New York
Blankenship L (1986) The hacker manifesto. https://en.wikisource.org/wiki/The_Hacker_Manifesto
Breur H (1966) Dictionary for computer languages. Academic Press for the Automatic Programming Information Centre, Brighton College of Technology, Brighton
Calcutt A (1999) White noise: an A-Z of the contradictions in cyberculture. Macmillan, Basingstoke
Carr M (1997) Internet dictionaries and lexicography. Int J Lexicogr 10(3):209–230. https://doi.org/10.1093/ijl/10.3.209
Chandor A (1968) A short introduction to computers. Barker, London
Chandor A, Graham J, Williamson R (1970) A dictionary of computers. Penguin, Harmondsworth
Chandor A, Graha J, Williamson R (1985) Dictionary of computers (3e). Penguin, Harmondsworth
Chantler AN (1995) Risk: the profile of the computer hacker. PhD Thesis, School of Information Systems, Curtin Business School, Australia
Coate J (1998 [1992]) Cyberspace innkeeping: building online community. http://johncoate.com/Building%20Online%20Community.html
Coleman J (2009) A history of cant and slang dictionaries: volume III: 1859–1936. Oxford University Press, Oxford
Coleman J (2010) A history of cant and slang dictionaries: volume IV: 1937–1984. Oxford University Press, Oxford
Collin SMH (1997) Dictionary of personal computing and the internet. Fitzroy Dearborn, Chicago
Cornwall H (1985) The hacker's handbook. Century Communications, London
Cotton B, Oliver R (1994) The cyberspace lexicon: an illustrated dictionary of terms from multimedia to virtual reality. Phaidon, New York
Covington MA, Downing DD (1986) Barron's dictionary of computer terms. Barron's, Hauppauge NY
Crumlish C (1995) The internet dictionary. SYBEX, San Francisco
Crystal D (2001) Language and the internet. Cambridge University Press, Cambridge
Crystal D (2003) The ideal dictionary, lexicographer and user. In: Hartmann PRK (ed) Lexicography: critical concepts. Routledge, London, pp 319–327
de Schryver G-M, Joffe D, Joffe P, Hillewaert S (2006) Do dictionary users really look up frequent words? On the overestimation of the value of corpus-based lexicography. Lexikos 16:67–83. https://doi.org/10.5788/16-0-648
Dery M (1992) Cyberculture. South Atlantic Q 91(3):501–523. https://doi.org/10.1215/00382876-91-3-501
Dery M (ed) (1994) Flame wars: the discourse of cyberculture. Duke University Press, Durham NC
Dery M (1996) Escape velocity: cyberculture at the end of the century. Grove, New York
Devost M (1997) A hacker primer. President's Commission of Critical Infrastructure Protection, Washington DC. https://www.oodaloop.com/wp-content/uploads/2019/06/Hacker-Primer-PCCIP.pdf
Downing DA, Covington MA, Covington MM (1996) Dictionary of computer and internet terms. Barron's, Hauppauge NY
Eagleton T (2000) The idea of culture. Blackwell, Oxford
Ellsworth JH, Ellsworth MV (1994) The internet business book. Wiley, New York

Etzioni A (1993) Spirit of community: the reinvention of American society. Touchstone, New York
Etzioni A (ed) (1998) The essential communitarian reader. Rowman & Littlefield, Lanham MD
Fahey T (1994) net.speak: the internet dictionary. Hayden, Indianapolis IN
Flaubert G (1968) Dictionary of accepted ideas (trans: Barzun J). New Directions, New York
Florin F (dir) (1984) Hackers: wizards of the electronic age (documentary film). https://archive.org/details/hackerswizardsoftheelectronicage
Foldoc (Free Online Dictionary of Computing) website: http://foldoc.org/programming+language
Fuertes-Olivera PA (ed) (2018) The Routledge handbook of lexicography. Routledge, London
Fuertes-Olivera PA, Bergenholtz H (eds) (2010) E-lexicography. The internet, digital initiatives and lexicography. Continuum, London
Galland FJ (ed) (1982) Dictionary of computing: data communications, hardware and software basics, digital electronics. Wiley, Chichester
Granger SG, Paquot M (eds) (2012) Electronic lexicography. Oxford University Press, Oxford
Grudin J (1993) Interface: an evolving concept. Commun ACM 36(4):110–119. https://doi.org/10.1145/255950.153585
Hacker's dictionary website: revision history: http://hackersdictionary.com/html/Revision-History.html
Hafner K (2000) In world of hackers, good guys and bad guys are often a blur. New York Times, 12 February. https://www.nytimes.com/2000/02/12/business/in-world-of-hackers-good-guys-and-bad-guys-are-often-a-blur.html
Hale C (ed) (1996) Wired style: principles of English usage in the digital age. HardWired, San Francisco CA
Halliday MAK, Teubert W, Yallop C, Čermáková A (2004) Lexicography and corpus linguistics: an introduction. Continuum, London
Hammersley M (2019) The concept of culture: a history and reappraisal. Palgrave Macmillan, Cham
Hauben M, Hauben R (1997) Netizens: on the history and impact of Usenet and the internet. IEEE Computer Society Press, Los Alamitos CA. Online at http://www.columbia.edu/~hauben/book-pdf/
Hayward P (ed) (1990) Culture, technology and creativity in the late twentieth century. John Libbey, London
Heilbroner RL (1966) The limits of American capitalism. Harper & Row, New York
Heslop B, Angell D (1994) The internet business companion: growing your business in the electronic age. Addison-Wesley, Boston
Hilton AM (1964) An ethos for the age of cyberculture. In: AFIPS '64 (Spring): proceedings of the April 21–23, 1964, Spring joint computer conference, pp 139–153. https://doi.org/10.1145/1464122.1464136
Hipgrave R (1985) Computing terms and acronyms: a dictionary. Library Association, London
'History of Wikipedia' webpage: https://en.wikipedia.org/wiki/History_of_Wikipedia
Holden R (2023) Digital. OED Word Stories. https://www.oed.com/public/digital/loginpage
Howard W. Sams and Co (1962a) Pocket dictionary of computer terms. Howard W. Sams, Indianapolis IN
Howard W. Sams and Co (1962b) Computer basics volumes 1–6. Howard W. Sams, Indianapolis IN
Hyman A (1976) Computing: a dictionary of terms, concepts and ideas. Arrow, London
IEEE Computer Society, Standards Coordinating Committee (1990) IEEE standard computer dictionary (610). The Institute of Electrical and Electronics Engineers, New York. https://ieeexplore.ieee.org/document/182763
IEEE Computer Society, Standards Coordinating Committee (1995) IEEE standard glossary for computer networking technology (IEEE Std. 610.7-1995). The Institute of Electrical and Electronics Engineers, New York. https://ieeexplore.ieee.org/document/467542
Ihnatko A (1997) Cyberspeak: an online dictionary. Random House, New York
Illingworth V (ed) (1983) A dictionary of computing. Oxford University Press, Oxford
Ince D (2001) Dictionary of the internet. Oxford University Press, Oxford

Internet Slang website: https://internetslang.com/
Jansen E, James V (2002) NetLingo: the internet dictionary. NetLingo, Ojai CA
Kachru BB, Kahane H (eds) (1995) Cultures, ideologies, and the dictionary. Max Niemeyer, Tübingen
Kelly-Bootle S (1981) The devil's DP dictionary. McGraw-Hill, New York
Kelly-Bootle S (1995) The computer contradictionary. MIT Press, Cambridge MA
Kymlicka W (1989) Liberalism, community and culture. Oxford University Press, Oxford
Levy S (1984) Hackers: heroes of the computer revolution. Anchor Press/Doubleday, New York
Lévy P (2001 [1997]) Cyberculture (trans: Bononno R). University of Minnesota Press, Minneapolis MN
Lew R, de Schryver G-M (2014) Dictionary users in the digital revolution. Int J Lexicogr 27(4):341–359. https://doi.org/10.1093/ijl/ecu011
Liu A (2004) The laws of cool: knowledge work and the culture of information. University of Chicago Press, Chicago
Longley D, Shain M (1986) Macmillan dictionary of personal computing and communications. Macmillan, London
Longo B (2021) Words and power: computers, language, and U.S. cold war values. Springer, Cham
Ludlow P (2013) What is a "Hacktivist"? New York Times, January 13. https://archive.nytimes.com/opinionator.blogs.nytimes.com/2013/01/13/what-is-a-hacktivist/
MacDonald L (2005) The Meaning of "e-": neologisms as markers of culture and technology. ETopia:82–90. https://doi.org/10.25071/1718-4657.36746
Machovec GS (1993) Telecommunications, networking and internet glossary. Library and Information Technology Association, American Library Association, Chicago
Malkin GS (1996) Internet users' glossary RFC 1983. Network Working Group. https://datatracker.ietf.org/doc/html/rfc1983
Malkin GS, LaQuey Parker T (1993) Internet users' glossary RFC 1392. Network Working Group. https://datatracker.ietf.org/doc/rfc1392/
McCulloch G (2019) Because internet: understanding the new rules of language. Riverhead, New York
Meadows AJ (1984) Dictionary of computing and new technology. Kogan Page, London
Moore DW (1995) The emperor's virtual clothes: the naked truth about internet culture. Algonquin, Chapel Hill NC
Nelson TH (1974) Computer lib/dream machines: new freedoms through computer screens—a minority report. Online at https://archive.org/details/computer-lib-dream-machines
NetLingo website: https://www.netlingo.com/
Online Slang Dictionary website: http://onlineslangdictionary.com/
Ooi VBY (1998) Computer corpus lexicography. Edinburgh University Press, Edinburgh
OpenThesaurus website: https://www.openthesaurus.de/
Palmer CC (2001) Ethical hacking. IBM Syst J 40(3):769–780. https://doi.org/10.1147/sj.403.0769
Peckham A (2005) Urban dictionary: fularious street slang defined. Andrews McMeel, Kansas City MO
Penley C, Ross A (eds) (1991) Technoculture. University of Minnesota Press, Minneapolis MN
Pfaffenberger B (1990) Que's computer user's dictionary. Que, Carmel IN
Pfaffenberger B, Wall D (1995) Que's computer and internet dictionary. Que, Indianapolis IN
Porter D (ed) (1996) Internet culture. Routledge, New York
Proffitt M (ed) (1997) OED additions to the second edition, vol 3. Oxford English Dictionary, Oxford
Quentin RD (1987) Longman illustrated dictionary of computing science: computers and their application. Longman, Harlow
Raymond ES (ed) (1991) The new hacker's dictionary. MIT Press, Cambridge MA
Raymond ES (ed) (1993) The new hacker's dictionary, 2nd edn. MIT Press, Cambridge MA
Raymond ES (comp) (1996) The new hacker's dictionary, 3rd ed. MIT Press, Cambridge MA
Resnick R, Taylor D (1994) The internet business guide: riding the information superhighway to profit. Sams, Indianapolis IN

Rheingold H (1993) The virtual community: homesteading on the electronic frontier. Secker & Warburg, London
Ross A (1991) Hacking away at the counterculture. In: Penley and Ross (eds), pp 107–134
Rushkoff D (1994) Cyberia: life in the trenches of hyperspace. HarperOne, San Francisco CA
Schell B, Martin C (2006) Webster's new world hacker dictionary. Wiley, Indianapolis IN
Schell B, Dodge JL, Moutsatsos SS (2002) The hacking of America: who's doing it, why, and how. Quoram, Westport CT
Seargeant P (2010) Lexicography as a philosophy of language. Lang Sci 33(1):1–10. https://doi.org/10.1016/j.langsci.2010.06.002
Selznick P (1992) The moral commonwealth: social theory and the promise of community. University of California Press, Berkeley CA
Shantz J, Tomblin J (2014) Cyber disobedience: re://presenting online anarchy. Zero Books, Alresford
Silver D (2004) Internet/cyberculture/digital culture/new media/fill-in-the-blank studies. New Media Soc 6(1):55–64. https://doi.org/10.1177/1461444804039915
Silver D, Massanari A (eds) (2006) Critical Cyberculture Studies. New York University Press, New York
Simon HA (1965) The shape of automation for men and management. Harper & Row, New York
Simpson JA, Weiner ESC (eds) (1989) The oxford english dictionary, second edition, 20 volumes. Oxford University Press, Oxford
Simpson JA, Weiner ESC (eds) (1993) OED additions to the second edition, Volumes 1 and 2. Oxford University Press, Oxford
Sinclair IR (1986) Collins Dictionary: Computing. Collins, London
Sinclair IR (1988) Collins dictionary of personal computing. Harper Collins, Glasgow
Sippl CJ (1966) Computer dictionary. Howard W. Sams, Indianapolis IN
Sondak NE, Sondak E (1973) The Layman's dictionary of computer terminology. Hawthorn, New York
Steele GL, Woods DR, Finkel RA, Crispin MR, Stallman RM, Goodfellow GS (1983) The hacker's dictionary: a guide to the computer underground. Harper & Row, New York
Sterling B (1992) The hacker crackdown: law and disorder on the electronic frontier. Bantam, New York
Sussman GJ (1973) A computational model of skill acquisition. Artificial Intelligence Laboratory, MIT, Cambridge MA. http://hdl.handle.net/1721.1/6894
Thaddeus J (2000) The confessions of a white hat hacker. Computerworld, 29 December. https://www.computerworld.com/article/2783116/the-confessions-of-a-white-hat-hacker.html
Urban Dictionary website: https://www.urbandictionary.com/
US Government (1985) Activities of the committee on governmental affairs, report of the committee on governmental affairs, United States senate and its subcommittees for the ninety-eighth congress. US Government Printing Office, Washington DC
US Government (1994) Telecommunications network security: hearings before the subcommittee on telecommunications and finance of the committee on energy and commerce, house of representatives, one hundred third congress, first session, April 29 and June 9, 1993. US Government Printing Office, Washington
van den Bragt W (1986) Book review: computing dictionaries. Eur J Oper Res 27(3):387–388. https://doi.org/10.1016/0377-2217(86)90342-5
Vollnhals O (1984) Elsevier's dictionary of personal and office computing: in five languages, English, German, French, Italian and Portuguese. Elsevier, Amsterdam
Weizenbaum J (1976) Computer power and human reason: from judgment to calculation. W.H. Freeman, New York
Wells RA (1973) Dictionaries and the authoritarian tradition. Mouton, The Hague
Williams R (1983) Keywords: a vocabulary of culture and society. Fontana, Glasgow
Williams R (1993) Jargon: an informal dictionary of computer terms. Peachpit, Berkeley CA

Chapter 6
'Internet of Things' and 'Social Networking': Containment

Abstract Moving to the post-2000 period, or the post-formation Internet Polity, this chapter begins with the implications of the internet becoming the centred repository of sources, medium of investigation, and object in historicist accounts of recent and contemporary events. Debates on 'technological determinism' are considered here. As events, 9/11 and the 2000 dot-com crash are pegged as turning points. A broad argument is proposed about the condition of the Internet Polity thereafter. It is suggested that it became *contained* in two moves during the 2000s. This containment involved, first, a space of the internet opening beyond the scope of the Internet Polity. This space incorporated data exchanges between 'smart' objects, unsupervised systems, and machine-learning systems. Second, much of the Internet Polity discourse and collective life became concentrated in very large platforms, which have global reach, local penetration, and data-management standards. This move facilitated the burgeoning data market and fed into the first move. The two moves are outlined by focusing on two catchwords and related terms. The first is addressed via the connotations of 'Internet of Things' and 'smart' objects, and the second by pausing on 'social networking' (on 'sites' or 'platforms'). This chapter, and the study, concludes by briefly reconsidering the formative first principles of the Internet Polity, and pinpointing areas for further investigations.

6.1 Post-formation

Thus far, this study has given an account of the *formation*—the coming together—of the Internet Polity through the later twentieth century. This concluding chapter turns to the Internet Polity in the twenty-first century, or, so to speak, its *post-formation* phase. This study is not rounded off and closed here but kept open. Accordingly, an argument is sketched out here with an eye on relatively recent developments in the Internet Polity's principles and discourse, which we are still amidst.

I begin by stating the gist of this argument, then proceed to some contextual details, and finally move towards substantiating the argument's two main strands.

S. Gupta, *Collective Principles and the Formation of the Internet*, Springer Series on Cultural Computing, https://doi.org/10.1007/978-3-031-90470-7_6

Previous chapters described the emergence of the Internet Polity as a collectivity with a social orientation towards the internet—as a technological structure, facility, and space. Two paths have been taken to that end in two parts. Part I (Chaps. 2 and 3) focused on norms which steered the development of Internet Technology and came to be assumed as social and political first principles of the Internet Polity. Those included protocols and minimal-gradual-mechanical standardization, hypertext systems and precedent individuation, and security controls and targeted collective regulation. Part II (Chaps. 4 and 5) then traced the development of an Internet Polity discourse and emergent cultural practices in terms of catchwords and an everyday vocabulary. Together these two paths coalesce to characterize the Internet Polity as a cohesive and distinctive collective formation by the beginning of the twenty-first century.

Through the early decades of the twenty-first century, the scale of the Internet Polity expanded to global proportions, with numbers of users worldwide being tracked continuously. In 2023, it was estimated that there are 5.3 billion users, around 65.7% of the global population (Petrosyan 2023). Of late, this scaling up has not been driven as much by developments in Internet Technology (the software dimension) as developments across Internet Infrastructure (especially the hardware dimension). Naturally, every move in the latter has been attended by corollary upgrading and reorientation of Internet Technology. For the Internet Polity, the most material of these developments took place at the line where users and inhabitants access the internet as facility and space. This line gradually incorporated a proliferation of devices for voluntarily accessing the internet, from increasingly portable personal computers to games consoles and smart TVs to, especially, smartphones and tablets. Moreover, the line of access has gradually incorporated a wide range of networked appliances and implements which are habitually used for everyday and professional purposes ('smart' objects or things). That could include home/office or industrial communication, upkeep of spaces, record-keeping, energy-supply, security, accounting, finance and management, health, entertainment, employment systems ... almost any regularly employed mechanical affordance. Such access points are not for voluntarily linking to the internet, but for facilitating the employment of mechanical affordances via the internet. Alongside materially extending the line of voluntary and involuntary access, the internet has also gradually incorporated automated Internet Technology systems, some with sophisticated machine-learning capacities. These typically work at some distance from the line of voluntary or involuntary access by internet users and inhabitants, but nevertheless bear upon them in numerous ways. These increasingly play a salient role in shaping the Internet Polity.

In synch with the global reach of the Internet Polity and the extended line of voluntary and involuntary access, the internet has been capitalized as a repository and generator of very large-scale data ('big data') on users and inhabitants, and concomitantly on their environments. A burgeoning market for data commerce centred on the internet has developed in the early decades of the twenty-first century, attended by regulatory and governance apparatuses for data maintenance, trading, and capitalization. At least three levels of data work are grounded in Internet Technology. First, the internet naturally enables the bringing together and collation of all kinds of datasets elicited from outside its facilities but recorded within its technological structure. Second, the usage and doings of the internet as facility and space, and moreover the usage of networked appliances and implements, produces a constant flow, recording, and accrual of data—the internet itself could be regarded as a data-generation system. Third, by introducing appropriate standards and specifications in Internet Technology, the data found and generated on the internet could be purposed for various ends, including testing and consolidating the automated systems and machine-learning capacities incorporated into the internet.

The condition that has obtained for the Internet Polity amidst these developments could be thought of as one of becoming *contained* while being scaled up. I choose the word 'contained' advisedly. It indicates that the Internet Polity is no longer co-extensive with the internet as facility and space. The Internet Polity's life has by degrees become confined within a relatively circumscribed space and a limited provision of facilities. In other words, the technological structure that is the Internet—the scope of Internet Technology and Infrastructure—extends well outside what is apprehended as the Internet Polity's space and facility. The Internet Polity's collective may putatively direct its political orientation towards the internet as such, but the internet is now inevitably larger than and significantly outside the reckonings of that collective. Moreover, that unreckoned outside bears upon and is woven into the Internet Polity.

What such containment of the Internet Polity consists of is considered in this chapter, in the manner of a prolegomenon which could lead to further investigations. The notion that the internet has become larger than the scope of the Internet Polity sounds paradoxical; some moves towards unpacking this paradox are suggested here. The Internet Polity's formative first principles and discourse discussed earlier serve to grasp the developing condition of the post-formation Internet Polity.

It is proposed here that there are two mutually supporting sides to this containment.

- On the one hand, the post-2000 developments in Internet Infrastructure limit the voluntary and intentional scope of the Internet Polity. The internet appears as not merely a structure which persons use for their purposes and inhabit for their doings, but one through which purposes and doings are designed or structured from above. This happens to a significant degree *despite* the Internet Polity rather than in its terms. Extended thus, the internet as space and facility serves to make social activity increasingly productive in a dual sense. First, such activity becomes more efficient, enhanced, convenient, remunerative, controlled, policed, etc. in users' and service-providers' terms; and second, such activity provides fodder—data—for the networked appliances and automated processes to be reproduced and proliferated.
- On the other hand, the collective life of the Internet Polity is concurrently concentrated within increasingly regulated and regularized settings. The circulations of Internet Polity discourse, and the interweaving of actually existing and online collectivity, are largely zoned accordingly now. To begin with, the mass of communications, doings, activities that characterize the Internet Polity converge upon a limited number of mega platforms ('social networking sites' or 'social media platforms'). These mega platforms allow for all those activities to be largely conducted

within coherent Information Technology substructures, i.e., within the remit of a small number of computer languages and networked programmes. That also facilitates large-scale data collection. Further, insofar as a great many activities still occur on smaller platforms (formal or informal), involving a considerable diversity of Internet Technology substructures, coherent standards and interoperable mechanisms have been embedded. These allow those diverse platforms to be garnered for large-scale data elicitation too.

These two aspects of the Internet Polity's containment operate within a continuous cycle of production and reproduction. The political economy that motivates and drives this cycle is grounded in real-world interests, especially governmental and commercial. How those interests play within and upon the Internet Polity is a pressing question and much discussion is directed to this at present, though mostly in a piecemeal fashion. Anxious discussion has focused on such issues (and catchwords) as 'digital divides', 'platform capitalism', 'big data' in relation to privacy and surveillance, 'information bubbles' and 'disinformation', the relation of these to the changing nature of employment and social stratifications, etc. Urgent as the issues are, a considered account of them is outside the scope of this book. However, the twofold containment of the Internet Polity is the ground upon which those hotly debated concerns have arisen. Even this chapter's cursory description of such containment will speak to current anxieties and deliberations.

The cursory description of the Internet Polity's containment here continues with the method followed to describe its formation in Part II. The two mutually supporting sides of the containment can be traced via two sets of catchwords: one clustered around 'Internet of Things' or 'smart' objects and the other clustered around 'social networking'. The shifting connotations and careers of these catchwords in relation to others trace the process through which the Internet Polity's containment has crystallized. The latter two sections of this chapter are devoted by turn to these. Terms surrounding these catchwords are intricately interconnected, and modifications in the Internet Polity's social and political first principles can be discerned.

Before focusing on those catchwords, I present a section with brief observations on the twenty-first century social contexts through which the post-formation condition of the Internet Polity emerged. To be precise, instead of contextualizing these developments as conditioned by social junctures, I pause on a distinctive dynamic involved in contextualizing or historicizing itself apropos of the internet in the twenty-first century. These observations are necessarily given in an impressionistic manner—their import is too weighty to be succinctly covered here.

6.2 Social Junctures: The 2000s

Earlier in this study, I have introduced various facets of the Internet Polity's emergence with brief accounts of socio-historical junctures: the Cold War in Chap. 2, the student and civil liberties protests and militarization of academic research in Chap. 3, late 1980s and early 1990s privatization policies in Chap. 4. These were based on the received historicist assumption that social phenomena—including the technological—are consequent upon political, economic, and cultural determinants, and are significantly at the behest of actually existing interests and power structures. That also gels with my passing observation that governmental and commercial agendas have driven the containment of the Internet Polity.

However, such a historicist assumption now immediately recalls debates about 'technological determinism'. One is reminded of arguments asserting that rather than being determined by social factors, technological innovations determine social developments. Historians should therefore approach these accordingly. Views on this have generally been divided between 'soft' and 'hard'. 'Soft' technological determinism holds that technology should be put alongside and in some horizontal relationship with economic, political, and cultural factors in accounting for social change and the historical process. 'Hard' approaches maintain that technology has a precedent thrust and itself determines economic, political, and social circumstances. On the whole, historians of technology and society have favoured a range of 'soft' approaches. When undertaken, collective scholarly reckonings have gone that way, such as, with a historicist emphasis, Merritt Smith and Leo Marx eds., *Does Technology Drive History?* (1994) and, with a sociological emphasis, Jan Servaes ed., *Technological Determinism and Social Change* (2014). Such reckonings were themselves responses to the growing popularity of technological determinism in political and economic discourses since the 1980s, notably with the advent of computing and the internet. Contributors to Smith and Marx (1994) took a long view of the concept in historiographical and historicist terms. The volume itself, as the editors noted, was of the moment:

> we need only look at the world of the 1990s to revivify the intuitively compelling idea that technological innovation is a major driving force of contemporary history, if not the primary driving force. [...] 'technological determinism' has been redefined; it now refers to the human tendency to create the kind of society that invests technologies with enough power to drive history. If any particular form of human power now has an outstanding claim to that distinction, it probably is technological power. Indeed, one of our chief reasons for collecting these essays is our sense of the increasingly strong hold of that claim on the public imagination. People seem all too willing to believe that innovations in technology embody humanity's choice of its future. (Smith and Marx 1994, xiv)

The edited volume appeared at the height of enthusiasm about 'information superhighway' policies and commercial drives (discussed in Chap. 4). Though developments in computing were mentioned only in passing, that motivating background for this volume was not circumstantial. Servaes's (2014) edited collection a couple of decades later showed how inextricable the internet as facility and space had become in considering arguments about technological determinism.

In fact, talking about, referring to, and studying the internet constituted a discourse that was peculiarly concentrated on deterministic expectations of technology through the 1990s. That was not just in the legislative pushes by governments in public-interest areas (especially education and information/knowledge management) or in the all-embracing financialization of internet services by commercial enterprises. It was only to be expected that promotional zeal focused on the internet would be infused with such deterministic convictions in governmental and commercial circles. Beyond that and more widely, technological determinism was variously infused in the Internet Polity discourse that came together, in the enthusiastic cadences of its vocabulary (see Chap. 5). Moreover, insofar as the internet became a focus of academic investigations outside technological disciplines, both exuberant anticipation of and gloomy disquiet about its impact acknowledged the power of its social determinations. A curious indicator here was the appearance of the *future* as an explicit horizon in general histories of the internet, giving this area of historicizing an unabashedly teleological character. Thus, in Michael Hauben and Rhonda Hauben's *Netizens* (1997), the history of USENET/Internet in Parts II and III glided smoothly into prognostications in Part IV; John Naughton's history was entitled *A Brief History of the Future* (1999) and John Ryan's entitled *A History of the Internet and the Digital Future* (2010); the influential article by Barry Leiner et al. (2009) giving 'A Brief History of the Internet' ended with a 'History of the Future' section. Books, reports, academic papers, policy documents, journalistic articles, etc. on the future of the internet and the future moulded by the internet are now legion. By the twentieth century *fin de siècle*, talking about the internet without subscribing to some kind of technological determinism seemed a challenge (Deva 1997; Daly 2000). Since then, it has occasionally seemed that the very concept of technological determinism was being honed by and on the internet. For instance, Tim Jordan's *Hacking* (2008) argued that the conceptual lines of technological determinism could be sharpened by contemplating hacking—thus reviving something of the 1980s glamour that attached to hackers (discussed in Chap. 5):

> Hackers are warriors of technological determinism through a dual movement. They identify where a technology is determining them in ways they dislike – from having to pay for phone calls to having email spied on – and they engage in altering that technology, which thereby automatically produces new ways in which technology can determine action. By engaging with the everyday determinations of technology, hackers enact the sociality of technology; we will constantly find hackers reconstructing the nature of a particular technology, recasting what that technology will enable a user to do, and in doing so providing living proof of the social criticism of technological determinist arguments. But, at the same time, we see that there is a constant subjection to everyday determinations of technology. (Jordan 2008, 14–15)

Put in other words, by referring to 'hacking' as a real activity and using it as a synecdoche, Jordan presented the internet as a site for negotiating technological determinism. He argued that the lines of determinations can be produced, resisted, and reproduced constantly, which paradoxically reiterates technological determinism via the internet continuously.

Despite my brief accounts of formative social junctures for the internet in earlier chapters, this historicist study has neither discounted nor affirmed the validity of technological deterministic convictions. To account for the construction of the technological structure that is the internet, and the formation of the Internet Polity with its collectivizing first principles and discourse, it has been expedient to take a conventional historicist approach at times. But once the internet was established as facility and space, it became difficult to gauge the Internet Polity as merely acted upon by political, economic, and cultural forces that are meaningfully extrinsic to the internet. A subsuming conviction in technological determinism simply characterizes the twenty-first century Internet Polity as such. It has become engrained in its discursive context, grounded in its political first principles, and subjugates its post-formation collectivity. The containment of the Internet Polity may well be coterminous with its subsumption in technological determinism.

There are other reasons for being circumspect about taking a conventional historicist approach to the twenty-first century Internet Polity. The very resources and practices of historicizing have been drawn into the internet's facilities and space, so that historical accounting of the internet inextricably implicates the mediation of its object of study. To some degree this has to do with the process of doing history—the practice of historical research—itself, as with the practices of other academic disciplines. Digitization of historical archives, the accrual of digital-born sources, shifts in searching and associative linking. digital platform-based presentation and communication of historical knowledge, growing interest in more numerate approaches to history (cliometrics and cliodynamics) facilitated by digital data collocations, etc. are all now established aspects of the practice of history and are all mediated by the internet. When the internet is itself the object of historical research, the process of research finds itself grounded in its object. The internet is, after all, recorded most intensively from its inception and that record is on the internet. History itself seems implicit in that which it holds up to scrutiny when its object is the internet.

Besides shifts in the practice of history, from the beginning of the twenty-first century the identification of historically significant events generally became imbricated with the mediation of the internet. In other words, the narrative of history-in-the-making seemed to be routed through the internet, and history as it was made appeared to consolidate the Internet Polity. In this respect, the terrorist attacks of 11 September 2001 (9/11), which were immediately pegged as a world historical event, are worth pausing on. It was variously noted soon after that perceptions of this event were significantly set through the internet. Or, to flip that, it was pegged as the global event after which it became natural to look to the internet to set perceptions. For several decades before that, it had become commonplace to consider that such world historical events were the instant productions of mainstream print and broadcast mass media, structured by a corporate logic of spectatorship and consumption. Memorably, in a series of essays in 1991, Jean Baudrillard (1995 [1991]) had observed that the 1990–1991 Gulf War was presented through the mainstream media in so preconceived a manner, in terms of stereotypes and advertising routines, that it became difficult to feel it was happening at all: 'the media promote the war, the war promotes the media, and advertising competes with the media' (31). By and large, 9/11 was narrated and presented similarly at the time, and was immediately received with a touch of Baudrillardian doubt (Gupta 2002; Schechter 2003; Silberstein 2004). However, a year later the Pew Internet and American Life Project published a report entitled *One Year Later: September 11 and the Internet* (2002). This was among the earliest to consider the public record of the global event aside from mainstream media—and also, for that matter, from what used to be alternative media then, which meant mainly regional broadcast and print media. The internet offered an alternative to mainstream news circulation, and yet with a global reach. Moreover, it opened an alternative mode for public responsiveness, by, for instance, having communication facilities that could be used to organize campaigns and protests. The internet appeared as a means for both circulating news and intervening in the news.

Accordingly, the Pew report (2002, Part 3) was particularly attentive to the evidence for do-it-yourself journalism and disclosure or non-disclosure of information on official websites. The most revealing dimension of the report, however, was not in what it documented but in its structuring assumption. The assumption was that a global event like 9/11 becomes such through collective engagement with the internet as facility and space. Put otherwise, the global importance of 9/11 is pinned down by patterns of internet usage *before* and *after*. The global event is a defining juncture because it is marked as a blip or step-change across the various dimensions of internet usage. So, for the Pew report (2002), 9/11 was the juncture which led to intense and widespread online communications beyond the formal: personal reassurances, information and guidance sharing, organizing mutual help, assistance and advocacy actions, etc. The notion that 9/11 provides a defining juncture in internet engagement then settled into academic and professional discourse. The historical record of 9/11 spiralled out towards presenting the internet as not only reflective of social conditions before and after, but as generative or productive of social conditions thereafter. The record began to track the effect of internet connectivity itself on responses to 9/11 (Kim et al. 2004 onwards), and to peg the internet as playing a distinct part in terrorism and counter terrorism after 9/11 (e.g., Janbek and Williams 2014) or in citizen protests and activism after 9/11 (e.g., Rohlinger and Brown 2009). The path was paved towards conceiving of the internet as both the repository of the newsworthy record and as a tool for manipulating that record. Historicizing seemed set to become subject to the facilitating and spatial dimensions of the Internet Polity, through future world historical events—the 2003 USA-led invasion of Iraq, the 2007–2008 financial crisis, Arab Spring and anti-austerity movements from 2010 onwards, rise of right-wing alignments worldwide, the growing urgency of climate-change activism, the COVID 19 pandemic in 2020–2021, the Russian invasion of Ukraine from 2022 and the Israeli invasion of Gaza after the Hamas attack in October 2023 and onwards. In being reported and recorded, each of these was tracked as disturbances in the space and facility of the internet, and as nodes in the collective life of the Internet Polity.

In this respect, let me pause on the significance of the internet itself becoming a theme in global news around the twentieth century *fin de siècle*, with the dot-com crash of 2000. Rapid stock-market growth from internet ventures and start-ups through the later 1990s till 10 March 2000 (Ankerson 2018: 160) was followed by precipitous decline. A bursting of the 'dot-com bubble' followed, with consequent closure of businesses, ruthless downsizing, bailouts, and job losses. Numerous studies reconsidered the internet as a business facility and space in view of this decline (Castells 2001; Kuo 2001; Malmsten et al. 2001; Lewis 2001; Laurel 2001; Perkins and Perkins 2001; Cellan-Jones 2001 among others). Reviewing a number of these, Geert Lovink (2002) observed:

> These very different narratives all share a desire to convey the excitement of their historical moment [...]. Their continuing dedication to network technologies and trust in commercial applications is overwhelming. Remarkably, in all these works, authors writing from divergent perspectives, the ideological origins of the dotcom model remain uncontested. (Lovink 2002, 130)

Instead of ideological doubts, in the aftermath of the dot-com crisis technology investors and developers focused on consolidating the industry on more sustainable grounds. One such investor, Roger McNamee (2004) influentially announced an emerging 'New Normal' of steady profit-making for investors in the e-commerce sector (on this, see Gupta 2022: 31–32). In fact, the onward career of the internet as a commercial facility and space seemed so certain that the direct fallout of the doc-com crisis on Internet Technology and the Internet Polity has received only bitty attention since. For instance, in her history of website design Megan Ankerson (2018) gave a useful account of the discourses leading up to and after the dot-com crisis, and marked a change in the character of website designs. Whereas before the crisis, the emphasis was on experimental and ostentatious designs, exemplified by the early versions of Flash web-design platform, after the crisis there was a shift towards staid usability:

> As the notion of the web auteur came under fire for stylistic excess, a new dominant discourse of 'usability' gained traction, a discourse that downplayed the designer and emphasized the user. In this moment, quality web design was less a cinematic experience for viewers or an experimental venue for designers; it was easy, efficient, and above all, usable. Whether tempering the wild excesses of the market or the interface, the 'return to fundamentals' that followed the bust involved disciplining overindulgence and hysteria with new sets of rules for evaluating worth. In the world of stock-market speculation and the world of web design alike, emotion and affect were to be toned down in favor of rationality, science, and user testing. (Ankerson 2018, 163)

Ankerson exemplified this observation with reference to the later career of Flash towards gradual disinvestments from it, and the functionalities offered by Web 2.0. However, such observations present but a surface apprehension of the impact of the dot-com crash of 2000. It seems likely that the consolidation of e-commerce and the internet as a facility and space after that juncture was implicit in—was a quiet driver for—all the moves outlined earlier towards the containment of the Internet Polity. The profound changes that have taken place in Internet Infrastructure were crucial for that consolidation and continued expansion.

The development of the 'Internet of Things' and 'smart' implements/systems and of 'social networking sites' with global reach took place after the dot-com crisis, and were arguably motivated by it. I turn to these in the next two sections. The integration of automation and Artificial Intelligence into the internet also followed accordingly, which I just about touch upon below. Perhaps most importantly, the underpinning rationale of data mining and the commodification of data that are woven through these developments emerged in degrees after the dot-com crash. When it took place in the very early 2000s, the former were an abstract possibility. The architecture for undergirding e-commerce systems with data-mining algorithms was beginning to be contemplated in digital technology forums (e.g., Dhond et al. 2000; Ansari et al.

2001) when the crash took place. Forming a functional market for data, or managing and transacting with data as commodity, was naturally a comparatively slow process. And yet, given the scale of legislative and governmental systematizing involved, it developed remarkably quickly after the crash. The market for data formed as quickly, in fact, as developments in Internet Infrastructure, the 'Internet of Things' and global 'social networking sites'. Contemplating the legal implications of data mining at an early stage, Kirsten Wahlstrom et al. (2006) mainly focused on ethical issues like privacy, accuracy, and stereotyping. They noted in passing that the commodification of data was beginning to raise the stakes for all of these:

> Recently, there has been an emerging trend to use personal data as a resource and offer it for sale. Information is easy to copy and re-sell many times. The phrase *data mining* uses the metaphor of the exploitation of natural resources, further contributing to the perception of *data as commodity*. (Wahlstrom et al. 2006, Section 3.1, Legal Context)

The useful pointer to the role played by the metaphor of 'mining' has a significant history since the early 1990s (Kerssens 2019 discussed the rich stew of metaphors that attach to 'data', especially 'mining'). In another paper at the time, H.M. Davis and J.N. Vickery (2007, 27) considered changing norms in scholarly research, publication, and ownership given what they called the emerging 'commoditization' of 'datasets'. These were the early glimmerings of a data-centred phenomenon which was set to explode within the next decade, with innumerable publications about 'data brokers', 'data warehousing', 'enterprise data', 'Big Data optimization' … In a pervasive way, the Internet Polity came to be both comprehended by and subjected to machinations upon its 'datafication' (a neologism introduced shortly afterwards, see Mejias and Couldry 2019; Edmond et al. 2022; Burkhardt et al. 2022).

By way of outlining the containment of the Internet Polity, I turn now to brief concluding observations on the phrases 'Internet of Things'/'smart' technologies and 'social networking', and other catchwords associated with these.

6.3 'Internet of Things'/'Smart' Objects

'Internet of Things' has been a runaway catchphrase from around 2004, and its usage-frequency continues to increase (Graph 6.1).

My impression is that though used intensively in management, governmental, and certain academic areas, it is not quite a popular catchphrase. The phrase is mainly confined to professional circles. It appears rarely, for instance, in general news broadsheets and websites, but frequently in newsletters for professional communities, policy and commercial reports and briefings, and condition-of-the-field research reviews. It is not a technical term that engineers or computer programmers use often in their ground-level research. The phrase draws together a diverse range of technologies for strategic purposes. It is mostly a top-down term, less meaningful at the bottom, however that bottom is understood—whether at the rock face of focused technology research and development, or whether at the baseline of everyday communications.

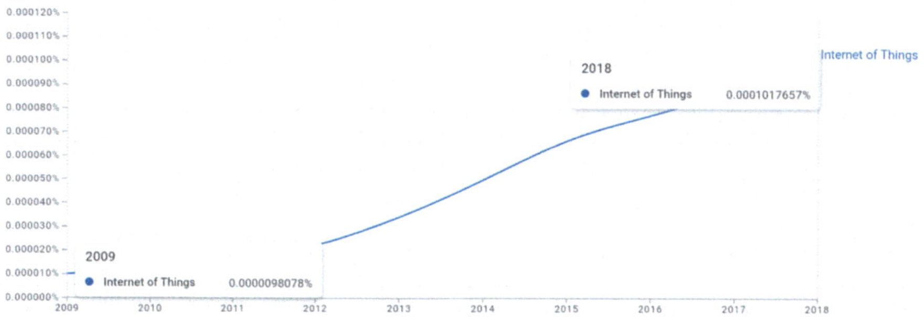

Graph 6.1 Google Ngram Viewer graph: usage-frequency of 'Internet of Things' (case insensitive), 2009–2018, showing over a tenfold increase in this period

Nevertheless, it features now in several general language dictionaries, including the online OED: 'A proposed development of the internet in which many everyday objects are embedded with microchips giving them network connectivity, allowing them to send and receive data'. This definition, however, says very little about its connotations in the professional circles where it is a catchphrase.

In fact, in this instance the business of defining says much about the catchphrase's thrust. In the relevant professional circles, the act of defining 'Internet of Things' itself serves several functions. First, definitions are designed to be inclusive of recent technological developments in different areas, often expressed in diverse registers, under a joined-up strategy and policy rubric. Usually such defining negotiates with such prior definitions to come up with a consolidated one. Second, every given definition flattens the chronological steps that are implicit in the phrase's career, suggesting that it has now acquired a consensual, standardized, and ahistorical validity. To this end, such definitions are most influentially given by regulatory bodies and professional associations (in this case, beginning with the International Telecommunication Union 2005). Third, each new definition suggests coordinated directions of application and implementation from the juncture at which it is offered. Defining 'Internet of Things' involves stock-taking labour and negotiation between a wide range of research fields and applications.

The struggle to define 'Internet of Things' accordingly—and also 'smart' technologies, on which more below—is well presented in publications on the issue. In this vein, Jorge Ibarra-Esquer et al. (2017) gave a considered account of existing definitions of 'Internet of Things', noting three consecutive phases: an early phase (later 1990s to 2005), focusing on what gets connected to the internet; an establishment phase (2009 to 2011), with the emphasis on the 'things' that get connected; and a further phase (from 2012 onwards), turning towards 'the role of things as data producers and the network as enabler of new services' (10). The definition which seems to cover the current phase of the 'Internet of Things' appeared with the authorizing heft of IEEE (2015), in a report giving a fulsome account of the many areas and registers involved. These were condensed here into two definitions, one for less complex systems (generally under one management), and the other for more complex systems (usually involving multiple managements) of the 'Internet of Things' (IoT). For the former, the IEEE definition is:

> An IoT is a network that connects uniquely identifiable 'Things' to the Internet. The 'Things' have sensing/actuation and potential programmability capabilities. Through the exploitation of unique identification and sensing, information about the 'Thing' can be collected and the state of the 'Thing' can be changed from anywhere, anytime, by anything. (IEEE 2015, 74)

And for the more complex:

> Internet of Things envisions a self-configuring, adaptive, complex network that interconnects 'things' to the Internet through the use of standard communication protocols. The interconnected things have physical or virtual representation in the digital world, sensing/actuation capability, a programmability feature and are uniquely identifiable. The representation contains information including the thing's identity, status, location or any other business, social or privately relevant information. The things offer services, with or without human intervention, through the exploitation of unique identification, data capture and communication, and actuation capability. The service is exploited through the use of intelligent interfaces and is made available anywhere, anytime, and for anything taking security into consideration. (IEEE 2015, 74)

The terms in these were carefully chosen, arrived at through numerous qualifications and resolutions of differentiated usage. The decision to have two definitions, at different levels of complexity and management responsibility, is itself testimony to the challenges faced here. Generally, one might expect the more complex definition to include the less complex, but here that evidently seemed a step too ambitious. The difference in complexity seems to rest in their implied levels of autonomy. In the less complex, the 'thing' can be controlled 'from anywhere, anytime, *by* anything'; in the more complex, the 'thing' offers 'services' that are controlled via 'intelligent interfaces' and 'made available anywhere, anytime, *for* anything'. The 'intelligent interfaces' is where significant degree of control is autonomized. Also, of interest here are the eloquent quotation marks around 'thing', the significance of which comes up below.

Evidently, given the predominantly strategic and policy purposes they serve, such definitions emphasize the technological content encompassed by the phrase at a given juncture. By content, I mean, the definitions give a succinct enumeration of the parts and relationships which form the whole of the 'Internet of Things'. Insofar as these have effects on collective life, typically such definitions of content have led to discussions of beneficent applications in social areas: such as, domestic setups, urban planning, health provision, education delivery, environmental sustainability, trading and markets, security and defence. The kinds of benefits in question were usefully summarized as follows by Friedemann Mattern and Christian Floerkemeier (2010), quite early in the passages of the phrase:

> from a *commercial point of view*, increased efficiency of business processes and reduced costs in warehouse logistics and in service industries (by automating and outsourcing to the customer), improved customer retention and more targeted selling, and new business models involving smart things and associated services. Of interest from a *social and political point of view* is a general increase in the quality of life due to consumers and citizens being able to obtain more comprehensive information, due to improved care for people in need of help

> thanks to smart assistance systems, and also due to increased safety, for example on roads. From a *personal point of view*, what matters above all are new services enabled by an Internet of Things which would make life more pleasant, entertaining, independent and also safer, for example by locating things that are lost, such as pets or even other people. (Mattern and Floerkemeier 2010, 247)

All these 'points of view' seem to be expressive of an overarching technocratic perspective, i.e., the area-wise perspectives that an entrepreneur, policymaker, manager, etc. may put on a Gannt chart of 'benefits' apropos of investments in the content of the Internet of Things.

While these definitional features say much about where the phrase 'Internet of Things' has purchase, they do not say much about what it signifies for the Internet Polity. The Internet Polity does not quite possess such coherent 'points of view'. Rather, the Internet Polity has a collective orientation towards the Internet as facility and space, structured by its first principles and discourse. To get to what the phrase 'Internet of Things' implies for the condition of the Internet Polity, a somewhat unorthodox question seems worth posing: *If the 'Internet of Things' qualifies what is, so to speak, internetted (i.e., 'things'), what is the 'internet' without qualification regarded as internetting*? Or, put differently: *when we say 'Internet of Things', we know that 'Things' are cross-connected in some way; when we simply say 'internet', what do we understand as being cross-connected?* Evidently, the 'internet' that the Internet Polity developed a collective orientation towards was grounded in an understanding of internetting some-*thing*, in relation to (in comparison with, in contrast to) which the 'Internet of Things' is understood. If this qualifying term of earlier implication can be sharpened, some reasonable inferences can be made about what the qualifier 'of Things' suggests for the principles and discourse of the Internet Polity.

This question does not have a straightforward answer, and to many it would sound somewhat naïve—almost a fool's question. The technically valid answers are obvious, and come pat. One is stated in the title of Mattern and Floerkemeier's (2010) paper, just quoted: 'From the Internet of Computers to the Internet of Things'. Thus, 'of computers' seems the obvious answer. And yet the first visionary sentences of that early explanation of 'Internet of Things' complicated matters already:

> The Internet of Things represents a vision in which the Internet extends into the real world embracing everyday objects. Physical items are no longer disconnected from the virtual world, but can be controlled remotely and can act as physical access points to Internet services. (Mattern and Floerkemeier 2010, 242).

Here, the internet seems to become the active subject that *extends* and *embraces* everyday objects in the real world; whereas if it were merely a system of connected computers, one might say it is composed also of objects, 'computers'—which, by 2010, were on the way to becoming everyday objects. A more considered answer appeared in the same year in a paper by Ding et al. (2010), defining three kinds of 'clustering' networks which are variously woven together: 'Internet', 'Internet of Things', 'social networks':

> The Internet is a network with plenty of data based on fast transmission hardware and software. [...] The first generation of Internet, now called Web 1.0, is a kind of media publisher. [....] The main characteristic of Web 2.0 is personal publishing and interaction. [...] Internet of Things (IoT) is a network of objects. The name of IoT came from two meanings. One is that its core and basis is the Internet and it is a kind of extension of the Internet. The other is that its users are extended to any objects and things. In IoT, objects are connected with each other by wire or wireless equipments. [...] Social network is a network of people. (Ding et al. 2010, 417)

The 'Internet' is then 'of data' which is published/communicated by users (also taken thus in Santucci 2009, of the European Commission), whereas the 'Internet of Things' is 'of objects'.

The characterizations of the 'internet' as 'of computers' and 'of published/communicated data' are technically accurate and yet seem to tiptoe around the Internet Polity's orientation towards it as facility and space. That is to say, the political principles and discourse that formed a collective with reference to the 'internet' had it pegged powerfully as an 'Internet of Humans' (for the Internet Polity) or 'Internet of Users' (from a producer perspective, see Grudin 1993). 'Computer' was conceived as inevitably engaged by persons; 'data' as emanating from and expressing persons. It seems reasonable to consider that the phrase 'Internet of Things' made sense by implicitly taking the existing 'internet' as being an 'Internet of Humans'. 'Humans' was the counterpoint in terms of which 'things' were named as such. In fact, this thrust was clearly traced in the early negotiations of the idea underpinning and then the early emphases put on the phrase 'Internet of Things'.

The seminal moves towards the concept of 'Internet of Things' traced a path of reducing human engagement in the facility and space of the internet. Along this path, Mark Weiser's (1991) formulation of 'ubiquitous computing', whereby remotely controlled microcomputers could be embedded in all sorts of appliances, is an obvious starting point. This was conceived as realizing 'technologies [that] disappear in the background' (80), so that at least a reduction of active human awareness of computer usage takes place. Shortly afterwards, Reza Raji (1994) envisioned an integration of data networks with an increased place for control networks, which would reduce the space for user control and regulation of networks. The line of conceiving reduced human control and engagement with networked computers can be traced from there, in various specialist areas, to the popular exposition in Neil Garshenfeld's *When Things Start to Think* (1999):

> For all of the coverage of the growth of the Internet and the World Wide Web, a far bigger change is coming as the number of things using the Net dwarfs the number of people. The real promise of connecting computers is to free people, by embedding the means to solve problems in the things around us. (Garshenfeld 1999, 9–10)

With the actual centring of the phrase 'Internet of Things', the relationship thereof to the (by implication) 'Internet of Humans' was pretty clearly articulated there. This was especially so in the influential International Telecommunication Union (ITU) report (2005). It appeared first and foremost as a market rationale, always an inevitable mover in capitalist economies:

> Today, in the 2000s, we are heading into a new era of ubiquity, where the 'users' of the internet will be counted in billions and where humans may become the minority as generators and receivers of traffic. Instead, most of the traffic will flow between devices and all kinds of 'things', thereby creating a much wider and more complex 'Internet of Things', the core subject of this report.
>
> If humans are the only internet users of the future, then the total user base cited above might conceivably double, but is unlikely to go beyond two billion active users in the near future. On the other hand, if 'things' become active internet users on behalf of humans, then the number of active connections could be measured in terms of tens or hundreds of billions. (ITU 2005, 1)

The expansion from humans to 'things' as internet users was conceived, then, as a matter of numbers. Notably, the 'things' would be 'active internet users *on behalf of humans*', so that ultimately the economy of consumption would still be focused on human consumption. The numbers indicate a market building turn, a way of getting past a saturated market. This was noted more quietly in the report, as a kind of aside:

> On the commercial side, [...] operators and equipment vendors are 'running out' of consumers to whom they can sell current telecommunication services and equipment, that don't already have it, at least in the developed economies. Thus, the prospects of a new emerging market for thing-to-thing communications are both exciting and essential to sustain future growth prospects. (ITU 2005, 7)

Much of the report was devoted to explaining why this would be useful apart from being profitable for those 'operators and equipment vendors', i.e., elaborating strenuously on the services and benefits, pointing out conveniences and advantages that the ultimately human consumers are not aware of or demanding yet (Chaps. 3 to 6). Alongside building awareness of consumable needs that are not yet felt, it observed that the 'Internet of Things' promises to expand by paradoxically reducing awareness of how those needs would be served. The latter would, after all, work *on behalf of* humans rather than *at their behest*, or they could be thought of as agents working for humans. Weiser's (1991) idea of 'ubiquity', which works by technology disappearing in the background, was given full scope—in the report, a box was devoted to the usage of the word 'ubiquitous' (2), seemingly to push it to the foreground of Internet Polity discourse.

On that last point, another interesting turn is found in the ITU report (2005), which came to be elaborated variously in later years. Some of the report (Chap. 2) was devoted to giving an overall sense of what the technological content of the 'Internet of Things' would be, in much the way it came to be realized. In brief, this involved:

- an identification/tagging mechanism for 'things', RFID (radio-frequency identification);
- incorporating wireless sensors in 'things' to gauge environments and 'smart materials' to respond to environmental changes;
- miniaturing 'things' and distributing them more extensively or intensively;
- and, of course, setting up arrangements for such 'things' to gather and share data of their usage with each other via the internet.

The last critical step was considered in a relatively cursory manner in the ITU report (2005), with a gesture towards 'next-generation networks'. A more developed imagining of this aspect as the core of the 'Internet of Things' was offered earlier by Gershenfeld et al. (2004), proposing an 'Internet-0' where each 'thing', now effectively a basic computer-in-itself, would be linked upon the Internet Protocol (IP). They anticipated some distinctive layers being added in the protocol stack for processing the explosion of data transmissions between 'things'. Since then, to this fundamental structure ever greater degrees of complexity and differentiations have been adduced, especially by incorporating machine-learning capacities (AI) at various levels ... The point I am reaching towards is that simply with this basic structure of 'Internet of Things', the 'things' in question came to be conceived as rather more than simply inanimate objects or implements. They seemed to become imbued with, in a catchy way, 'smartness' (in the American English sense) or 'intelligence'. In the ITU report (2005), 'things' were envisaged as set to became not just agents for humans but more or less autonomous communicators and users alongside human, where the internet itself becomes a sort of embodiment of the systemic intelligence of 'things' *and* humans:

> The internet as we know it is set to transform radically. From an academic network for the chosen few, it will become a fully pervasive, interactive and intelligent system. Real-time communications will be possible not only by humans but also by objects at anytime and from anywhere. (ITU 2005, 123)

The internet in a general way was now re-envisaged as a technological structure composed of two interwoven dimensions, an 'Internet of Things' and an 'Internet of Humans', which are co-dependent, cooperative, and independently zoned at the same time. But the political economy of this structure remained grounded in the 'Internet of Humans'—towards which, we may add, the collective of the Internet Polity confines its orientation, or its first principles and discourse. This is one of the nubs of the Internet Polity's containment. We may say that the internet (of 'things' and humans) had simply been taken outside the scope of internet as facility and space apropos of which the Internet Polity had formed. This renewed vision of internet appeared *despite* the Internet Polity's first principles and discourse.

Various moves to garner the 'Internet of Things' according to this vision, by ensuring convergence in technological production and consumption and by agreeing market standards, were energetically underway before long. The Internet Protocol for Smart Objects (IPSO) Alliance was formed in 2008 (see OMASpecWorks website 'About' page) to promote the Internet Protocol for communications between 'things'. The Web of Things initiative by the World Wide Web consortium, especially from around 2014 onwards, worked 'to counter the fragmentation of the IoT by using and extending existing, standardized Web technologies' (W3C Web of Things website; for an overview of the architecture, see Guinard and Trifa 2016). The Industrial Internet Consortium was formed in 2014 by a number of large corporations, becoming the Industrial Internet of Things (IoT) Consortium in 2021, to coordinate investment and strategy for industrial productions and applications (on the remit of the 'Industrial Internet of Things' see Misra et al. 2021). More indicatively for this study, even as those moves at the level of developing Internet Technology and Internet Infrastructure were forming, concepts of a 'Social Internet of Things' (SIoT) were proposed. These effectively upped the separateness and counterpoint of the 'Internet of Things' apropos of the 'Internet of Humans' by envisaging—or rather instilling—principles of *social* relationships, powerfully grounded in human collectivity, into networks of 'things'. Introducing the 'paradigm', Luigi Atzori (2011) envisaged three possibilities arising out of doing so:

- Give the IoT a structure that can be shaped as required to guarantee network navigability, so as that object and service discovery is effectively performed and scalability is guaranteed like in human social networks [...].
- Extend the use of models designed to study social networks to address IoT related issues (intrinsically related to extensive networks of interconnected objects).
- Create a level of trustworthiness to be used for leveraging the level of interaction among things that are 'friends'. (Atzori 2011, 1193)

These were soon expanded in Luigi Atzori et al. (2012), and the idea has been gradually fleshed out in papers and several edited journal special issues and books. The insidious animating of 'things' in the 'Internet of Things' apropos of humans has effectively been collectivized in the way human socialness and society have conventionally been apprehended.

Way more pervasively than the rarefied circles in which the SIoT is discussed, the animating of 'things' has been popularly disseminated through the catchword or catch-prefix 'smart'. It is, of course, particularly strongly associated with 'smartphones' since the mid-1990s, initially as a brand name and then as the networked mobile device we cannot quite do without now (of which more in the next section). But pervasively, in everyday exchanges the prefix has come to be attached to all kinds of appliances, material systems, and infrastructures, mainly through product branding and advertising and various future-gazing policy/strategy manifestos. Through those fluid associations and disseminations, the term has also gradually been harnessed to technical precision and definition. Noting its growing popularity in relation to technological applications, a paper by Goddard et al. (1997) was the first to attempt a scientific definition for 'smart technologies'. They built upon it with a definition for 'smart systems', as possessing '*an inherent ability to gather information on its operating environment or history, to process that information in order to draw intelligent inferences from it and to act on those inferences by changing its characteristics in an advantageous manner*' (130, italics in original). This was usefully in the direction of cohering with the 'Internet of Things'. In fact, subsequent scientific definitions have not departed far from that, and mainly depended upon negotiating with the fluidity of the term (as in Gutiérrez et al. 2013; Alter 2020). Unsurprisingly, it has come to be correlated with the 'things' in the 'Internet of Things', explicitly in Manuel Silverio-Fernández et al. (2018) via a review of usage in recent publications:

> Ultimately, the key features considered by this study for a device to become "Smart" are connectivity, autonomy and context-awareness. Being connectivity [sic] the most relevant based on the amount of mentions obtained from the literature. (Manuel Silverio-Fernández et al. 2018, 5)

The convergence of popular and scientific usage on 'smart' has tended to focalize 'things' in the 'Internet of Things' as more or less self-actuating, just as the 'internet' actualizes human usage. That also serves, one may argue, to obscure the part of all-too-human control that every account of the 'Internet of Things' leaves a tacit and unremarked space for. This implicit space both preserves and underplays the controlling role of organizational managers in corporate, governmental, and other bodies.

The containment of the Internet Polity, despite itself and through its own consuming power, in this larger internet (of 'things' and of humans) has, obviously, other dimensions than that of the 'Internet of Things' technological structure. A distinctive model of this internet outside the ken and behest of the Internet Polity is, for instance, found in the decentred Blockchain ledgering system for cryptocurrencies. Large spaces in the operation of the internet are opening up with machine-learning capacities sewn in (conceivable as AI entities in legal and discursive senses) which are rather more animate and flexibly serviceable than 'things'. These are beyond the scope of the current study, though very much out there already. The shape of the expanding internet that contains the technological structure, facility, and space that the Internet Polity had formed upon is only impressionistically conveyed by focusing on the catchphrase 'Internet of Things'. Nevertheless, the catchphrase allows for a reasonable grasp of what this kind of containment means, or on what is being contained and in relation to and by what.

6.4 'Social Networking'

Arguably, the containment of the Internet Polity apropos of the 'Internet of Things' was built upon another kind of containment that was enacted and performed within the 'Internet of Humans' already, mainly in the first decade of the twenty-first century. Another catchphrase traces its unfolding: 'social networking' (Graph 6.2).

The broader conceptual shifts behind the extraordinary proliferation of 'social network' (especially where a verb or past participle form of 'network' is foregrounded, as in 'networking' or 'networked') can be variously traced through media discourses of the time. In an economical manner and with the scholarly register in view, Barry Wellman's substantial publications in the area are useful. In the latter part of the 1990s, he and his co-authors got down to bringing 'social network theory' in sociological terms to bear upon examining group and community formation via internet facilities (Wellman et al. 1996; Wellman 1997). The agenda Wellman (1997) set up initially was of mapping computer-aided social networks to preceding and existing forms (categories) of social networks in human collective life: 'to discuss how computer networks support a variety of social networks at work and in the community' (182). The idea was to present internet-based collectivity or 'computer networks' (in the sense I have been calling an 'Internet of Humans' above) as reflecting and accentuating 'social networks' (always of humans), without dramatically reconceptualizing the latter. Accordingly, different kinds of social networks

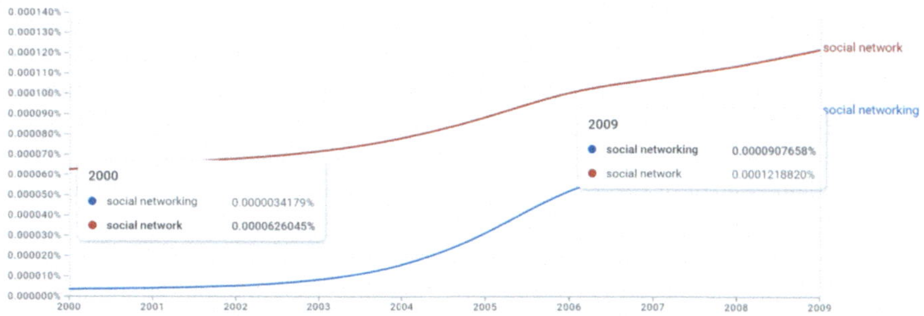

Graph 6.2 Google Ngram Viewer graph: usage-frequency of 'social networking' and 'social network' (case insensitive), 2000–2009, showing respectively a 26-fold increase in this period. 'Social network' has been in used reasonably frequently since the mid-1960s; the verb-form, closely associated with internet activity, took off mainly from the early 2000s

('dense, bounded' and 'sparse, unbounded'/'work' and 'community'), and with different features (boundedness, density, range, etc.), were compared with computer networks as more or less co-extensive. This line was maintained in Wellman's coedited volume with Caroline Haythornthwaite, *The Internet in Everyday Life* (2002a; b). The editors firmly rejected any compromise with technological determinism and averred that computer-mediated social networks had become a mundane part of everyday life:

> We are moving from a world of Internet wizards to a world of ordinary people routinely using the Internet as an embedded part of their lives. It has become clear that the Internet is a very important thing, but not a special thing. (Wellman and Haythornthwaite 2002a, b: 6)

A decade later, Lee Rainey and Wellman in *Networked* (2012) took a quite different turn. This enthusiastically described three 'revolutions': in social networks (computer mediated), internet, and mobile (mainly cell phones to smart phones). This volume averred that received concepts of social networks (human) were modified in significant ways, in terms of work-home demarcations, social hierarchies, privacy and availability, etc. Social networks grounded in technological systems and devices now seemed to be 'transformative' compared to the social networks conceived hitherto. Amidst some weak nods to arguments against technological determinism, this book found that the technology has generated a new phenomenon of 'networked individualism':

> This is the era of free agents and the spirit of personal agency. But it is not the World According to Me – it is not a world of autonomous and increasingly isolated individualists. Rather, it is the World According to the *Connected* Me, where people armed with potent technology tools can extend their networks far beyond what was possible in the past and where they face new constraints and challenges that are outgrowths of networked life. (Rainey and Wellman 2012, 19)

This emergence of 'networked individualism' seemed to be *produced* by technological means and could be thought of as a technologically determined social phenomenon. The revolution-declaring tone of the book was a throwback to writings about the internet in the mid-1990s, and far from the sober sense of the internet being 'not a special thing'. Looking to future developments, Rainey and Wellman were lyrical about the prospects of the 'Internet of Things' for enhancing human social engagements (279–281). Apart from some observations on digital divides, they evinced little interest in the political economy of production and consumption, ownership and control of services and platforms, and the distribution of public and private interests therein.

With the collective orientation of the Internet Polity in mind, let me sketch out some features of the 'social networking' terrain that Wellman and co-authors did not make much of. Brief observations on two features of that terrain follow by turn. These concern, first, 'social networking sites' (or 'social media platforms'), which is in the area of Internet Technology; and second, the smartphone as that has developed to its current form, in the area of Internet Infrastructure.

Conceptually, any facility accessed through the internet where a number of users are able to exchange messages with each other or share information, form groups, and address an open audience could be regarded as a 'social networking site'. That could include bulletin boards, gaming forums, chat and chatroom services and the like. Such sites could focus either on a specific kind of interest (gaming, shopping, education, advocacy, entertainment, etc.) or be open to more fluid everyday exchanges, and be designed for using different media (text, images, films, podcasts, etc.). In this sense, 'social networking sites' have been available at every stage of the internet's development and were seminal in the formation of the Internet Polity in the 1990s. The excitement about these in the 2000s, when the phrase as such became popular, seemed connected to the emergence of a core form amidst distinctive offerings in such sites. The features of the form came to define such sites, put thus by Danah Boyd and Nicole Ellison (2008):

> We define social network sites as web-based services that allow individuals to (1) construct a public or semi-public profile within a bounded system, (2) articulate a list of other users with whom they share a connection, and (3) view and traverse their list of connections and those made by others within the system. The nature and nomenclature of these connections may vary from site to site. [...]
>
> What makes social network sites unique is not that they allow individuals to meet strangers, but rather that they enable users to articulate and make visible their social networks. (Boyd and Ellison 2008, 211)

This form, in other words, was not merely designed for facilitating communications at various levels but for making visible and managing connections for communications. Social networking sites mapped a network of connections and placed users/participants within these mappings. They were designed, in other words, to make communicating seem ostentatiously networked.

The excitement about these in the 2000s was also because, with this core form, several social networking sites had extraordinary global uptake and local penetration, beginning with MySpace. These were all in the domain of the international private or corporate sector, outside and extending beyond the reach of states or transnational governmental entities. Their spread had a narrowing-down pattern, with a relatively small number gradually concentrating uptake. Those that dominate uptake and penetration globally now are household names, taking in over half the world's population: Facebook, YouTube, WhatsApp, Instagram, TikTok, WeChat, Telegram, LinkedIn, etc. Between the form of such sites, mapping networks user-by-user, and the concentration of widening social networking in a relatively small number of mega sites, the life and space of the 'Internet of Humans' seems to become crystallized within them. To a significant extent, the form of social networking sites seems to shape the Internet Polity and become its form. The collective orientation towards the internet of the Internet Polity is increasingly focused on the facility and space of social networking sites, so that its first principles and discourse are negotiated most obviously within these sites. At the same time, the form of the social networking sites confers clearly articulated parameters and boundaries for the Internet Polity, renders its collective life trackable and measurable on massive scales. By largely containing the Internet Polity's discourse and principles within the measurable precincts of social networking sites, the commerce and exploitation of data elicited from that collective engagement with the internet, and the feeding of data into the 'Internet of Things', could take place without gratingly interfering with the Internet Polity—by circumventing the larger 'Internet of Humans'.

I turn briefly now to the main development in Internet Infrastructure that coincided with the emergence of the 'Internet of Things' and social networking sites: smartphones. The appearance of the first modern mass-market smartphones, Apple's Iphone in 2007 and the Android smartphone in 2008, has mainly been discussed as technological achievements, and entrepreneurial and cultural phenomena. Along those lines, the various features that had developed since the early 1990s and been integrated into this one gadget have been historicized (e.g., Woyke 2011; Merchant 2017; Garcia-Swartz and Campbell-Kelly 2022); the extent to which smartphones have been culturally adapted and shaped social and everyday life considered (e.g., Vincent and Haddon 2017; Reid 2018; Miller et al. 2021; Roholt 2023); and their usage in various enterprises and industries examined (e.g. Berry and Schleser 2014; Giachetti 2017). However, there is little in such discussions that throws light on what smartphones have meant for the Internet Polity's principles and discourse. In this respect, the following are noteworthy.

First, the direction of the development of and adaption to smartphones (and other portable mobile networked gadgets) has been to tie in specific gadgets with specific users so that they are continuously mutually implicated. That is to say, the smartphone operates as a continuous record-maker of its user's presence and activities, and the phone number works as an electronic identity number and locator for the user. Portability and convenience ensure that the smartphone is constantly by the body of the user, at rest or in motion. GPS receptors give a universally recognizable location. The user's recourse to various apps allows those to be linked to the user's activities in real time. Data-sharing facilities between apps enhance such linkedness. Moreover, data sharing depends on synchronization, which also allows for a specific user's gadgets for accessing the internet, if more than one (such as, smartphone, smartwatch, desktop, and laptop), to all be linked to each other and tagged to that user. In brief, smartphones have enabled the ultimate global identity number system. To echo Benedict Anderson's (2006 [1983]) terms to describe colonial governance, the uptake of smartphones has actuated a kind of universal bounded 'serialization', producing 'a human landscape of perfect visibility; [where] the condition of this visibility was that everyone, everything, had (as it were) a serial number' (185).

Second, the smartphone—synched with other devices—is a profiling device in relation to its user. To some extent it is a self-profiling device for the user and in some respects a profiling device despite the user. Insofar as the apps allow continuous access to social networking facilities (with posting, sharing, recommending, copying and modifying, etc.), it enables continuous self-profiling. Social networking sites are, as observed, designed for users to articulate their networks, map and manage them, and perform their selves on those platforms. Insofar as the apps facilitate any other activity—shopping, banking, gaming, entertainment, bookings, dating, health monitoring, energy consumption, etc.—that produces records (which can be joined up) that are more in the region of being produced despite the user. To the extent that a user can customize or choose some of these other app features, they are still within the domain of self-profiling, but to more significant degrees these are records of user profiles that the user has little control over. Some such uncontrolled records can nevertheless be formally consensually garnered (e.g., by accepting cookies before use), a great many more need no consent (e.g., work as default settings for usage of an app). These two dimensions of profiling could be thought of as akin to recording what Erving Goffman (1959) had characterized as signals that are *given* because the user wishes to and signals that are *given-off* despite the user's intentions:

> The expressiveness of the individual (and therefore his capacity to give impressions) appears to involve two radically different kinds of sign activity: the expression that he *gives*, and the kind of expression that he *gives off*. The first involves verbal symbols or their substitutes which he uses admittedly and solely to convey the information that he and others are known to attach to these symbols. [...] The second involves a wide range of action that others can treat as symptomatic of the actor, the expectation being that the action was performed for reasons other than the information conveyed in this way. (Goffman 1959, 14)

Similarly, we may say that to some degree the smartphone is used for self-profiling in terms of the signals its user *gives*, and to a significant degree profiling takes recourse to signals its user *gives off*.

Third, the smartphone is increasingly the preferred bridge in everyday life between the 'Internet of Things' and the 'Internet of Humans'. Insofar as consumers opt in for apps to avail services offered via networked 'things'—e.g., to run their living and working spaces, to facilitate their productive and transactive commitments—the 'things' involved are fed by the profiling records, especially of the signals given-off variety. To a considerable extent, this is a one-way bridge. The exchange of and responsiveness to data within the'Internet of Things' is largely unsupervised by humans, at least by the great majority who consume internet-mediated services. There might however be shadowy human producers who have their unremarked supervisory place within the 'Internet of Things'.

Between the concentration (along with widening uptake) of social networking on a limited number of platforms, the fixing of the relationship between smartphones (and other mobile networked gadgets) to users, the possibilities of eliciting user profiles (especially from signals given-off), and the bridging to the 'Internet of Things', a reasonable sense is conveyed of the boundaries within which the Internet Polity has come to be confined in the twenty-first century.

6.5 Post-formation Principles

The implications of these developments for the formative social and political first principles of the Internet Polity described in Part 1 are considerable.

For the contained Internet Polity, its collectivity remains structured upon those principles and active in the 'Internet of Humans'. This collectivity is powerfully concentrated on internet-mediated services—the accessible facilities and space—wherein users have an ostensible life. The social and political life of this collective, insofar as oriented towards the internet as facility and space, is undertaken accordingly and expressed in its ever fluid vocabulary. This is a social life which bears constantly upon real-world commitments and engagements via the internet and vice versa. In fact, the distinction between actually existing world and internet as political terrains are so woven into each other that they are difficult to separate. As discussed at the beginning of this chapter, the internet has become implicated in attempts to historicize it, social junctures are conceived as being determinative upon and yet sieved through the internet, and technological determinism of at least a 'soft' sort has become endemic in the Internet Polity discourse. A host of catchwords attests to this: 'netroots', 'Twitter/Facebook revolutions', 'hashtag activism', 'Twiplomacy', 'online campaigning', 'algorithmic radicalization', 'e-governance', 'open-source government', 'digital democracy', 'digital citizen', 'digital constitutionalism', 'platform capitalism', 'surveillance capitalism', 'platform economy', 'platform co-op', 'platform evangelism', 'filter bubbles', 'algorithmic curation', 'algorithmic bias', 'net neutrality', 'net bias', 'dataveillance', 'dataism', 'datafication', 'Googlization', 'internet privacy', 'digital integrity', 'virtual politician' ... to name a few. Such terms describe the continuing burgeoning of the Internet Polity discourse in the twenty-first century, growing upon the general discourse features described in Chap. 5. Insofar as these articulate a collective political orientation towards the internet as facility and space, the debates continue to be premised—either to reiterate or to contest—those formative first principles discussed in Chaps. 2 and 3. Within this sphere of the 'Internet of Humans', the technological structure is collectively apprehended principally in terms of minimal-gradual-mechanical standardization, precedent individuation, and targeted collective regulations.

If the 'Internet of Things' (including within that phrase integrated AI systems and automated processing like Blockchain) is thought of as a domain that sits alongside and in relation to the 'Internet of Humans'—i.e., so that the internet is larger than what users and inhabitants apprehend—then these first principles are, however, inevitably inflected without being disavowed in the Internet Polity. Minimal-gradual-mechanical standardization remains substantially the underpinning principle in the uptake of internet services at the market end (insofar as 'end-users' and consumers are concerned). The accessed surface of Internet Technology that is encountered directly within the precincts of the Internet Polity offer piloting and market-testing, various consumer choices (customization features, privacy settings, consent and agreement checks, pricing options, etc.), and add-ons and alternative pathways in the spirit of that principle. Correspondingly, the Internet Polity's ethical and political discourses are shaped at this surface. Collective contestations and anxieties are expressed as departures from or contraventions of a common-sense ethics and rationale that is grounded at this surface of Internet Technology. They all seem to be addressable at the surface itself, in the access and usage features of this 'Internet of Humans', in line with minimal-gradual-mechanical standardization. Commitments to internet democracy, user/consumer power and rights, net neutrality and digital citizenship, etc. are expressions of the minimal-gradual-mechanical standardization principle working at this surface.

Effectively, however, the formative first principle of the Internet Polity has shifted ground. The formative principle was built upon the innards of Internet Technology, in the protocol specifications that link discrete networks and enable the management of I-information. Increasingly, this is now more on, to stress again, the *surface* rather than the *innards*—the innards of Internet Technology have grown more capacious, beyond the remit of the 'Internet of Humans'. Insofar as that extension takes in the 'Internet of Things', within this extension a quite different corresponding principle applies. This could be thought of as a *principle of axiomatic standardization* that articulates the 'Internet of Things'. This aspect of Internet Technology is constituted through standard-setting from the get-go. In fact, the technology consists functionally in agreeing and setting standards among technology producers. These standards are akin to axioms for the very possibility of the 'Internet of Thing' structure; in other words, standards are the technological substructure. The relationship between the principle of axiomatic standardization in the 'Internet of Things' and of the principle of minimal-gradual-mechanical standardization in the 'Internet of Humans' is a matter of considerable complexity and needs careful unpacking. Insofar as it resonates with anxious expressions in present-day Internet Polity discourse, it seems that the former compromises or conflicts with the latter. But the processes at work between are not easily disentangled into clear binaries. A careful exploration of this relationship lies ahead of this study.

In the 'Internet of Humans', the principle of precedent individuation holds insofar as hypertext facilities and associative linking through the field of I-information are still available. In the 'Internet of Things', a corresponding *principle of logical synchronization* appears to be emerging upon the substructure of axiomatic standards. Not only is this different from 'associative thinking' and the principle of precedent individuation in the 'Internet of Humans', this is also different from what I had characterized as 'assimilative knowledge' in Chap. 3. No throwback is afoot towards information-to-knowledge processing based on hierarchical layers, usually disposed in indexical form. The principle of logical synchronization is premised on a relatively narrow and unremittingly consistency-seeking mode of logical synthesis and analysis. That means it enables processing of I-information into functional knowledge forms insofar as condensable into algorithms, while avoiding the indeterminacies indicated, for instance, by Turing Machine circularity or Kurt Gödel's incompleteness theorem (relevantly and succinctly outlined by Peter Tu in Gupta and Tu 2023: Chap. 9). In a way, this situation could be regarded as the realization of Tim Berners-Lee's (1999) early vision of the 'semantic web' (discussed earlier in Chap. 3). The 'Internet of Things' appears as a sort of segregated and automatized zone of the 'semantic web', carrying out 'the day-to-day mechanisms of trade, bureaucracy, and our daily lives [being] handled by machines talking to machines', following the principle of logical synchronization, For Berners-Lee, that effectively leaves 'humans to provide the inspiration and intuition' (158) according to the principle of precedent individuation and associative linking in the 'Internet of Humans'. And yet, the emerging situation for the Internet Polity is not quite as clearcut. The 'Internet of Things' is not segregated from the 'Internet of Humans'; rather, the former feeds back into and bears upon the latter. The Semantic Web resources or the WWW Consortium's setting of standards bring active interventions—massaging of messages—from the'Internet of Things' and AI-assistants into the doings and life of the 'Internet of Humans'. How the principle of logical synchronization is accommodated with the principle of precedent individuation is a murky area yet, and the post-formation shape of the Internet Polity in this respect calls for sustained scrutiny.

The principle of collective regulation via security controls continues to be the most pervasive shaper of the Internet Polity, with constantly proliferating legislations and policy formulations at all levels, and an ever-expanding cybersecurity industry. Such collective regulation is most obtrusively in the eye of the collectivity with a social orientation towards the internet. Subscriptions to political freedom and authoritarianism continue to be predominantly expressed in terms of this principle. Collective regulation of the internet is seen as both the panacea and the aggravator of all issues that trouble the Internet Polity. Nevertheless, here too there is a significant shift. In a reverse direction from the principle of minimal-gradual-mechanical standardization, the principle of collective regulation seems to have moved from the *surface* of the technological structure—from layerings over the core protocols—towards the *innards*, or rather towards the expanded depths of the 'Internet of Things'. Ostensibly, of course, collective regulation is so energetically at the behest of actually existing political authorities that it must be seen to be activated in the 'Internet of Humans', operationalized by governmental and corporate agencies. But that has not quite kept the 'Internet of Things' at arm's length, quite the contrary. Corresponding to the principle of collective regulation for the 'Internet of Humans' a somewhat distinct *principle of automated self-regulation* is widely attributed to the 'Internet of Things'. That is to say, the 'Internet of Things' is conceived as being constitutively a regulated system and in no need of after the-the-fact regulation. In fact, it is this attribution of automated self-regulation to the 'Internet of Things' which is increasingly pushed as offering correctives to the challenges of collective regulation in the 'Internet of Humans'. In particular, the literature on e-governance, fintech, and cybersecurity is replete with setting automatic networked systems and using AI capacities to eliminate 'human error', 'corruption' and 'self-interest', human 'bias' and 'prejudice', etc.—or at the least as having the potential to do so with salutary social effects. The flows between systems set by the principle of collective regulation in the 'Internet of

Humans' and the principle of automated self-regulation in the 'Internet of Things' will keep researchers busy in the foreseeable future. Much will be clarified thereby about the emerging condition of the Internet Polity.

Insofar as the 'Internet of Humans' goes, a final impressionistic thought with an eye to further investigation. Internet Polity discourse premised on the principle of collective regulation has been powerfully centred on the bureaucratic catch-phrase 'privacy and security' (as observed in Chap. 3). This continues to be so. The presumption that 'privacy' and 'security' are conjoined or co-dependent terms are of considerable interest. The phrase 'privacy and security' sets a preconceived binary conjunction that focalizes, on the one hand, individual selves whose privacy needs to be protected and, on the other hand, top-down authorities who provide protective security. The coherences of or contradictions at this conjunction largely structure the discursive field, and subsumes the life of the Internet Polity in the 'Internet of Humans'. However, it is also becoming constantly clearer that this conjunction is underpinned by something other than individual selves and collective governance. This conjunction is structured by and manoeuvred through an underpinning rationale of ownership. Shrouded under 'privacy and security' claims, there are pressing questions: Who owns the facilities and space that are the 'Internet of Humans'? Who owns the 'things' and processing mechanisms that are the 'Internet of Things'? Who owns data from social networking?

Very little of the internet is free in any considered sense. However, ownership is itself a contested concept here, balanced between distributed modes of control and distributed means for being capitalized. These are issues which have been surfacing with a steady urgency from scholarly and activist circles for a while into the wider sphere of the Internet Polity. Contested concepts and initiatives referred through terms such as 'open source', 'dark web', 'platform capitalism', 'data commons', and so on come to mind … Indeed, the conundrums and realities of ownership are in the interstices of all the anxious recent studies of the internet this book began with. Ultimately, the shape and condition of the post-formation Internet Polity depends upon how the political economy of the current internet—'Internet of Humans' and 'Internet of Things'—is conceived and engaged, both ideologically and practically. This political economy has not been addressed systematically in this study. The political economy of the Internet Polity is yet awaiting a rigorous and sustained investigative effort. It is possible that through this effort, the Internet Polity may move towards being released from containment. The spectre of an Internet Polity which refuses containment might well come to haunt the dominant global digital order in due course.

References

Alter S (2020) Making sense of smartness in the context of smart devices and smart systems. Inf Syst Front 22:381–393. https://doi.org/10.1007/s10796-019-09919-9

Anderson B (2006 [1983]) Imagined communities: reflections on the origin and spread of nationalism. Verso, London

Ankerson MS (2018) Dot-Com design: the rise of a usable, social, commercial web. New York University Press, New York

Ansari S, Kohavi R, Mason L, Zheng Z (2001) Integrating e-commerce and data mining: architecture and challenges. In: ICDM '01: proceedings of the 2001 IEEE international conference on data mining, November, 27–34. https://doi.org/10.1109/ICDM.2001.989497

Atzori L (2011) SIoT: giving a social structure to the Internet of Things. IEEE Commun Lett 15(11):1193–1195. https://doi.org/10.1109/LCOMM.2011.090911.111340

Atzori L, Iera A, Morabito G, Nitti M (2012) The Social Internet of Things (SIoT)—when social networks meet the Internet of Things: concept, architecture and network characterization. Comput Netw 56:3594–3608. https://doi.org/10.1016/j.comnet.2012.07.010

Baudrillard J (1995 [1991]) The gulf war did not take place (trans: Patton P). Indiana University Press, Bloomington IN

Berners-Lee T, Fischetti M (1999) Weaving the web: the original design and ultimate destiny of the World Wide Web by its inventor. HarperCollins, New York

Berry M, Schleser M (2014) Mobile media making in an age of smartphones. Palgrave Macmillan, Cham

Boyd DM, Ellison NB (2008) Social network sites: definition, history, and scholarship. J Comput-Mediat Commun 13(1):210–230. https://doi.org/10.1111/j.1083-6101.2007.00393.x

Burkhardt MDvG, Gerlitz C et al (2022) Introduction. In: Burkhardt MDvG, Gerlitz C et al (eds) Interrogating datafication: towards a praxeology of data. Transcript, Bielefeld, pp 9–38

Castells M (2001) The internet galaxy: reflections on the internet, business, and society. Oxford University Press, Oxford

Cellan-Jones R (2001) Dot.Bomb: the rise and fall of Dot.Com Britain. Aurum, London

Daly JA (2000) Studying the impacts of the internet without assuming technological determinism. ASLIB Proc 52(8):285–300. https://doi.org/10.1108/EUM0000000007023

Davis HM, Vickery JN (2007) Datasets, a shift in the currency of scholarly communication: implications for library collections and acquisitions. Ser Rev 33(1):26–32. https://doi.org/10.1016/j.serrev.2006.11.004

Deva Y (1997) Internet: a paradigm shift in technological determinism. IETE Tech Rev 14(4–5):317–323. https://doi.org/10.1080/02564602.1997.11416689

Dhond A, Gupta A, Vadhavkar S (2000) Data mining techniques for optimizing inventories for electronic commerce. In: KDD '00: Proceedings of the sixth ACM SIGKDD international conference on knowledge discovery and data mining, August, 480–486. https://doi.org/10.1145/347090.347188

Ding L, Shi P, Liu B (2010) The clustering of internet, Internet of Things and social network. In: 3rd International symposium on knowledge acquisition and modeling, 20–21 October. https://ieeexplore.ieee.org/abstract/document/5646274

Edmond J, Horsley N, Lehmann J, Priddy M (2022) The trouble with Big Data: how datafication displaces cultural practices. Bloomsbury, London

Garcia-Swartz DD, Campbell-Kelly M (2022) Cellular: an economic and business history of the international mobile-phone industry. MIT Press, Cambridge MA

Garshenfeld N (1999) When things start to think. Henry Holt, New York

Gershenfeld N, Krikorian R, Cohen D (2004) The Internet of Things. Scientific American, October, 76–81. https://doi.org/10.1038/scientificamerican1004-76

Giachetti C (2017) Smartphone start-ups: navigating the IPhone revolution. Palgrave Macmillan, Cham

Goddard NDR, Kemp RMJ, Lane R (1997) An overview of smart technologies. Packaging Technol Sci 10(3):129–143. https://doi.org/10.1002/(SICI)1099-1522(19970501/30)10:3%3C129::AID-PTS393%3E3.0.CO;2-C

Goffman E (1959) The presentation of self in everyday life. Doubleday, Garden City, NJ

Grudin J (1993) Interface: an evolving concept. Commun ACM 36(4, April):110–119. https://doi.org/10.1145/255950.153585
Gutiérrez C, Garbajosa J, Diaz J, Yagüe A (2013) Providing a consensus definition for the term "Smart Product". In: 20th Annual IEEE international conference and workshops on the engineering of computer based systems (ECBS), 22–24 April. https://doi.org/10.1109/ECBS.2013.26
Guinard DD, Trifa VM (2016) Building the Web of Things. Manning, Shelter Island NY
Gupta S (2002) The replication of violence: thoughts on international terrorism after September 11, 2001. Pluto, London
Gupta S (2022) Political catchphrases and contemporary history: a critique of new normals. Oxford University Press, Oxford
Gupta S, Tu P (2023) The practical philosophy of AI-assistants: an engineering-humanities conversation. World Scientific Europe, London
Hauben M, Hauben R (1997) Netizens: on the history and impact of Usenet and the Internet. IEEE Computer Society Press, Los Alamitos CA. Online at http://www.columbia.edu/~hauben/book-pdf/
Ibarra-Esquer JE, González-Navarro FF, Flores-Rios BL, Burtseva L, Astorga-Vargas MA (2017) Tracking the evolution of the internet of things concept across different application domains. Sensors 17(6):1379. https://doi.org/10.3390/s17061379
IEEE (2015) Toward a definition of the Internet of Things (IoT). https://iot.ieee.org/images/files/pdf/IEEE_IoT_Towards_Definition_Internet_of_Things_Revision1_27MAY15.pdf
ITU (International Telecommunication Union) (2005) The Internet of Things. ITU, Geneva. https://www.itu.int/net/wsis/tunis/newsroom/stats/The-Internet-of-Things-2005.pdf
Janbek D, Williams V (2014) The role of the internet post-9/11 in terrorism and counterterrorism. Brown J World Affairs 20(2):297–308. https://www.jstor.org/stable/24590989
Jordan T (2008) Hacking: digital media and technological determinism. Polity, Cambridge
Kerssens N (2019) De-agentializing data practices: the shifting power of metaphor in 1990s discourses on data mining. J Cult Anal 4(1). https://culturalanalytics.org/article/11049-de-agentializing-data-practices-the-shifting-power-of-metaphor-in-1990s-discourses-on-data-mining
Kim Y-C, Jung J-Y, Cohen EL, Ball-Rokeach SJ (2004) Internet connectedness before and after September 11 2001. New Media Soc 6(5):611–631. https://doi.org/10.1177/146144804047083
Kuo JD (2001) Dot.Bomb: inside the Internet Goliath—from lunatic opinion to panic and crash. Little, Brown and Company, New York
Laurel B (2001) Utopian Entrepreneur. MIT Press, Cambridge MA
Leiner BM, Cerf VG, Clark DD et al (2009) A brief history of the internet. ACM SIGCOMM Comp Commun Rev 39(5):22–31. https://doi.org/10.1145/1629607.1629613
Lewis M (2001) The future just happened. Hodder and Stoughton, London
Lovink G (2002) After the dotcom crash: recent literature on internet, business and society. Cult Stud Rev 8(1):130–154. https://doi.org/10.3316/ielapa.200310819
McNamee R (2004) The new normal: great opportunities in a time of great risk. Portfolio, London
Malmsten E, Portanger E, Drazin C (2001) boo.hoo: a dotcom story from concept to catastrophe. Random House, New York
Mattern F, Floerkemeier C (2010) From the Internet of computers to the Internet of Things. In: Sachs K, Petrov I, Guerrero P (eds) From active data management to event-based systems and more. Springer, Berlin, pp 242–259
Mejias UA, Couldry N (2019) Datafication. Internet Policy Rev 8(4). https://doi.org/10.14763/2019.4.1428
Merchant B (2017) The one device: the secret history of the Iphone. Little, Brown and Company, New York
Miller D, Rabho LA, Awondo P et al (2021) The global smartphone: beyond a youth technology. UCL Press, London
Misra S, Roy C, Mukherjee A (2021) Introduction to industrial Internet of Things and Industry 4.0. CRC Press, Boca Baton FL

Naughton J (1999) A brief history of the future: the origins of the internet. Phoenix, London
OMASpecWorks website: https://omaspecworks.org/about/
Perkins AB, Perkins MC (2001) The internet bubble: the inside story on why it burst-and what you can do to profit now. HarperCollins, New York
Petrosyan A (2023) Number of internet and social media users worldwide as of October 2023. Statista, 25 October. https://www.statista.com/statistics/617136/digital-population-worldwide/#:~:text=Worldwide%20digital%20population%202023&text=As%20of%20October%202023%2C%20there,percent%20of%20the%20global%20population
Pew Internet and American Life Project (2002) One year later: September 11 and the internet. Pew Internet and American Life Project, Washington DC. https://www.pewresearch.org/internet/2002/09/05/one-year-later-september-11-and-the-internet/
Rainey L, Wellman B (2012) Networked: the new social operating system. MIT Press, Cambridge MA
Raji RS (1994) Smart networks for control. IEEE Spectr 31(6):49–55. https://doi.org/10.1109/6.284793
Reid AJ (2018) The smartphone paradox: our ruinous dependency in the device age. Palgrave Macmillan, Cham
Rohlinger DA, Brown J (2009) Democracy, action, and the internet after 9/11. Am Behav Sci 53(1):133–150. https://doi.org/10.1177/0002764209338791
Roholt TC (2023) Distracted from meaning: a philosophy of smartphones. Bloomsbury Academic, London
Ryan J (2010) A History of the Internet and the Digital Future. Reaktion, London
Santucci G (2009) From the Internet of Data to the Internet of Things. https://docbox.etsi.org/erm/Open/CERP-IoT20090518/Santucci%20paper%20on%20IoT%20for%20Internet%20conference_Luxembourg_28-01-2009.pdf
Schechter D (2003) Media wars: news at a time of terror. Rowman and Littlefield, Lanham MA
Servaes J (ed) (2014) Technological determinism and social change in a tech-mad world. Lexington, Lanham MA
Silberstein S (2004) War of words: language, politics and 9/11. Routledge, Abingdon
Silverio-Fernández M, Renukappa S, Suresh S (2018) What is a smart device? A conceptualisation within the paradigm of the Internet of Things. Visual Eng 6. https://doi.org/10.1186/s40327-018-0063-8
Smith M, Marx L (eds) (1994) Does technology drive history? The dilemma of technological determinism. MIT Press, Cambridge MA
Vincent J, Haddon L (eds) (2017) Smartphone cultures. Routledge, Abingdon
W3C Web of Things website: https://www.w3.org/WoT/
Wahlstrom K, Roddick JF, Sarre R, Estivill-Castro V, deVries D (2006) On the ethical and legal implications of data mining. Technical Report SIE-06-001, School of Informatics and Engineering, Flinders University, Adelaide
Weiser M (1991) The computer for the 21st century. Scientific American, 1 September. https://doi.org/10.1038/scientificamerican0991-94
Wellman B, Salaff J, Dimitrova D et al (1996) Computer networks as social networks: collaborative work, telework, and virtual community. Ann Rev Sociol 22:213–238. https://www.jstor.org/stable/2083430
Wellman B (1997) An electronic group is virtually a social network. In: Kiesler S (eds) Culture of the internet. Lawrence Erlbaum, Mahwah NJ, pp 179–208
Wellman B, Haythornthwaite C (eds) (2002) Moving the internet out of cyberspace: the internet in everyday life: an introduction, pp 3–44
Wellman B, Haythornthwaite C (2002b) The internet in everyday life. Blackwell, Malden MA
Woyke E (2011) The smartphone: anatomy of an industry. New Press, New York

Index

S. Gupta, *Collective Principles and the Formation of the Internet*, Springer Series on Cultural Computing, https://doi.org/10.1007/978-3-031-90470-7

The manufacturer's authorised representative in the EU is Springer Nature Customer Service Centre GmbH, Europaplatz 3, 69115 Heidelberg, Germany. If you have any concerns regarding our products, please contact ProductSafety@springernature.com

Printed and bound by CPI Group (UK) Ltd, Croydon, CR0 4YY
01/10/2026
02225922-0001